ARISTOTLE

PARVA NATURALIA

with *ON THE MOTION OF ANIMALS*

I0809094

MERCER UNIVERSITY

MERCER UNIVERSITY PRESS

Endowed by

TOM WATSON BROWN

and

THE WATSON-BROWN FOUNDATION, INC.

ARISTOTLE

PARVA NATURALIA

with *ON THE MOTION OF ANIMALS*

Translated by David Bolotin

MERCER UNIVERSITY PRESS
Macon, Georgia

H 1003
P 622

Copyright © 2021 by David Bolotin

All rights reserved. No part of this book may be reproduced, stored in a retrieval system, or transmitted, in any form or by any means, electronic, mechanical, photocopying, recording, or otherwise, without the prior permission of Mercer University Press.

Printed and bound by Friesens in Canada.

1 2 3 4 5 6 26 25 24 23 22 21

Library of Congress Cataloging-in-Publication Data
Aristotle.
[Parva Naturalia / with On the Motion of Animals. English]
Short Works Having to Do with Nature / with On the Motion of Animals / Aristotle; translated by David Bolotin.
Macon, Georgia: Mercer University Press, 2021.
Includes bibliographical references.
ISBN 978-088146-783-3 (hardback)
ISBN 978-088146-784-0 (paperback)
Additional Cataloging-in-Publication Data is available from the Library of Congress.

∞ The paper used in this publication meets the minimum requirements of the American National Standard for Information Sciences Permanence of Paper for Printed Materials, ANSI Z39.48–1984.

The typefaces used in this book are Monotype Ehrhardt and GFS Porson.
Cover image: a 10th-century folio that includes the beginning of *On Sense Perception and Sense-Perceptibles*, in the Bibliothèque nationale de France, Departement des manuscrits, Grec 1853, used with the permission of the Bibliothèque nationale de France, Paris
Cover design by Burt&Burt Studio
Interior design by Susan P. Johnson

Published by
Mercer University Press
1501 Mercer University Drive
Macon, Georgia 31207
www.mupress.org

Contents

Introduction

Although the title *Parva Naturalia* (*Short Works Having to Do with Nature*) dates only from the Latin Middle Ages, it is clear from the texts themselves that the treatises known collectively by that name do belong together, and that Aristotle intended them to be read, in the order in which they traditionally appear, as a sequel to *De Anima* (*On Soul*).[1] Most of these treatises are devoted to particular states and activities of living beings, and of animals in particular, that were not treated thematically in *De Anima*, but Aristotle makes it clear that these are all connected with sense perception,[2] which is both the topic of the initial treatise and also the one that he had treated more extensively than any other in that prior work. And it is especially clear with regard to this key topic that the treatises in the *Parva Naturalia* are not mere appendages to *De Anima*, but that they help to perfect the account of soul, and of its relation to the world as a whole, that is given there. Aristotle indicates from the very beginning that these treatises will concern activities that involve body and soul together,[3] and by paying more attention than in *De Anima* to the bodily aspect of sense perception, he gives a fuller, and to that extent truer, account of it. In particular, the treatise *On Sense Perception and Sense-Perceptibles* adds an important discussion of what the senses perceive, i.e., what it is in the world that becomes manifest as color, for instance, or as odor, a discussion that also goes more deeply into the question of how these objects produce actual perception. In this initial treatise, moreover, Aristotle's concluding

---

1 Cf. *On Sense Perception and Sense-Perceptibles* 436a1–17, 449b1–4; *On Sleep and Awakeness* 453b11–24; *On Prophecy from Sleep* 464b16–18; *On Long-Livedness and Short-Livedness* 464b31–465a2, 467b5–9.

2 Cf. *On Sense Perception and Sense-Perceptibles* 436b3–4.

3 Cf. *On Sense Perception and Sense-Perceptibles* 436a6–8, 436b1–8.

examination of the question of whether it is possible to perceive two objects at the same time involves a continuation and a deepening of his two separate discussions in *De Anima* of how we perceive that the objects of different senses are indeed different.[4] And to mention only two examples from the other treatises of important additions to the treatment of sense perception, in the discussion, in the treatise on sleep, of the modification that the power of sense perception as a whole undergoes in sleep, Aristotle brings out more clearly than he had before how the senses are all bound up with one another; and in his discussion, in the treatise on dreams, of the illusory perception that belongs to them, he brings out more clearly than he had before what is involved in the waking perception of an object that is truly what it presents itself as being.

The treatises traditionally known as the *Parva Naturalia* do not include *On the Motion of Animals*. But I have chosen to include it in this volume, immediately after *On Prophecy from Sleep*, since there is strong textual evidence that Aristotle intended it to be included there. For *On Prophecy from Sleep* concludes, according to the preponderance of the manuscripts, with the words, "And the motion that is common to animals must be spoken about," and these are clearly a pointer to this treatise.[5] Moreover, *On the Motion of Animals* concludes with a sentence stating that the causes have been given "concerning each of the parts of the animals, and concerning soul, and furthermore, concerning sense perception and sleep and memory and the motion in general [of the animals]," a summary statement confirming that this treatise is the immediate sequel to the preceding treatises of the *Parva Naturalia*, whose leading themes are indeed sense perception, sleep, and memory. Now this final sentence of *On the Motion of Animals* continues with "and it remains to speak about coming into being," which, in the context of Aristotle's writings on living beings, must be a pointer to the treatise *On the Generation of Animals*. And especially since *On the Generation of Animals* contains several clear backward references to *On Sense*

---

4 *On Sense Perception and Sense-Perceptibles* 447a12–449a20; cf. *De Anima* 426b8–427a14, 431a20–b1.

5 *On Prophecy from Sleep* 464b18a. That *On the Motion of Animals* belongs in general to the *Parva Naturalia* is also indicated in *De Anima*, as one can see by comparing *De Anima* 433b19–21 with *On the Motion of Animals* 701a33–b10 and 703a4–b2, together with the passages from *On Sense Perception and Sense-Perceptibles* referred to in n. 3.

Perception and Sense-Perceptibles (779b21–23, 786b23–25, 788a34–b2), a probable one to *On Sleep and Awakeness* (779a4–7), and also a forward reference to *On Long-Livedness and Short-Livedness* (777b6–8), a good case could be made for including it after *On the Motion of Animals*, and for returning only then to *On Long-Livedness and Short-Livedness* and the other remaining treatise of the *Parva Naturalia*. But the length of *On the Generation of Animals* makes it impractical for me to include it in this volume, and so I have chosen to return, directly after *On the Motion of Animals*, to the final two treatises of the *Parva Naturalia*.

This translation is a sequel to my previously published translation of *De Anima*.[6] And as with that one, I have again chosen not to use the standard English edition of the Greek text, the one edited by W. D. Ross, as the basis for my translation.[7] For Ross is, in my judgment, if to a lesser extent than in his edition of *De Anima*, too ready to introduce modern conjectural emendations into his text,[8] often in passages where a greater effort to make sense of admittedly difficult manuscript readings would have helped bring to light the true Aristotle, whose thought is more subtle and penetrating than modern scholars generally recognize. As a result, I have based my translation of the first two of the treatises here, *On Sense Perception and Sense-Perceptibles* and *On Memory and Recollection*, on the text of the *Parva Naturalia* established by Wilhelm Biehl in his 1898 Teubner edition.[9] This remains the best of the modern editions, in my view, and Biehl's Greek text of these first two treatises is available in G. R. T. Ross' *Aristotle* De Sensu *and* De Memoria.[10] However, Biehl's edition itself is not so reliably available, and so I have used as the basis for my translation of the remaining treatises of the *Parva Naturalia* the Budé edition of René Mugnier,[11] in which the Greek text, as Mugnier himself

6 *Aristotle* De Anima (On Soul), trans. David Bolotin (Macon, Ga.: Mercer University Press, 2018).

7 *Aristotle* Parva Naturalia, ed. Sir David Ross (Oxford: Clarendon Press, 1955).

8 Cf. the review of Ross' edition by D. J. Furley, *Classical Review* 6, no. 3–4 (1956): 227.

9 *Aristotelis* Parva Naturalia, ed. Guilelmus Biehl (Leipzig: B. G. Teubner Verlag, 1898).

10 *Aristotle* De Sensu *and* De Memoria, ed. G. R. T. Ross (Cambridge: Cambridge University Press, 1906/2014).

11 *Aristote,* Petits traités d'histoire naturelle, ed. René Mugnier (Paris: Les Belles Lettres, 1953/2010).

acknowledges, is substantially the same as Biehl's.[12] Finally, I have used the Budé edition of Pierre Louis as the basis for my translation of *On the Motion of Animals*.[13] I have chosen this edition in preference to either of the two more recent editions of it, the 1978 edition by Martha Nussbaum[14] and the 2018 edition of Oliver Primavesi (with Klaus Corcilius),[15] since both of these, in my view, also include in their Greek texts too many conjectural emendations by modern scholars. Primavesi's edition does contain dozens of unique readings from authentic sources,[16] readings that are for the most part the result of his having collated several previously neglected manuscripts, which belong, as he has convincingly shown, to a family of manuscripts with a different ancient archetype than that of the manuscripts that had been most relied on by modern editors. But while many of the readings that Primavesi and Corcilius have chosen on the basis of these manuscripts have some initial plausibility, it seems to me that in almost every case the traditional readings that appear in Louis' text are to be preferred. And I suspect that the family of manuscripts that Primavesi has brought to light stems from some medieval scribe or scribes who, like too many modern editors, tried to smooth over passages in which Aristotle deliberately challenges his readers with difficult thoughts.

Although I have used the three editions mentioned here as the basis for my translations, I have not always agreed with these editors' readings. Editions of ancient Greek works standardly include, along with the Greek text, a critical apparatus that reports alternative readings from manuscripts other than the one that the editor has chosen to rely on for each particular passage. I have examined all of these alternative readings, and I have sometimes chosen to base my translation on one or another of them. Also, I have examined both the text and the critical apparatus in the other editions that I have mentioned, as well as in the Siwek edition of the *Parva*

---

12 Mugnier, 16.

13 *Aristote*, Marche des animaux, Mouvement des animaux, ed. Pierre Louis (Paris: Les Belles Lettres, 1973/2002).

14 *Aristotle's* De Motu Animalium, ed. Martha Craven Nussbaum (Princeton: Princeton University Press, 1978).

15 *Aristoteles* De Motu Animalium, Über die Bewegung der Lebewesen, ed. Oliver Primavesi, trans. Klaus Corcilius (Hamburg: Felix Meiner Verlag, 2018).

16 Cf. Primavesi, cxxxiv–cxxxix.

Naturalia and the Bloch edition of *On Memory and Recollection*,[17] all of which involve the study of more manuscripts than those taken into account by the editors I have preferred, and I have sometimes chosen to base my translation on the text of one of these editions or on an alternative reading that it reports. However, in order to allow the reader to make an independent judgment, whenever I have translated a reading different from the one that appears in my primary text, I have added a footnote that includes, along with a transliteration of the reading that I have chosen, and sometimes my reason or reasons for choosing it, a transliteration and also a translation of the one in the text.

In translating these texts I have tried to convey Aristotle's meaning as accurately as I could, while also providing as literal a translation as is compatible with good English. And especially because Aristotle is such a terse and even elliptical writer, the only way I could combine these two aims was to supplement the literal translation with many additions of my own, which I have included within square brackets. These bracketed suggestions, though they are sometimes extremely minor and necessary only to give the translation a normal English style, do however frequently involve interpretive judgments regarding the passage in question. And though there are so many of these additions that no reader could possibly ignore them, those readers who question my judgment regarding this or that passage can at least measure my full translation against the literal version that excludes the bracketed words. Yet even the amplified translation leaves many difficulties and raises many questions, and to help guide the reader through some of these, I have also included quite a few footnotes. Some of these, as I have said, give textual variants for the manuscript readings I have chosen to translate, and I sometimes add such notes even in passages where I have agreed with the editor whose text I am primarily working from. Others identify passages from the works of other authors that Aristotle either quotes or refers to, or they specify the passages he has in mind when he refers to what he has said earlier, what he will say later, or what he has said in other works. Still others give transliterations of the Greek originals for various English words that appear in the translation, along

17 *Aristotelis* Parva Naturalia, ed. Paulus Siwek, S.J. (Rome: Desclée & C.^{i}, 1963); *Aristotle on Memory and Recollection*, ed. David Bloch (Leiden: Brill, 2007).

with a brief discussion of these Greek words and of my reasons for translating them as I do.[18] But many of the footnotes are frankly interpretive, and although I have not attempted anything approaching a full commentary on these texts, the notes do provide pointers toward my own interpretation of each of them. Still, I have tried scrupulously not to allow these interpretations to influence my literal translation, and even in the case of my bracketed additions, I have tried as hard as I could to include only as much elaboration as a particular passage requires, elaboration meant to be persuasive even to readers who would disagree with my overall interpretation of the work in question.

I have accepted the traditional division into chapters of the treatises translated here, although it is not present in the oldest manuscripts, since it seems intelligent for the most part, and since it would be too jarring for the contemporary reader not to have chapters. But though it is now customary for editors and translators to divide each chapter into paragraphs, I have not done so, since the ease of reading they provide does not seem to me to be worth the risk of making inappropriate divisions within Aristotle's presentation of his thought.

Finally, I want again to express my gratitude to Christopher Bruell, who checked the penultimate version of this translation against the Greek original with meticulous care and who brought to bear on it his deep understanding of Aristotle. His suggestions have led to hundreds of improvements to the translation, and they showed me the way to understanding many passages that I had seriously misunderstood.

September, 2019
Santa Fe, New Mexico

---

18 I have also included transliterations of particularly important Greek words in parentheses within the text, and I have sometimes even substituted the transliterated Greek for any attempt at a translation.

ON SENSE PERCEPTION AND SENSE-PERCEPTIBLES

Chapter 1

Since determinations have been made [in *De Anima*] concerning 436a soul in itself and concerning each of its powers part by part, next [in order] is to make our examination concerning the animals and all the [beings] that have life, [as to] which of their activities (*praxeis*) are peculiar and which are common. So then let what (pl.) has been said concerning soul be assumed, and let us speak concerning what (pl.) remains, and first concerning what (pl.) is first. And it is manifest that the most important [things], both those that are common [to all] of the animals and those that are peculiar [to some], are common to the soul and the body, for instance sense perception and memory and spiritedness and desire and appetite in general, and in addition to these, pleasure as well as pain; and in fact these [all] belong to nearly all the animals. And in addition to these [i.e., to the most important things], some [others] are common to all the [beings] that share in life, whereas others [are peculiar] to some of the animals. And the most important of these are in fact pairs [that are] four in number, namely, awakeness and sleep, and youth and old age, and breathing [in] and breathing out, and life and death; concerning which one must contemplate what each of them [is] and on account of what causes it occurs. And [it belongs] to a student of nature to see the first causes also concerning health and disease; for it is not possible for either health or disease to come to be in the [beings] that are without life. Therefore, the majority, roughly, of those [whose study is] concerning nature, and of the doctors, those who pursue their art more philosophically—the former come to the end [of their study] in the [matters] that concern the medical [art], while the latter begin concerning the medical [art] 436b from the [principles] concerning nature. And that the [things] that have been spoken of belong to the soul and the body in common is not unclear. For they all occur either with sense perception or else through sense perception; some are in fact affections (*pathē*)[1] of this, some are states (*hexeis*)[2] [of it], some are protections and preservations [of it], and some are destructions and deprivations [of it]. And that sense perception comes into being for the soul through the body is clear both through speech (*logou*)[3] and apart

---

1 The word *pathē*, which I translate as "affections," and which is the plural form of the word *pathos*, comes from the verb *paskhein*, which means "to suffer," in the sense of being acted upon, having something done to one, or having something happen to one, and also to be in a state or condition that results from such happenings, or more generally to be in some state or condition. The conditions that it refers to can be either quite temporary or more long-lasting, and in some cases they are even permanent attributes of what they belong to. The word sometimes also refers to passions, such as anger and fear, as well as to sufferings or misfortunes that happen to people. But in general, and especially as it is used in these treatises, there is no adequate English equivalent for the word *pathos*. I have chosen the translation "affection" here, using the word in its older sense of a condition of being affected by something, or one that results from being affected by something. And I will generally translate it as "affection," as "attribute," or as "suffering," and I will usually add in parentheses a transliteration of the Greek, as I do here. Finally, in more than a few cases I will merely transliterate the Greek word, without any attempt at translation.

2 The Greek word *hexis*, of which *hexeis* is the plural form, comes from the verb *ekhein*, which means "to have," and it often refers to a more or less lasting state of something, i.e., to a state in which that something is, as health or sickness are states of the body. But the word also can have the different, but related, meaning of "having." And Aristotle will later speak of memory as a certain kind of *hexis*, i.e., a certain "having" of an appearance that persists as a result of an earlier sense perception (*On Memory and Recollection* 450a27–30, 451a14–16). Accordingly, I might well have chosen the translation "havings" in the passage before us rather than "states." At all events, I will translate the word *hexis* either as "state" or as "having," and I will often add in parentheses a transliteration of the Greek.

3 The word *logou* is a form of *logos*, whose meanings include "speech," "argument," "account," "explanation," "definition," and "reason," as well as "ratio" or "proportion." On account of the importance as well as the breadth of meanings of this word, I will often, as here, add a transliteration of the Greek in parentheses.

from speech. But concerning sense perception and [the act of] perceiving by sense, what it is and on account of what this affection (*pathos*) happens to animals has been said before in what (pl.) [was said] concerning soul. And it is necessary that sense perception belong to animals, insofar as each is an animal; for by this we distinguish [between] being an animal and not [being] an animal.[4] But now as regards each [sense] in particular, touch and taste go with all [animals] by necessity, touch on account of the cause spoken of in the [things said] concerning soul,[5] and taste on account of nourishment; for by means of it they discriminate between the pleasant and the painful concerning nourishment, so as to avoid the one and pursue the other, and in general flavor is an attribute (*pathos*) of what is nutritive. But the senses [that operate] through external [media], such as smell and hearing and sight, [go with] those of them that have locomotion, [and] they belong to all those that have [these senses], for the sake of preservation, so that they might pursue their nourishment, perceiving it beforehand, and might avoid what (pl.) is inferior and destructive, but [they belong] to those that also attain understanding (*phronēsis*), for the sake of the good; for they [i.e., these senses,] give notice of many differentiae, from which understanding of the intelligibles as well as of what [actions] are to be done comes to be in [them]. And of these [senses] themselves sight, in itself, is superior with a view to what (pl.) is necessary, but with a view to [the] intellect and by concomitance, hearing [is superior]. For the power of sight informs [us] of many and all sorts of differentiae because of all bodies sharing in color, so that also the common [perceptibles, as well as colors,] are perceived through this [sense] above all (I mean by "common [perceptibles]"[6] shape and magnitude, motion, number); but hearing [informs us] only [of] the differentiae of sound, and, for [the benefit of] a few

4 Cf. *De Anima*, Book Two, Chapter 2, 413b1–4.

5 *De Anima*, Book Three, Chapter 13, 435a11–b3.

6 Cf. *De Anima*, Book Two, Chapter 6, 418a16–20 and Book Three, Chapter 1, 425a14–21ff.

[among the animals], also those of voice.[7] But by concomitance hearing contributes the greatest share toward understanding. For speech (*logos*) is responsible for learning, being audible, not in itself, but by concomitance; for it is put together from [audible] words, but each of the words is a token [for something not audible]. Therefore, among those who from birth have been deprived of one or the other of these senses, the blind have more understanding than the deaf and dumb.

Chapter 2

Now it has been spoken earlier[8] concerning the power that each of the senses has. But [concerning] the body [that constitutes the] sense organs in which [the senses] naturally come into being, [students of nature] now investigate by recourse to the elements of the bodies; but since they don't succeed in matching [the senses], which are five, with [the] four [elements],[9] they scramble concerning the fifth one. They all make sight[10] [consist] of fire, on account of their being ignorant of the cause of a certain *pathos*;[11] for when the eye is pressed and moved, fire appears to flash forth; and this naturally happens in the dark, or when the eyelids are closed; for also then there comes to be darkness. And this [*pathos*] contains a perplexity, also a different one [from the question of why it occurs at all]. For if, when one is perceiving, i.e., seeing, it isn't possible to be unaware of some seen [object], it is necessary, then, for the

7 Cf. *De Anima*, Book Two, Chapter 8, 420b5–421a6.

8 *De Anima*, Book Two, Chapters 7–11.

9 The four elements of bodies, to which Aristotle is referring here, are earth, water, air, and fire. Each of these elements was thought of as possessing one from each of the two fundamental pairs of contrary qualities, hot and cold and wet and dry. Thus, earth was understood as cold and dry, water as cold and wet, air as hot and wet, and fire as hot and dry. Cf. *On Coming into Being and Perishing* 330a30–b7.

10 The word for sight is *opsin*, a form of *opsis*, which can also refer to the organ of sight, or the eye—a meaning that should be kept in mind throughout.

11 On the Greek word *pathos*, cf. n.1 above.

eye itself to be seeing itself.[12] Why, then, does this not happen [to it] when it is at rest? Now what (pl.) is responsible for this [*pathos*], and for the perplexity and for sight being thought (*dokein*) to be fire, must be grasped from the following. For smooth [things] are of a nature to shine in the dark (and yet they do not produce light), and what is called "the black," i.e., the middle, of the eye appears 437b
smooth. And this [flashing] appears when the eye is moved, on account of the happening [then of what is] like the one [thing] becoming two. The speed of the motion produces this, so that that which sees and that which is seen seem (*dokein*) to be different. Wherefore also [the flashing] doesn't come about unless [the eye is moved] quickly and [unless] this happens in the dark; for what is smooth is of such a nature as to shine in the dark, for instance the heads of certain fish and the ink of the cuttlefish; and when the eye changes slowly it doesn't happen that that which sees and that which is seen seem (*dokein*) to be one and two at the same time. But [when it changes] in that way [i.e., quickly and in the dark], the eye itself sees itself, as [it] also [does] in reflection, since if it were fire, as Empedocles asserts[13] and as it has been written in the *Timaeus*,[14] and if[15] seeing happened because of light going out as

12 By "some seen [object]," Aristotle means something that can be touched as well as seen, i.e., not just a color or a flash of light, and his argument assumes that since it is dark there is nothing else, other than the eye itself, that this object could be. Aristotle also implicitly rejects the alternative that on these occasions one isn't really seeing, but merely imagining.

13 Empedocles, frag. 84, in *Die Fragmente der Vorsokratiker*, vol. 1, ed. H. Diels, 6th ed. rev. W. Kranz (1903; Berlin: Weidmann, 1951); quoted at 437b26–438a3.

14 Plato, *Timaeus* 45b4–d3, 67e4–68b1.

15 By adding this second condition, Aristotle leaves unaddressed the claim that the eye consists of fire but that seeing does not happen because of light going out from it. Now he presumably does so at least partly because the thinkers whom he is opposing in fact argue that seeing occurs because of light going out from the eye. But especially since he has not given an account of why things that are smooth, like the middle of the eye, shine in the dark (cf. also *De Anima* 419a2–7), the question remains whether he didn't think that fire, or whatever it is that produces light, plays a role, at least, in the constitution of the eye (cf. *De Anima* 425a5–6). How else, indeed, could he have accounted for what he takes here to be the case, namely, that the eye sees itself, in a sense, in the dark?

from a lantern, why wouldn't sight [i.e., the eye,] see also in the dark? And to assert that it [i.e., sight, or its visual ray,] is extinguished when it goes out in the dark, as Timaeus says,[16] is completely empty; for what "extinguishing" is there of light? For what is hot and dry—as the fire in charcoal, as well as flame, are thought (*dokei*) to be—is extinguished either by [what is] wet or [what is] cold; but neither of these [i.e., heat or dryness,] is manifest as belonging to light. But if perchance they do belong [to it], but escape our notice on account of [their being present only] to a slight degree, light ought to be extinguished during the day, in the rain, and [there ought] to come to be darkness in frosty weather more [than at other times]; flame, at any rate, and bodies that have been set on fire suffer this; but as it is, nothing of such a sort happens. Empedocles sometimes looks as if he holds that seeing [takes place] because light goes out [from the eye], as was said before;[17] he speaks, at any rate, as follows:

> As when someone, planning a journey, equips himself with a lamp,
> A flame of fire burning through the stormy night,
> Having fitted lantern plates as screens against all sorts of winds,
> And these scatter the breath of the blowing winds,
> But the fire leaping out through [them], insofar as it is thinner,
> Shines over the threshold with its unyielding beams;
> So the primeval fire hid itself, confined in membranes
> 438a [With] their fine tissues, in the round pupil [of the eye];
> And these [membranes] shut out the depth of the water that flowed around it,
> But the fire leapt out through [them], insofar as it was thinner.[18]

---

16 Plato, *Timaeus* 45d3–7.

17 At 437b10–13.

18 Empedocles, frag. 84 Diels-Kranz.

Sometimes he asserts that seeing [takes place] in this way, but sometimes by means of effluences from the things seen. Democritus, in that he asserts that [sight, or the eye] is water, speaks finely, but in that he supposes that seeing is [the having of] the appearance [that appears] in [the eye], not finely; for this happens because the eye is smooth, and [the appearance] is not in that [i.e., the eye], but in the one who sees [it]; for the affection (*pathos*) [in question] is reflection. But in general, as it looks, it was not yet clear [to students of nature] concerning the [things] that appear in [smooth surfaces] and [concerning] reflection. And it is strange also that it didn't occur to him to be perplexed why the eye alone sees, but none of the other [things] in which [such] likenesses appear. Now that sight [i.e., the eye,] is [constituted] of water is true, yet seeing doesn't happen insofar as [it is] water, but insofar as [it is] transparent, [a property] that is common also to air. But water is more easily kept in and more compressed than air; wherefore the pupil, i.e., the eye, is of water. And this is clear also in the facts (*ergōn*) themselves; for manifestly it is water that flows out from [eyes] that are decomposing, and in the earliest embryos it is exceedingly cold and bright; and the white of the eye in the [animals] that have blood is fatty and oily, which it is on account of this, [namely,] that what is wet may remain unfrozen. And on account of this the eye is, of the [parts of the] body, the [one] most resistant to cold; for no one has yet felt cold on the inside of his eyelids. And the eyes of the bloodless [animals] have a hard skin, and this makes their protection. And [to speak] generally, it is unreasonable that sight should see by means of something going out [from it, i.e., from the eye], and [for that something] to extend as far as the stars, or for it to go out up to a certain [distance] and to coalesce [with something], as some say.[19] For [it is] better than this [to say] that it coalesces [with something coming from its object] in the beginning (*en arkhē*) [i.e., in the ruling part,] of the eye. But even this is simple-minded; for what is it for light to coalesce with light? Or how can [coalescence] belong [to light]? For not [just] anything

19 Cf. Plato, *Timaeus* 45c2–d3.

438b whatsoever coalesces with [just] anything whatsoever. And how does the [light] inside [the eye coalesce] with that outside? For the membrane [of the eye] is in between. Now it has been spoken in other [speeches] concerning [there] not [being] seeing without light;[20] but whether it is light or air that is between what is seen and the eye, it is the motion through this that produces seeing. And reasonably, the inside [of the eye] is [composed] of water; for water is transparent. And [an object of sight] is seen, just as indeed outside [the eye] not without light, so also inside [it];[21] therefore it has to be transparent. And it is necessary for it to be water, since [it is] not air. For the soul or the perceptive [faculty] of the soul is not at the extremity of the eye, but evidently inside; wherefore [it is] necessary for the inside of the eye to be transparent and receptive of light. And this is clear also in the [things] that happen; for in fact to some [men], when in war they have been struck on the temple in such a way that the channels of [or from] the eye were severed, it seemed that there had come to be darkness, just as if a lamp had been extinguished, [and this happened] on account of the transparency that is called the pupil, like a sort of lantern, being cut off [from the ultimate sense organ]. So that if any of these [things] happens in the way we say, it is manifest that one must in this manner assign and attach each of the sense organs to one of the elements:[22] one must take that [part] of the eye which is

20 *De Anima* 418a31–b10. Aristotle defines light there as the actuality of what is transparent, insofar as it is transparent, a definition that helps to explain why his argument here presupposes that where there is light, there must be something transparent.

21 This clause is usually translated, "And [an object of sight] is seen, just as indeed not without light outside [the eye], so also [not without light] inside it"; but the Greek word order suggests the translation I have given. If my translation is correct, this clause may be referring to Aristotle's discussion earlier in this chapter of the flashing that is seen inside the eye when it is set in rapid motion in the dark (437a22–b10); and he may be making the additional point that there must be some light inside the eye, even when it is dark outside of it, for such flashing to be seen. Cf. n.15 above.

22 At 438b17, I read *hōs dei*, with manuscripts E, M, and Y, rather than *hōs ei dei*, with Biehl, who follows manuscripts L, P, S, and U. According to Biehl's text, the part of this sentence after the comma would be translated, instead

capable of seeing [to be] of water, that which is capable of perceiving sounds [to be] of air, and smelling[23] [to be] of fire. For what smelling is in actuality, this is what that which is capable of smelling is potentially; for what is perceptible [by sense] makes the sense work in actuality, so that it is necessary for it [i.e., the sense,] to be present [as] what [it was] in its potentiality before. And odor is a smoke-like exhalation, and smoke-like exhalation is [composed] of fire. Wherefore also the sense organ of smelling is proper to the place around the brain; for [it is] the material belonging to the cold [that] is potentially hot. And the coming into being of the eye is in the same manner; for [the eye] is constituted from the brain; for this is the wettest and coldest of the parts in the body. And that which is capable of touch is of [i.e., is perceptive of,] earth.[24] And that which is capable of taste is a certain form of 439a

---

of as "it is manifest that one must in this manner assign and attach each of the sense organs to one of the elements: one must take...," as "it is manifest that if one must in this manner assign and attach each of the sense organs to one of the elements, one must take...." But it seems to me that Biehl's reading, which is also the reading of nearly all the more recent editors, doesn't give sufficient weight to the words translated as "in this manner." Moreover, the doubt that Biehl's text raises, as to whether Aristotle truly accepts that it is possible to assign each of the sense organs to one of the elements, is implicit in the passage in any case. One can see this, for instance, from the fact that instead of assigning the sense organ of smelling to fire, as he will assign (part of) the organ of seeing to water (and part of the organ of hearing, as it seems, to air), Aristotle will say that the act of smelling, like its object odor, is (i.e., consists) of fire; and he will have to admit that the organ of smelling is itself cold, and hence not fiery. Compare *De Anima* 425a5, where he suggested, at any rate, that the organ of smell is composed chiefly of water or air.

23 The Greek word translated as "smelling" is *osphrēsis*, which can mean the organ of smelling (as in this context one expects it to mean at first). But it can also mean the sense of smell, and even the sense of smell in actuality, namely, the act of smelling; and this last meaning, as the continuation of the passage makes clear, is what must be intended here.

24 It would appear at first that this sentence means that the organ of touch is constituted of earth, i.e., the element that is cold and dry. But from the sequel, where Aristotle suggests, at any rate, that this organ is quite hot (since it is near the heart), it is more likely that he means here what I suggest with my bracketed addition, namely, that the object of the organ of touch (and thus, more immediately, of the act of touching) is (composed of) earth, just

touch. And on account of this, their sense organ, [that] of taste and of touch, is near the heart;[25] for this is opposed to the brain, and it is the hottest of the parts. And concerning the parts of the body that are capable of sense perception, let things have been determined in this manner.

Chapter 3

Concerning the perceptibles[26] in accord with each sense organ—I mean, namely, color and sound and odor and flavor and touch[27]—

---

as he meant above that the object of smelling is (composed of) fire. As for the objection to this interpretation—an objection already raised by the ancient commentator Alexander—that the sense of touch perceives the qualities of all four of the elements, and not just of earth, one might reply that Aristotle has to jump through hoops in order to assign each sense to one of the elements, and that earth and its qualities (i.e., cold and dry) are at any rate among the objects of the sense of touch, as they are not among the objects of the senses of sight, hearing, and smell.

25 Cf. *De Anima* 423b1–26.

26 The Greek word (*aisthētōn*) that I translate here as "perceptibles" is the same word that I translated as "sense-perceptibles" in the title of this treatise. Although the English word "perceptible" can have a wider meaning than "perceptible through the senses," and although Aristotle sometimes uses the Greek word for "to perceive" with a wider meaning than "to perceive through the senses," he uses this adjectival form only, so far as I can tell, for what is perceptible through the senses. Having made this limitation explicit in my translation of the title, I will continue to translate the term more simply as "perceptible" or "perceptibles" in the text itself.

27 Instead of naming a perceptible object of touch, as he has just named those of sight, hearing, smell, and taste, Aristotle speaks here of touch itself, rather than its object. This anomaly is presumably related to the fact that, as he said in *De Anima*, Book Two, Chapter 11 (422b32–33), it isn't clear what the one [kind of object] is that underlies the various pairs of touchable contraries, as sound is in the case of the audible ones (and color in the case of the visible ones, etc.). He did go on to say, later in that chapter, that the touchables are the differentiae of body as body (*De Anima* 423b27), but he never presented "body" as the answer to the question of what it is that underlies the various pairs of touchable contraries, and he didn't speak of it there, just as he does not here, as the perceptible object of the sense of touch. On the other hand, he does speak here of the sense of touch as a single sense, even though the

it has been spoken in general in our [speeches] about soul, what their work (*ergon*) is and what their being actual (*energein*) is in relation to each of the sense organs.[28] But whatever [it is that] one should say any one of them [is], for instance what color [is] or what sound [is] or what odor or flavor [is], and likewise also concerning touch, we must examine, and first concerning color. Now each [of these] is spoken of in two ways, as [it is] in actuality (*energeiāi*) and as [it is when it is] potentially [that]. Color in actuality, and sound, how they are [each] the same as or different from the senses in actuality, namely, from seeing and hearing, has been said in our [speeches] about soul.[29] But being what, each of them will produce sense perception, i.e., its actuality, let us say now.[30] Now as it has been said concerning light in those [speeches], that it is the color of the transparent by concomitance[31]—for whenever there is some-

---

difficulty that he raised in *De Anima* regarding the unity of the various pairs of touchable contraries had led him to suggest that what we call the sense of touch might in fact be several different senses.

28 *De Anima*, Book Two, Chapter 5 (416b32–418a6) and Chapter 12 (424a17–b18). Note that the word *energein*, which I have translated here as "being actual," might also be translated as "being at work."

29 *De Anima*, Book Three, Chapter 2 (425b26–426a26).

30 Aristotle has said in *De Anima*, Book Two, Chapter 7 (418a31–b2, 419a17–20), that color is capable of causing motion in a transparent medium, such as air, which in turn acts on the organ of sight, so as to produce (actual) seeing of that very color. But he hasn't yet said, at least not as adequately as he thinks possible, what it is in a being that is its color.

31 *De Anima*, Book Two, Chapter 7 (418b9–13), where Aristotle says that light is like the color of the transparent. In that passage, Aristotle's fuller claim was that "light is as it were the color of the transparent, when it is transparent in the complete sense through the agency of fire or of such a thing as the body up above." Here, by contrast, he does not say that light is the color of the transparent when it is "transparent in the complete sense," but instead speaks of it as the color of the transparent "by concomitance." Now the expression "by concomitance" seems to point to what he will say next, something that he had indeed made clear in *De Anima*, namely, that light is the presence in the transparent of something else, of something fiery, that sometimes belongs to it but sometimes does not. And his failure to repeat the *De Anima*'s reference to the transparent "in the complete sense" might be in keeping with what he had indicated at the beginning of this chapter, namely, that the perceptibles are what they are, in the complete sense, only as actually

thing fiery in a transparent [body], its presence is light, whereas its being lacking is darkness; but what we mean (*legomen*) by "transparent" is not peculiar to air or water, nor to [any] other of the bodies that are spoken of (*legomenōn*) in this way [i.e., as "transparent"], but it is a sort of common nature and power, which is not separable, but is in these, and [which] is present [also] in the other bodies, in some more so and others less so;[32] accordingly, as it is necessary that there be some extremity of bodies, [so] also [must there be some extremity] of this [nature]—so then the nature of light is in the transparent [that is] indeterminate [in shape]; and of the transparent in bodies,[33] that there would be some extremity [is] clear;

---

perceived. But a more important difference between the statements in the two treatises may be indicated by Aristotle's dropping the qualifier "as it were" (*hoion*) in speaking here of light as the color of the transparent. For in the sequel he will go on to state, and even stress, something that the treatment of color in *De Anima* had never quite said, namely, that transparent media, such as air and water, are themselves colored (439a33–b14).

32 It is striking that Aristotle chooses to use the word "transparent" for bodies that are not transparent in the ordinary sense of the word, which would be bodies through which one can see the color of something else. But if we look back at his definition of the transparent in *De Anima* (418b4–6), we note that even there he spoke of it in an unusual way. For rather than defining it as that through which one can see the color of something else, he defined it as "what is visible, but not visible in itself, to speak simply, but [visible] on account of a color belonging to something else (*di'allotrion khrōma*)." Now in his discussion in *De Anima* he never developed, at least not so far as I can see, the suggestion that the transparent is itself visible. But he will do so in this treatise, not only by speaking of it as possessing color, as he has just done (cf. n. 31 above), but in other ways as well (e.g., 445a8–13). But of more immediate importance is the fact that the definition of the transparent in *De Anima* can be seen to apply not only to bodies that are transparent in the ordinary sense of the word, but also to opaque bodies (cf. the reference to "all" bodies at 439b8–9). For those bodies are indeed visible on account of—or "through," as one can also translate Aristotle's preposition *dia*—a color belonging to something else, since they are visible on account of light (which Aristotle has just spoken of as a color), which belongs to something else, i.e., to the transparent in the ordinary sense of the word "transparent."

33 Here Aristotle seems to be using the word "bodies" to refer only to those bodies which, unlike air and water, hold their own shape, rather than adapting themselves to the shape of their containers. And some of his uses of this word later in the chapter (e.g., 439b5, b17) clearly refer only to such bodies. In his

while that this is color [is] manifest from what (pl.) happens. For color is either in the limit [of bodies] or [it is] the limit; wherefore also the Pythagoreans used to call the surface [of a body] "color,"[34] for it [i.e., color,] is in the limit of the body; but it is not at all the limit of the body[, which limit is, instead, its surface]; rather, one must hold that the same nature [i.e., the transparent,] that is colored outside [i.e., in the air and water that surround the determinately shaped bodies,] [is present] inside [them] as well. And both air and water are manifestly colored; for their brightness is [something] of this sort. But in those cases, on account of its [being] in [something] indeterminate [in shape], neither the air nor the sea has the same color (*khroian*) from close by and to those who are approaching and from far away; but in bodies, unless the surrounding [medium] makes [it] change, the appearance (*phantasia*) too of the color (*khroas*) is defined/determined. It is clear, then, that the same [something] is receptive of the color (*khroas*) both in those cases and in these. The transparent, then, insofar as it is present in bodies (and it is present, more so or less so, in [them] all), makes them share in color. And since the color (*khroa*) is in the limit, it would be in the limit of this. So that the limit of the transparent in a body that is defined/determined [in shape] would be color. And it is present equally in all [bodies], the transparent [ones] themselves, for instance water and if there is anything else of this sort, and in as many as appear to have a color peculiar [to them] at their extremity. Now it is possible for that which in air produces light to

---

discussion of the transparent in *De Anima*, Aristotle had referred to (some of) these bodies as "solids" (*De Anima* 418b6–7), but he never uses the term "solid" in this treatise. Indeed, the very fact that the fiery something that produces light in air and water can be present in these bodies but also absent from them (cf. 439b14–16) might lead one to wonder in what sense they are really solid.

34 The Greek word translated here as "color" is *khroian*, from *khroia* (or *khroa*), a word whose primary meaning is skin. The word that Aristotle had been using for color is *khrōma*. Although I cannot discern, in the continuation of this chapter, a clear pattern in his choice to use one word or the other, there may be one that I don't see, and so whenever he uses some form of the word *khroa*, I will include a transliteration of the Greek word in parentheses.

be in the transparent[, as it exists in determinately shaped bodies as well], but it is [also] possible [for it] not [to be in it], but to be lacking. So then just as there [e.g., in the air,] light, on the one hand, and darkness, on the other, [come to be], so in bodies the white and the black come to be.[35] But we must now speak about the other colors, distinguishing in how many ways it is admissible for them to come into being. For it is admissible that, when the white and the black are placed next to each other in such a way that, while each of them is invisible on account of [its] smallness, the [combination that results] from both is visible, [the other colors] come to be in this way. For this cannot appear either white or black; but since it is necessary that it have some color, whereas neither of these is possible, it is necessary that [the color] be something mixed and some different species (*eidos*) of color (*khroas*). So then it is possible to take it in this way that there are more colors (*khroas*) besides the white and the black, and [that they are] many because of the ratio [between the white and the black]; for it is possible that they have been placed beside each other [in ratios of] three to two, and three to four, and according to other numbers, and [it is possible] that some are [juxtaposed] according to no [numerical] ratio at all, but according to some incommensurable [relation of] excess and deficiency, and for them [i.e., the other colors,] to be in the same manner as the [musical] consonances;[36] for [it is possible that] the colors [with ratios of white to black] in easily calculable numbers, just as the consonances there,[37] are the ones of the colors that seem to be

35 This clause, by asserting a parallelism between the air becoming light and dark and bodies becoming white and black, suggests that a white body's whiteness depends on the presence of that fiery something that causes light to come to be in air or water. In other words, it suggests that a white body's whiteness does not belong to it simply in itself, but that it results from some kind of interaction between the body and that fiery something, an interaction that presumably takes place only when that fiery something has also produced light in the surrounding medium.

36 The term translated as "consonances" (*sumphōniais*) refers, in this clause, though not in those that follow, to dissonances as well.

37 The ratio of the string lengths that produce notes an octave apart is two to one, of those that produce a perfect fifth it is three to two, and of those that

most pleasant, for instance purple and crimson and a few such [colors], on account of which cause the [musical] consonances are also few, whereas those not in [ratios according to] numbers [are] the other colors; or [else] that indeed all the colors (*khroas*) are in numbers [i.e., composed of white and black juxtaposed according to numerical ratios], with some [being] well-ordered [in the juxtaposition of their elements], while others are disordered, and that these themselves [i.e., the colors that are in numbers], when they are not pure [instances of whatever color they are], come into being on account of not being such [i.e., not being pure,] in [their] numbers.[38] So then this is one manner of [accounting for] the coming into being of the colors, while another [is] that they appear through each other, as painters sometimes produce [them]—they smear one color (*khroan*) over a different, more vivid one, as when they wish to represent something appearing in water or in air—and as the **440a**

---

produce a perfect fourth it is four to three. These three intervals, and especially the octave and the perfect fifth, have long been regarded as the most consonant. The tritone, on the other hand (namely, the half-octave or the interval of three whole tones, which occurs, for instance, between C and F-sharp), is a particularly striking dissonance, and the ratio of its string lengths is the incommensurable ratio between the diagonal and the side of a square.

38 This account of how all the colors might consist of white and black in numerical ratios is difficult, and it has been interpreted in quite a few ways by editors and translators. My version differs from all the others that I have seen by taking "these themselves" to refer to all the colors, and not merely those that are disordered; and it differs from nearly all of them by translating the last clause as "come into being on account of not being such in numbers," rather than "come to be such on account of not being in numbers." That alternative translation has the obvious difficulty that it contradicts the premise of this whole account, namely, that all the colors are in numbers, and editors and translators have tried to resolve this contradiction in various ways. Biehl, for instance, suggests a possible emendation to the text so that the sentence would end with "come to be such on account of not being in <the same> numbers." But on my interpretation, colors that are not pure in their numbers would be, for instance, a shade of purple that tends toward green: if purple consisted of black and white in the ratio of three to two (or twenty-seven to eighteen), while green consisted of them in the ratio of four to three (or twenty-four to eighteen), the actual color might be an impure purple consisting of them in a ratio, say, of twenty-six to eighteen. Note that according to Aristotle there are only seven or so species of color. See 442a19–25 and 440b23–25.

sun, by itself, appears white, but, through mist and smoke, crimson. And there will be many colors (*khroai*) also in this way [of accounting for the intermediate colors], in the same manner as in the [one] spoken of before; for there would be a certain ratio between the [amounts of the color] on the surface and those [of the color] underneath, while some would not even be in a [numerical] ratio at all. Now to say, as also the ancient [thinkers did], that the colors (*khroias*) are effluences, and that they are seen on account of such a cause, [is] strange; for at all events [it is] necessary for them to make sense perception [take place] through touch [i.e., through touch or contact between the effluences and the sense organs], so that [it is] better to assert straightaway that sense perception comes into being by the medium between the sense [and its object] being set in motion by the perceptible, by touch [i.e., touch or contact between the perceptible object and the medium, and then between the medium and the sense organs,] but not the effluences.[39] Now in the case of the [white and the black colors] placed next to each other, as it is necessary to assume an invisible magnitude, so also [must one assume] an imperceptible time, so that the [single] motions might escape notice as they arrive and might seem to be one on account of their appearing together. But here [i.e., on the as-

39 Editors, including Biehl, and also translators, have thought that this sentence (beginning from "Now to say...") doesn't belong in the text, at least not here, on the grounds that it interrupts the account of the various ways of producing the colors other than white and black. On the other hand, it is present here in all the manuscripts, and so I have chosen to translate it. And assuming that it belongs here, it is striking that Aristotle would choose this particular context to remind us that all sense perception, and sight in particular, takes place through touch or contact of the medium with the organ of sense. Perhaps he saw a certain analogy between the different motions that the color on a painter's surface produces in the sense organ, depending on whether or not it is moved by another color underneath it (cf. 440a23–26), and the different motions that the medium of sight produces in the sense organ, depending on the different colors of the visible objects that set it in motion. And this analogy is made more perfect by the fact, to which Aristotle has called attention earlier in this chapter, that the medium itself (when there is light) possesses color. (On my use of the words "but not" here to translate the Greek *kai mē*, see Herbert Weir Smyth, *Greek Grammar*, rev. Gordon M. Messing [1920; Cambridge, Mass.: Harvard University Press, 1971], para. 2871.)

sumption of a surface overlay of one color upon another,] there is no necessity, but the color on the surface will not produce the same sort of motion when it is unmoved, as [it does] when it is moved, by what lies underneath it. Wherefore also it appears different and neither white nor black. So that if it is not admissible for there to be any invisible magnitude, but every [magnitude] is visible from some distance, still this [and without requiring the assumption of invisible magnitudes] would be a mixture, of a sort, of colors. And even in that [former] way, nothing prevents some color (*khroan*) [that is] common [and intermediate between white and black] from appearing to those [who are looking] from far away; [but only from far away,] for that there is no invisible magnitude must be examined in the [speeches that are coming] later.[40] But if there is a mixture of bodies, not only in this manner which some suppose, with the **440b** least [bodies] being placed next to one another, and [being] unclear to us [i.e., separately invisible,] through sense perception, but [if there is a mixture] altogether in every way completely, as has been said about all [mixtures] universally in our [speeches] concerning mixture[41]—for in that [other] way such [bodies] alone are mixed as admit of being divided into their least [parts], just as human beings, horses, or seeds; for a human being is the least [part] of [a multitude of] human beings, and a horse of [a multitude of] horses; so that by the placement of these next to one another the multitude [consisting] of both together has been mixed; but we do not say that one human being has been mixed with one horse; but as for such [bodies] as are not divided into the least [part], it isn't admissible for a mixture of these to come about in this manner, but [only] by being mixed in every way, [and it is bodies mixed in this way] that are also of a nature to be most mixed; and how this is able to come to be has been said before in our [speeches] about mixture[42]—

40 See 445b3–446a15.

41 *On Coming into Being and Perishing* 328a5–18ff.

42 *On Coming into Being and Perishing* 328a18–b22.

but[43] that it [is] necessary when [bodies are] mixed for the colors (*khroas*) also to be mixed [is] clear, and [also that] this is the sovereign cause of there being many colors (*khroias*), but not surface overlay nor placement next to one another; for [the] one color (*khroa*) of [the bodies] that are mixed doesn't appear [as one] from far away but not from nearby, but from everywhere. And there will be many colors (*khroai*) on account of its being admissible for [the bodies] that are mixed to be mixed with each other in many ratios, with some [being mixed] in numbers, and others according to excess alone. And with regard to the other [things that could be said about the possible arrangements], it is admissible to speak, also concerning the [bodies that are] mixed, in the same manner as [we spoke about] the colors placed next to each other or [with one] on the surface [of the other]. But on account of what cause there are determinately many, and not infinitely many, species (*eidē*) of colors, and of flavors and sounds, we will say later.

Chapter 4

What color is, then, and on account of what cause there are many colors (*khroai*) has been said. And what concerns sound and voice has been said earlier in our [speeches] concerning soul.[44] But we must speak now concerning odor and flavor. For they are nearly the same affection (*pathos*), but each of the two is not in the same [kinds

43 Here begins the main clause that completes the sentence that began with an if-clause at 440a31.

44 *De Anima*, Book Two, Chapter 8. Since Aristotle also spoke of color in *De Anima*, this remark implies that he regarded his account there of sound and voice as being adequate, for saying what these are, in a way that his account of color was not. And he is probably referring, in particular, to his assertion there that sound is a motion of air (or water) produced by one body striking against another, and that voice is a sound that some animals produce when they cause some of the air that they breathe in to strike against their windpipe. *De Anima* 419b18–20, 420a7–9; 420b27–29.

of bodies as the other].[45] The genus of flavors is more distinctly clear to us than that of odor. And the cause of this is that the sense of smell [that] we have [is] the worst among the animals and [the 441a
worst] of the senses in ourselves, whereas the sense of touch [that we have is] the most precise among the animals. And taste is a sort of touch. Now the nature of water wishes[46] to be flavorless; but it is necessary either for water to have in itself the genera of flavors, [with them being] imperceptible on account of the smallness [of the amounts], as Empedocles asserts,[47] or for it to be the sort of material as an aggregate of all the seeds of flavors [is], and for them all to come into being from water, but some from one part [of it] and others from another, or for water to have no differentiation [within itself] but for what acts [upon it] to be the cause [of flavors], for instance, if someone would assert [that] heat or the sun [is this cause]. And of these [alternatives], the falsity [of speaking] as Empedocles speaks is exceedingly easy to see at a glance; for we see that the juices[48] [of fruits] change [in flavor] through the action of heat when the fruits are picked [and placed] in the sun or exposed to fire, as [is to be expected] if they don't become of such a sort by drawing [their flavor] from the water [in the soil], but change in the fruit itself, and [we see] that when they are extracted [from the fruits] and kept in store, they become, on account of [the passage of] time, harsh, from [having been] sweet, and [also] bitter and of all sorts [of flavors], and that when they are boiled, they change into all the genera, so to speak, of flavors. And [it is] likewise also impossible for water, [understood as] consisting of an aggregate of

---

45 Aristotle will go on to say that flavor is an affection in liquid (and, in particular, water), but that odor is an affection in air and water alike (and insofar as it is perceptible by human beings, only in air). See 441b19–21, 442b27–29.

46 The Greek word translated as "wishes" is *bouletai*, which in Aristotle seems frequently to mean little more than "tends [in the direction of being]." However, his choice of the word *bouletai* might suggest—whether he is speaking only rhetorically or more seriously—an intention on the part of nature to achieve the end or goal that is referred to.

47 It is not known where Empedocles made this claim.

48 The Greek word translated as "juices" is *khumous*, a form of *khumos*, which is also the word for flavor.

all their seeds, to be [the] material [of flavors]; for we see that different flavors come into being from the same [water] as [their] nourishment. There remains, then, that the water changes by being acted upon in some way. Now it is manifest that [it is] not by the power of heat [that] it gets this power that we call flavor; for water is the thinnest of all the liquids, [thinner] even than oil itself; but oil spreads further than water on account of its stickiness, whereas water is non-cohesive; wherefore water [is] also harder to keep in one's hand than oil. And since water, [by] itself alone, is manifestly not thickened at all when it is heated, [it is] clear that there would be some different cause [of its becoming flavored]; for all the flavors/juices have thickness more [than it does]; but heat is a contributory cause. And as many flavors as [there are] in fruits, these
441b are manifestly present also in the earth. Wherefore also many of the old natural philosophers assert that water is [with respect to flavor] like whatever sort of earth it travels through. And this is especially clear in the case of salty waters; for salt is a certain form (*eidos*) of earth. And the [waters] that filter through ash, which is bitter, produce flavor [that is] bitter. And there are many springs, some bitter, others vinegary, and others having all sorts of other flavors. And as is reasonable, the genus of flavors comes into being most of all in the [things] that grow [from the earth, i.e., in plants]. For the wet, like the other [contraries], is naturally acted upon by its contrary; and contrary [to it] is the dry. Wherefore also it is acted upon in a way by fire; for the nature of fire is dry. But heat is [the] peculiar [attribute] of fire, whereas dryness [is that] of earth, as has been said in our [speeches] concerning [the] elements.[49] So then [fire] as fire and [earth] as earth are not at all of a nature [such as] to act and to be acted upon, nor [is] any other [element]; but insofar as a contrariety is present in each [of them] they all both act and are acted upon. So then just as those who wash away colors and flavors[50] in

49 *On Coming into Being and Perishing* 331a3–6. As for the dryness of fire, cf. 330b1–5 (and, as for what Aristotle means by "dryness," cf. 329b30–32).

50 Aristotle is perhaps referring here to the flavors in dry food. Cf. *De Anima* 422a10–11, a17–19.

what is wet make the water [in which they wash them] to be [of] such [a color or flavor], so also nature [does to] the dry and the earthy, and filtering the wet through the dry and earthy and causing motion/change[51] [in it] by means of heat, renders it of a certain sort. And this is flavor, the affection in the wet, coming into being through the agency of the aforesaid dry, [that is] capable of altering the sense of taste, [already present] as a potentiality, into actuality; for it brings the perceptive [faculty] into this [state, namely, perceiving], which was [already] present potentially before;[52] for perceiving corresponds not to learning, but to [actively] contemplating [what one already knows].[53] And that flavors are either an affection

51 The Greek word translated here as "causing motion/change" is *kinousa*, a participle related to the noun *kinēsis*. Now I have been translating *kinēsis* as "motion," and for the sake of consistency I will not stop doing so; but Aristotle uses the word not only for locomotion, or change of place, but also for growth and decay, or change of size, and for alteration, or change of quality. And since he is speaking in this passage of alteration in water that is being filtered, the most natural English translation would be "causing change," rather than "causing motion."

52 The Greek participle translated here as "which was [already] present potentially before" is *proüparkhon*, which I interpret as agreeing with the word I have translated as "this," which in turn I interpret as referring to "actuality" (*energeia*). But the participle might conceivably be construed instead with the Greek words that I have translated as "the perceptive [faculty]," so that the clause would be rendered, "for it brings the perceptive [faculty], which was [already] present potentially before, into this [condition, namely, perceiving]"; and this would imply, on the reasonable assumption that it is not a mere repetition of the first part of the sentence, that even the perceptive faculty as a potentiality [for actual perceiving] was only potentially present prior to the alteration produced by flavor. And since Aristotle could easily have excluded this alternative reading by using a feminine form, instead of the neuter, of the pronoun translated as "this"—which would indeed have been the normal form, since its referent, "actuality," is feminine in Greek—and a feminine form of the participle *proüparkhon*, so that it could not agree with the (neuter) words for "the perceptive [faculty]," I believe that he intended this reading, at least as a secondary one. As for what it might mean, see the following footnote, n. 53.

53 Cf. *De Anima* 417b18–19. Though this clause begins with the conjunction "for," it is not clear how it explains or justifies the previous one, since it would seem that the knowledge gained by learning also belonged to the soul potentially beforehand, though in a different sense of the word "potentially" than

or a lack [in the wet], not of every [sort of] dry, but of that which is nutritive, one must grasp from this, that neither the dry without the wet nor the wet without the dry [has flavor]; for not [either] one of them [is] nourishment for animals, but [only] what is mixed [from both of them is]. And of the nourishment taken in by the animals, [it is] the touchables, of the perceptibles [in it], [that] are productive of growth and wasting, for what is taken in is responsible for these insofar as [it is] hot and cold[, which are perceived through **442a** touch]; for these produce both growth and wasting; but the [nourishment] taken in nourishes insofar as it is tasteable; for all [things] are nourished by the sweet, either simply or as it is mixed [with other flavors]. We must make distinctions concerning these [things] in our [speeches] concerning generation,[54] but now [we must] touch upon them as much as [is] necessary. For heat makes [the animal] grow and works up the nourishment, and it draws [upward] what is light, while it leaves behind what is salty and bitter, on account of weight [i.e., the weight of the salty and bitter]. What external heat, then, does in external bodies, this the [heat] in the nature of the animals and plants [does in them];[55] wherefore they are nourished by what is sweet. And the other flavors are mixed into the nourishment in the same manner as [we add] the salty and vinegary, as relish. And these [things occur] in order to counter the sweet's

---

the knowledge that had already been acquired (cf. *De Anima* 417a21–30). And this difficulty is compounded by the fact that Aristotle speaks here of flavor as being capable of "altering" the potential sense of taste into actuality, whereas in *De Anima*, though he had spoken of learning as taking place through alteration in the learner, he had said that the transition from a state of knowing to the active contemplation of what one knows is not alteration, at least not of the usual sort (*De Anima* 417a31–b9). Could he be suggesting, then, that flavor acts upon the perceptive faculty in two stages, only the first of which is alteration, strictly speaking, and only the second of which is perceiving or tasting in the proper sense of the word? Cf. *De Anima* 417b17–18.

54 Cf. *On the Generation of Animals* 776a28ff.

55 Cf. *Meteorologica* 355a33–b12, where Aristotle says that the sweet and drinkable water in the sea is drawn up into the air, since it is light, whereas the salty and heavier water is left behind; and he then goes on to compare this process to what happens to the food taken in by living beings.

being excessively nutritive[56] and prone to lie on the surface [of the contents of the stomach]. And just as the [intermediate] colors are [constituted] from a mixture of white and black, so the [intermediate] flavors [are constituted] from sweet and bitter. And they are each, indeed, in a ratio, as [having] more [of one] and less [of the other], whether according to particular numbers of the mixing and motion/change or indeterminately [i.e., in a ratio of incommensurable quantities]. And the [flavors] that when mixed produce pleasure, these are in numbers. Now then only the flavor of the sweet is oily,[57] the salty and bitter [are] pretty much[58] the same, and the harsh and pungent and astringent and vinegary [are] in the middle. For the species of flavors and those of colors are pretty much (*skhedon*) equal. For there are seven[59] species of both, if someone puts grey, as is reasonable, to be a sort of black; for it remains that yellow is [a variety] of white, as the oily is [a variety] of the sweet, and that crimson and purple and green and blue [are] in the middle of the

56 At 442a10–11, I read *dia to antispan tōi lian trophimon einai to gluku*, with manuscripts L, S, U, and P, rather than *dia to anti pantōn lian trophimon einai to gluku*, with Biehl, who follows manuscript Y. According to Biehl's text, this passage could perhaps be translated, instead of as "to counter the sweet's being excessively nutritive," as "on account of the sweet being, compared with all [the other flavors], excessively nutritive."

57 Cf. 442a23, "the oily is [a variety] of the sweet."

58 The Greek word translated as "pretty much" is *skhedon*, which can also mean "nearly."

59 I read *hepta*, or "seven," in accordance with all the manuscripts, as opposed to *hex*, or "six," a nineteenth-century emendation accepted by Biehl. Biehl's reason for accepting this emendation is that one arrives at seven species of color only by treating grey as a variety of black or yellow as one of white, while treating the other of these pairs as two colors, and one arrives at seven flavors only by treating salty as a variety of bitter or oily as one of sweet, while treating the other pair as two flavors. Indeed, on the basis of Aristotle's discussion one could just as easily, if not more easily, come up with six, or eight, colors and flavors as with seven. But it seems better to me to accept the unanimous evidence of all our manuscripts and to read "seven." Moreover, Aristotle has said only that the species of flavors and those of colors are "pretty much," or "nearly" (*skhedon*), equal, and this suggests to me that he thought there was a (limited) degree of arbitrariness in the division of colors and flavors into species, and that he regarded seven as the most convenient definite number.

white and black, while the other [shades of color] are mixed from these. And just as black is a lack of white in the [determinately shaped] transparent [body], so the salty and bitter [are a lack] of the sweet in the nutritive liquid. Wherefore also the ash of all the [things] that burn [is] bitter; for what is drinkable has been extracted from them. Democritus and most of the natural philosophers, those who speak about sense perception, do something [that
442b is] most strange; for they make all the perceptibles touchables.[60] And yet if this is indeed so, [it is] clear that also each of the other senses is a sort of touch; but that this [is] impossible is not hard to see at a glance. Furthermore, they treat as proper [to this single sense] the [perceptibles that are the] common [objects] of all the senses; for magnitude and shape and the rough and the smooth, and furthermore, the sharp and the blunt in [bodily] masses,[61] are common [objects] of the senses, if not of all [of them], at any rate of sight and touch. Wherefore also [people] are deceived concerning these, but they are not deceived concerning the proper [perceptibles], for instance, sight [is not deceived] concerning color and hearing [is not deceived] concerning sounds. But these [thinkers] reduce the proper [perceptibles] to these [common ones], just as Democritus [does] the white and the black; for he asserts that the one is rough and the other smooth, and he reduces the flavors to the shapes [of the atoms]. And yet [it belongs] either to no one [sense] or more to sight to recognize the common [perceptibles, such as the shapes]. But if indeed [this belongs] to taste more [than to sight or to the other senses], it belongs to the most precise sense to discriminate among (*diakrinein*) the smallest [differences], at any rate, in each genus, so that taste ought both to best perceive the

60 Cf. 440a15–18.

61 The Greek words translated as "in [bodily] masses" are *en tois ogkois*. Perhaps Aristotle includes them because the word translated here as "sharp" can also mean "keen" or "high-pitched" or "vinegary," and the word translated as "blunt" can also mean "dull"; and taken in any of these ways they would not be common objects of the senses. And perhaps he uses the word "masses," rather than the more common word for "bodies," because bodies can also have flavors and characteristic pitches (cf. *De Anima* 420a26–29), in addition to the sharp edges and blunt surfaces that belong to them as masses.

other common [perceptibles] and to be most capable of judging (*kritikōtatēn*) shapes[, but it is not]. Furthermore, all the perceptibles have contrariety, for instance, in color the white [is contrary] to the black and in flavors the bitter [is contrary] to the sweet; but a shape doesn't seem to be contrary to a shape; for to which of the polygons [is] the circular contrary? Furthermore, since the [kinds of] shapes are infinite, [it is] necessary [according to this account] for the flavors also to be infinite; for why would one [flavor, i.e., shape,] produce sense perception, while another one would not produce [it]? And so it has been spoken concerning the tasteable and flavor; for the other affections (*pathē*) of flavors have their proper inquiry in the natural philosophy concerning plants.[62]

Chapter 5

In the same manner [as concerning flavors,] one must think also about odors; for just that which the dry does in the wet, [and which makes it flavored,] this the flavored wet[63] does in another genus, [which is] in air and water alike. We have been speaking now of the transparent as [what is] common to these [i.e., air and water],
but it is smellable not as transparent, but as able to wash or rinse 443a
flavored dryness; for the [object] of smell is not only in air but also in water. [This is] clear in the case of fish and the shell-skinned [animals];[64] for they manifestly do smell, although neither is there

62 Aristotle refers in a number of places to what he has said concerning plants, and so it is assumed that he wrote a treatise or treatises about them. But although we have two treatises on plants by his pupil Theophrastus, nothing of his own has survived.

63 Since a flavored body is necessarily a mixture of wet and dry (441b25–27; cf. 443a9–12), the flavored source of odor in the medium of odor can be called either "the flavored wet," as Aristotle calls it here, or "the flavored dry," as he will below (443a7; cf. 443a1–2). He may speak of it here as the flavored wet, immediately after having spoken of the wet as what has been flavored (by the dry), in order to give more emphasis to his claim that odor comes from something flavored.

64 The Greek word for "shell-skinned" is *ostrakoderma*, which derives from the word *ostrakon*, which means "an earthen pot" or "potsherd," and from *derma*,

air in the water (for air rises to the surface when it comes to be in [it]) nor do they themselves breathe. If, then, someone should put both air and water down [as] wet,[65] the nature of the flavored dry in a wet [medium] would be odor, and what is of such a sort [would be] smellable. That the affection (*pathos*) is from [something] flavored [is] clear from the [things] that have and that don't have odor; for the elements are odorless, namely, fire air earth water, on account of the wet as well as the dry [ones] of them[66] being flavorless, unless something mixed in produces [flavor]. Wherefore also the sea has odor; for it has flavor and dryness [mixed in]. And salt is more odorous than washing soda—[the] oil that exudes from it makes [this] clear—while washing soda is more [entirely] of earth. Furthermore, a stone is odorless, for it is flavorless, but logs are odorous, for they are flavored; and of these, those that are watery [are] less [so]. Furthermore, in the case of metals, gold is odorless, for it is flavorless, but bronze and iron are odorous. And when what is wet [in them] is burned [away],[67] the slag of all [of them] becomes more odorless. And silver and tin [are] more odorous than some [metals] and less so than others; for they are watery. To some [thinkers], the smoke-like exhalation, which is [constituted] of earth and air in common, seems to be odor. And all are led toward

---

which means "skin." It refers to invertebrates, such as oysters, clams, and snails, that have potsherd-like shells, as distinct from those with soft shells, such as crabs. They are mostly, though not exclusively, water animals. Cf. *On the History of Animals* 527b35–528b10; *On the Generation of Animals* 761a13–24.

65 Aristotle defines the word *hugron*, which I translate as "wet," as that which has no determinate boundary of its own, but which is easily bounded by whatever contains it (cf. *On Coming into Being and Perishing* 329b30–31). I might therefore have translated it as "fluid," except that Aristotle follows normal Greek usage in using it mostly to refer to what we call liquids, and in particular water, rather than to what we call gases (cf. 443a6–9). Thus, I have sometimes translated it as "liquid," and will continue to do so.

66 Aristotle characterizes the four elements in terms of the two pairs of contraries hot/cold and wet/dry, with earth being cold and dry, water cold and wet, air hot and wet, and fire hot and dry. Cf. n. 9 above.

67 Cf. *Meteorologica* 389a7–9.

this concerning odor.[68] Wherefore also Heraclitus spoke in that way, [saying] that if all the things that are became smoke, [our] nostrils would distinguish [them].[69] And since with regard to odor, all are led [in this direction], some [regarding it] as a vapor, some as an exhalation, and some as both of these—vapor is a certain wetness, while smoke-like exhalation, as has been said, is [constituted] of air and earth in common;[70] and water comes together from that one, while a certain form of earth [does] from this one—[it could seem that odor must be one of these]; but neither of these is likely [to be odor]; for vapor is [i.e., consists,] of water [dispersed into the air], while the smoke-like exhalation is incapable of coming into being in water; but the [animals that live] in water also smell, as has been said before.[71] Furthermore, exhalation is spoken of in 443b
the same manner as effluences [i.e., as bodies emitted by the perceived object and impinging on the sense organs]; so if that is not [spoken] finely, neither is this [spoken] finely. Now that it is admissible for the wet (*to hugron*), both that in the breath [i.e., the air breathed in,] and that in water, to gain [something] from and to be acted upon in some way by flavored dryness, [is] not unclear; for air too is [something] wet in its nature. Furthermore, if the dry, when washed out, as it were, acts in the same manner in liquids (*en tois hugrois*)[72] and in the air, [it is] manifest that odors ought to be analogous to flavors. Well, in some cases, surely, this happens. For odors are pungent and sweet and harsh and astringent and

68 This sentence, though it appears in all our manuscripts, is bracketed for exclusion by Biehl, along with all the other modern editors, since it seems inconsistent with what Aristotle will say two sentences later. Perhaps the modern editors are correct, but I don't know.

69 Heraclitus, frag. 7 Diels-Kranz.

70 In the *Meteorologica*, Aristotle distinguishes two sorts of exhalation that arise when the earth is heated by the sun, a more vapor-like one, which comes from the water within and upon the earth, and a more windy or smoke-like one, which comes from the earth itself. But he also calls the vapor-like exhalation vapor simply, as distinct from an exhalation, which of course is what he does here. *Meteorologica* 341b6ff.; 340b24–30.

71 443a3–6.

72 Cf. n. 65 above.

fatty, and someone might say that rotten [odors] are analogous to bitter [flavors]. Wherefore, just as those [i.e., liquids with bitter flavor,] are hard to swallow, the [things that are] rotten are hard to inhale. [It is] clear, therefore, that just what [is], in water, flavor, this [is], in air and water, odor. And on account of this, cold and freezing both dull flavors and obliterate odors; for cooling and freezing obliterate the heat that moves [them] and works [them] up. There are two species of the smellable; for [it is] not [the case], as some assert, [that] there are not [any] species of the smellable,[73] but there are. And we must distinguish how there are [species] and how there are not; for one [species] of them is ordered in accordance with the flavors, as we said,[74] and [these odors] have the pleasant and the painful by concomitance; for on account of their being affections (*pathē*) of [something] nutritive, the odors of these [things] are pleasant [to those desiring nourishment] when they desire [it], but [they are] not pleasant [to them] when they are full and in want of nothing, nor [are they pleasant] to any of those to whom the nourishment that has the odors is not pleasant. So that these [odors], as we have said,[75] have the pleasant and painful by concomitance; wherefore they are also common to all the animals; but others of the odors [are] pleasant in themselves, for instance those of flowers; for neither more nor less do they call [us] toward nourishment, nor do they contribute anything toward desire, but rather the contrary; for [it is] true, what Strattis[76] said in mocking Euripides, "When you're boiling lentil soup, don't
444a pour perfume in [it]." But those who now mix such powers into drinks force pleasure through habituation, until what is pleasant from two senses comes to be as if from one.[77] Now this smellable

73 Cf. Plato, *Timaeus* 66d1–4, 67a1–6.

74 443b7ff. See also *De Anima* 421a26–30, where, however, Aristotle observes that some things that have a certain sort of flavor have an opposite sort of odor.

75 443b19–21.

76 Strattis was an Athenian comic poet of the generation before Aristotle.

77 This apparently means that what is naturally pleasant to smell, on the one hand, and what is naturally pleasant to taste, on the other, come to be expe-

[species] is peculiar to human beings, whereas the [species of odor] ordered in accordance with [the] flavors [belongs] also to the other animals, as was said before.[78] And the species [i.e., subspecies,] of those [odors], on account of their having the pleasant by concomitance, have been distinguished in accordance with the flavors, but of this [odor] no longer [are there any such subspecies], on account of its nature being pleasant or painful[79] in itself. [The] cause of such odor being peculiar to man [is] on account of the condition around the brain. For since the brain is cold in its nature, and since the blood [that flows] around it in the blood vessels is fine and pure, but easily cooled (wherefore also the exhalation of nourishment, when it is cooled on account of the [coldness of that] place, produces morbid discharges), this species of odor has come into being for human beings as an aid for health; for there is no other function of it than this.[80] And it manifestly does this; for nourishment, though pleasant, both [the] dry and [the] wet, is often unwholesome, but the [action] from the odor that is fragrant in itself[81] is

---

rienced as if the pleasure comes only from (the anticipated and the actual) taste. Yet perfumes, according to what Aristotle says in the *Nicomachean Ethics* (1118a10–12), themselves belong to the class of odors that he here calls pleasant by concomitance, and so the quotation from Strattis is not strictly apposite to the point he is apparently making. Moreover, at least some perfumes, which are the ones Aristotle has chiefly in mind in the passage in the *Nicomachean Ethics*, are pleasant because of their association with sexual pleasures, i.e., with the sense of touch, rather than taste. Aristotle's failure throughout this chapter to discuss such odors explicitly might be due, at least in part, to the fact that he treats odor from the perspective of those in whom the natural pleasures have not been corrupted.

78 443b24–26.

79 This is Aristotle's first explicit mention of the fact that the species of odors that he has been speaking of as "pleasant in themselves" also includes odors that are painful in themselves.

80 Biehl would delete the words translated as "than this," in keeping with manuscripts E and M. They appear, however, in manuscripts L, S, and U, as well as in a number of others.

81 At 444a17–18, I read *hē d'apo tēs osmēs tēs kath'hautēn euōdous*, in accordance with manuscripts E and M, rather than Biehl's *hē d'apo tou euōdous osmē hē kath'hautēn*, which is a conjecture by Biehl himself. Biehl's text would be translated, instead of as "but the [action] from the odor that is fragrant in it-

always, so to speak, beneficial to those in any condition. And on account of this it comes to be through breathing [in], not for all [animals], but for human beings and, of the [animals] with blood, for the quadrupeds, for instance, and for as many as have more of a share of the nature of air;[82] for when the odors rise toward the

---

self," as "but the odor from what is fragrant, the [odor that is pleasant] in itself." There are a number of conjectures by various modern editors regarding the text of this passage, and I know of no modern edition or translation that accepts either the manuscript reading that I accept or any of the variants from the other manuscripts.

82 Here Aristotle qualifies his previous statement that the perception of odors that are pleasant in themselves is peculiar to man, and indeed, he has to do this, since the cause to which he attributes its being peculiar to man suggests in fact that it would belong to some of the other animals as well. Moreover, at 444a28–31 Aristotle repeats the claim that the genus of such odor is peculiar to the nature of man, and there his support for it, namely, that man has the largest and wettest brain in relation to his size, indicates explicitly that there is only a difference of degree rather than of kind between man and some of the other animals in this respect. Thus, his repeated claim that this sort of odor is peculiar to man, combined with his manifestly inadequate argument in support of that claim, suggests either that the claim is not true or that if it is true, there must be better support for it than that which he explicitly gives. And soon after making this claim for the second time, Aristotle does in fact again qualify it somewhat, saying only that "alone, *so to speak*, of the animals, man perceives and delights in the odors of flowers and those of [other] such [things]" (444a31–32; emphasis mine). On the other hand, his rephrasing of the claim suggests that it might still in a sense be true, since in saying that "man alone, so to speak, of the animals perceives and delights in the odors of flowers," he invites the thought that man, while not being the only animal to perceive these odors, is the only animal that delights in them as being pleasant in themselves (cf. the reference to the sense of smell possessed by bees at 444b11). And this suggestion is supported by what Aristotle will soon say, at 444b28–445a4, in connection with odors that are unpleasant in themselves. For he doesn't say there that man is the only animal that perceives these odors, but rather that man is the only animal that is offended by them, or that is in any way concerned with them, apart from their relation to some further consequences. And the reason for this uniqueness of man would not be the condition of his brain, but rather, as it seems to me, the fact that man is the only animal not simply at peace with his own nature as a mortal animal. Thus, for instance, man can be oppressed by animal desire, not merely because it is unsatisfied, but simply as being animal desire, so that the odor of flowers, which according to Aristotle leads to a diminishment of such desire (443b28–30), sometimes comes as a relief. Now if this suggestion

brain on account of the lightness of the heat in them, what (pl.) is around this place is healthier; for the power of odor is hot in its nature. And nature makes a twofold use of breathing: as [its main] function, for aid to the chest, but as a secondary function, for odor; for when one breathes [in], [the odor] makes its motion through the nostrils as from a side entrance. And the genus of such odor [i.e., odor that is pleasant in itself,] is peculiar to the nature of man on account of his having the largest and wettest brain of the animals in relation to his size; for on account of this, and alone, so to speak, of the animals, man perceives and delights in the odors of flowers and those of [other] such [things]; for their heat and mo- 444b
tion are commensurate with the excess of the wetness and coldness in the place [around the brain]. And to the other animals, as many as have a lung, nature has given sense perception through breathing[83] of the other genus of odor, so as not to make two sense organs;[84] for it suffices that when they breathe [in], the sense perception of those other [odors] alone is present to them, as [the per-

---

of mine is correct, the question arises as to why Aristotle does not state his position openly. And to this I would respond as follows: to state openly that the species of odors that are pleasant and unpleasant in themselves does not consist of odors that only man happens to be able to perceive, but rather odors that are perceived also by many other animals, but that man responds to in this unique manner, would require him to state openly that what he means by odor is what it is in relation to man in particular (and this despite the fact that the human sense of smell is, as he had said earlier, the worst among all the animals, 440b31–33; cf. *De Anima* 421a9–13). That man is the measure in this sense, and not only with regard to odor, is Aristotle's genuine view, as it seems to me, but it is not one that he wishes to obtrude.

83 At 444b3, I read *dia tou anapnein*, in accordance with manuscripts U, V, and W, rather than *dia to anapnein*, with Biehl, who follows manuscripts E, M, L, and X. According to Biehl's text, the beginning of this sentence would be translated, instead of as "And to the other animals, as many as have a lung, nature has given sense perception through breathing . . . ," as "And to the other animals, as many as have a lung on account of breathing, nature has given sense perception [through breathing] . . . ."

84 Since breathing is not a type of sense perception, and its organ not a sense organ, I think that this claim means "so as not to give the other animals an organ of smell that differs from the nose, through which human beings perceive odors pleasant in themselves."

ception] of both [classes of] smellables [is present] to human beings [when we breathe in]. And as for the [animals] that don't breathe, [it is] manifest that they have sense perception of the smellable; for both fish and the entire genus of insects perceive [their nourishment] accurately and from a distance, on account of the nutritive species of odor, [even] when they are far away from their proper nourishment, for instance bees as well as the genus of small ants, which some call "knipes," and, of the sea [animals], the purple murex; and many of the other such animals perceive their nourishment keenly on account of its odor. But that [organ] by which they perceive [it] is not equally manifest. Wherefore someone might also be perplexed [as to] what [sense it is] by which they perceive odor, if indeed smelling comes about in only one way for [animals], when they breathe [in], (for this manifestly [is what] happens in the case of all the animals that breathe), whereas none of those breathes, but yet they perceive [odor]—unless [there is] some different [sense] beyond the five senses. But this is impossible; for smelling is of the smellable, and those [animals] perceive this, but not perhaps in the same manner, but for those that breathe, the breath removes what lies upon [the sense organ] like a sort of lid (wherefore they don't perceive [odor] when they are not breathing [in]), but for those that don't breathe, this [lid] has been removed; just as in the case of the eyes, some of the animals have eyelids, [and] when these [coverings] are not removed, they are incapable of seeing, but the hard-eyed [animals] don't have [them]; wherefore they don't need anything that will remove [them], but they see at once from the [organ by] itself that is capable [of seeing]. Similarly also, none of the other animals is at all offended by the odor of the [things] that are foul-smelling in themselves, unless something happens to be destructive.[85] By these they

85 In *On the History of Animals* 626a24ff., Aristotle says that bees are a very clean (or the cleanest) animal, and that they are offended by foul-smelling odors, and he says this without any apparent limitation to odors that are also destructive. Perhaps this was not Aristotle's view at the time when he composed the present treatise, or perhaps he disregarded these thoughts about bees in order to help make the larger point that I suggested in n. 82 above.

are destroyed in like manner, just as human beings, too, get headaches from the vapor of charcoal and are often destroyed [by it]; so the other animals are destroyed by the power of sulfur and of asphalt-like [substances], and they avoid these on account of the **445a**
suffering (*pathos*) [that they cause]. But they aren't at all concerned with foul odor itself, by itself, even though many of the things that grow have [as their] odors foul ones, unless [this odor] contributes something with a view to their taste or eating.[86] It looks as if the sense of smelling, since the senses are odd [in number] and since an odd number has a middle, is also itself in the middle of the touching [senses, i.e., those that involve contact with their object], namely, touch and taste, and those that [are] perceptive through [something] other, namely, sight and hearing. Wherefore that which is smellable is a certain affection both of the [bodies that are] nutritive (and these are in the touchable genus) and of what is audible and what is visible; wherefore [animals] smell both in air and in water. So that what is smellable is common to both of these [classes], and [it] belongs to the touchable as well as to the audible and transparent;[87] wherefore it has reasonably been likened

---

86 The words that I have translated as "contribute something" are *ti sumballētai*. Other translators render them as "make some difference," and they presumably are thinking of odors whose foulness dissuades other animals from eating whatever emits them. But the normal meaning of the word *sumballein* is "to contribute" in a positive sense (cf. 443b29, 445a28), and it seems to me that, at least primarily, Aristotle is referring to odors that awaken the desire to eat. Concerning the possibility that other animals are not only aware of, but in some cases even attracted by, odors that Aristotle calls "foul-smelling in themselves," see again n. 82 above. The question also arises here as to why Aristotle refers to foul odors from plants in particular—"the things that grow" (*tōn phuomenōn*) at 445a2–3 are the things that grow from the earth, i.e., plants—and not to those from animals. It seems to me that he limits his discussion to plants because, if he were to include animal odors, he would have to acknowledge that such odors, even those that we find foul-smelling, can be strong inducements, in other animals, to sexual desire, and he would be compelled to say openly why he doesn't include a species or subspecies of odor that is ordered in accordance with the sense of touch, as well as one ordered in accordance with the sense of taste.

87 Now it is odd that Aristotle speaks here of what is "transparent," by which he presumably means the transparent medium of sight, rather than of what

to a sort of dipping and washing of dryness in [what is] wet and flowing. So then [as for] how one should speak of species of the smellable and how one should not, let it have been said to this extent. And what some of the Pythagoreans say is not reasonable; for they assert that some animals are nourished by odors. For in the first place we see that nourishment must be composite; for the [beings that are] nourished are also not simple; wherefore there also comes to be a residue of their nourishment, some inside them, and some outside, as in the case of plants.[88] Further, not even water, when it is unmixed [and] itself alone, is able (*ethelei*) to nourish; for that which is going to be put together [with a body] must be bodily in some respect. Further, it is much less reasonable for air

---

is "visible," as he said in the previous sentence, and by which he would clearly have meant the visible body. But could "transparent" refer to the air, i.e., the medium of sight for human beings, rather than to the distant bodies that are seen through it? And if this is so, "the audible" in the expression "the audible and transparent" would also refer to the air, rather than to the bodies that, by being struck together, produce a sound. And air is indeed smellable. For Aristotle has defined odor as "the nature of the flavored dry in a wet [medium]," i.e., in air (or water), and he has implicitly distinguished it from the flavored and odorous body that produces this affection (443a7–9). And if he is referring here to air, he would be reminding us that even and precisely in our smelling of bodies through this medium, we are in contact with their odor, which they have imparted to the air itself (cf. *De Anima* 424b14–16). Now if this is what Aristotle means, his expression "the audible and transparent," as a substitute for "what is audible and what is visible" in the previous sentence, would also be characterizing the air as audible and as visible. But this too makes sense, more obviously concerning its being audible, since what we perceive immediately is not the bodies that, by being struck together, produce a sound, but rather the air that they have set in motion (cf. *De Anima* 420a8–9, a21–23; 420b11). And even in the case of its being visible, Aristotle has reminded us in Chapter 3 that the transparent medium has color (cf. nn. 31 and 39 above), and he will later say explicitly that, in one sense, it is a motion of this medium that we each perceive when we see the color of a distant object, such as a fire (cf. 446b17–26; and consider 446a20–22). The question of how our perception of these motions of the air in contact with us is related to our hearing and seeing the sounds and colors of objects at a distance, as being the sounds and colors of those objects, is one that Aristotle leaves for the reader.

88 The ancient commentator Alexander suggests that by the "residue" of plants Aristotle is referring to such things as gum and bark.

to become body. And in addition to these [considerations], [we see] that for all animals there is a place [that is] receptive of nourishment, [a place] from which, when it has entered [there], the body takes it; but the sense organ of the smellable is in the head, and it [i.e., the smellable,] enters together with a breath-like exhalation,[89] so that it would go into the place that can take in breath. So then [it is] clear that the smellable, as smellable, doesn't contribute to nourishment.[90] However, that [it contributes] to health [is] manifest both from sense perception and from the [things we have] said, so that just what flavor [is] in the nutritive and in relation to the [beings that are] nourished, this the smellable is in relation to health.[91] So then let [the perceptibles] have been determined in 445b
this manner in accordance with each sense organ.[92]

---

89 Unless Aristotle is taking back, for smellable objects in air, at any rate, his rejection of the view that odor is an exhalation from the object smelled (443a21–b2; but see 438b24), he seems to be suggesting here that there is indeed some exhalation from the odorous object, but that this is associated with odor, rather than itself being odor.

90 Note that Aristotle concludes here only that it is the smellable, as smellable—as distinguished perhaps from odor simply—that doesn't contribute to nourishment. See 447a6–8.

91 The (implicit) subject of this sentence is the smellable, as smellable. And since Aristotle has been speaking here of odors associated with nourishment, and since, moreover, it would be odd for him not to conclude his account of odor with a statement about odor as such, he appears to be saying that it is not just the species of odors that are pleasant in themselves that contribute to health. [By this he would presumably not mean that all odors contribute equally to health, any more than all flavors contribute equally to nourishment (cf. 442a1–12), but rather that this is a normal effect of odor as such, one not limited to one of its two species.] And if this is indeed Aristotle's suggestion, by attributing to odor as such an effect that he had presented earlier only as resulting from the odors that are pleasant in themselves (but consider also 444a17–25 and context), he would be giving another sign that he did not regard that species of odors as simply distinct from those that are associated with nourishment, and another pointer to the question of in what sense, or from what perspective, they truly are a distinct species.

92 Aristotle has spoken explicitly in this treatise of the objects of sight, taste, and smell, and he has told us at the beginning of Chapter 4 that he had already treated the objects of hearing in *De Anima*. But he has not discussed the object of the sense of touch, even though he had explicitly promised to

Chapter 6

Someone might be perplexed, if every body is divided into infinitely many [parts]: [are] the perceptible affections (*pathēmata*) [of body], such as color and flavor and odor and weight and sound[93] and cold and hot and light and hard and soft, also [divided

---

discuss it in Chapter 3, at 439a10–12; and by asking us here to let what he has said so far count as a determination of the perceptibles in accordance with each sense organ, he calls attention to his silence about the object of touch. However, he has not been completely silent about it in fact. For in calling color the limit of the transparent in bodies, sound the motion of air, and flavor and odor affections that the dry produces in the wet (i.e., in water and air), Aristotle has been appealing implicitly to objects of the sense of touch as they are actually perceived. For he has told us in *De Anima* that the objects of the sense of touch include such qualities as hard and soft, and, more especially, what he calls the differentiae of body as body, namely, hot and cold and wet and dry, the qualities in terms of which the elements earth, air, fire, and water have been distinguished (*De Anima* 422b25–27, 423b27–29; and cf. nn. 9 and 66 above). Since, then, it is in terms of what is actually perceived through the sense of touch that we understand what the objects are that produce actual perception through the other senses, to try to say what the objects of touch are, in the way that Aristotle has spoken of the objects of these other senses, would seem to lead to a circular account. And by his indirect pointer here to his failure to give an account of the object of the sense of touch, Aristotle shows that he is well aware of this great difficulty.

93 At 445b5, I read *baros kai psophos*, with manuscripts E, M, Y, S, U, and W, rather than *psophos kai baros*, with Biehl, whose reading appears in manuscripts L, X, H[a], and P. These three words in Biehl's text would be translated, instead of as "weight and sound," as "sound and weight." In either case, weight and lightness (i.e., "light") are the only pair of tangible contraries that are not listed together here. But the anomalous position of the word translated as "weight" is slightly greater in the version I have chosen, since the six affections associated with the sense of touch do not all follow the four associated with the other senses, as they would in the other version. But in either case what seems to me most important is that Aristotle chooses to use the noun "weight" rather than the adjective "heavy," although the other five objects of the sense of touch are all characterized by adjectives. And from this it follows that weight is the only affection of the ten listed that can be regarded not merely as the affection of a body (e.g., "color," or indeed "weight"), or as a sort of body (e.g., "cold"), but as a body itself, i.e., a weight. In this way, it seems to me, Aristotle points to the question of the relation between a body and its affections. (Compare the use of the word "magnitude," or *megethos*, which can also be translated as "size," at 445b9–10 and at 445b18.)

into infinitely many parts]? Or [is this] impossible? For each of them is [what is] productive of sense perception [in actuality]; for by [dint of] it being capable of judging [them],[94] they are all spoken of [as being these affections]. So that [it would be] necessary[, if the perceptible affections are infinitely divisible,][95] for sense perception[96] to be divided into infinitely many [parts], as well as for every magnitude to be perceptible/perceived;[97] ([I say "every magnitude" instead of "every part of any sense perception,"] for [it is] impossible to see white, but not [to see it as being] so big.) For if

---

94 At 445b8, I read *krinein*, with manuscripts E and Y, rather than *kinein*, with Biehl, who follows the preponderance of the manuscripts. According to Biehl's text, this phrase would be translated, instead of as "for by [dint of] it being capable of judging [them]," as "for by [their] setting it [i.e., sense perception, or the sense organ,] in motion." I prefer the reading that I have chosen, since by calling attention to the fact that sense perception is not merely acted upon by the perceptible affections, but must also judge them, it brings out somewhat more forcefully that these affections are what they are only as objects of (possible) perception. As for the role of judgment in the activity of sense perception, see *Posterior Analytics* 99b34–35; *De Anima* 424a5–6, 426b10ff., 427a18, 428a3–4, and 431a20–25; as well as 445b15 and 447b25–27.

95 It appears at first that this sentence states only what would have to be the case on the assumption that the perceptible affections of body are infinitely divisible, and that it supports the claim that this alternative is impossible. But in the sequel—beginning with the sentence at 445b11, "For if [this were] not so..."—Aristotle argues in support of the necessity that he speaks of here, namely, that any sense perception must be divided into infinitely many parts, on the grounds that otherwise perceptible bodies would be composed, not from smaller perceptible bodies, but from imperceptible bodies, bodies which he then argues would be unknowable, thus suggesting the absurd conclusion that the perceptible bodies are unknowable themselves. In light of this subsequent argument, then, which prepares Aristotle's account of the way in which the perceptibles as perceptibles are indeed infinitely divisible (as is sense perception as well), the beginning of this sentence might also be translated as "So that [it is] necessary for sense perception to be divided into infinitely many [parts]...."

96 Note that according to what Aristotle says in *De Anima* (425b26–27), the actuality of sense perception and that of the perceptible are one and the same (although their being is different), so that when he speaks here about sense perception, by which he means sense perception in actuality, he is speaking also about the actuality of the perceptible, e.g., a perceived color.

97 Cf. 440a30–31.

[this were] not so [i.e., if any sense perception were not divided into infinitely many parts, each of which is perceptible], it would be admissible for there to be some body[, resulting from division of a perceptible body,] that had no color nor weight nor any other such affection (*pathos*); so that [it would] not even [be] perceptible at all; for these [are] the perceptibles. Therefore, the perceptible will be composed not from perceptibles[, but from imperceptibles]. But [it is] necessary [that it be composed from perceptibles]; for certainly it isn't from the mathematicals. Furthermore, by what will we judge these [imperceptible parts of the perceptibles] or come to know [them]? Or [perhaps it is] by the intellect. But [they are] not intelligibles, nor does the intellect think/apprehend what (pl.) [are] outside [of it] without sense perception. And at the same time, if these [things] are so [i.e., if the perceptible is not composed from perceptibles], it looks as if it gives support to those who make [i.e., fabricate,] the indivisible magnitudes [i.e., atoms]; for thus the argument (*ho logos*) could be resolved. But [the atoms are] impossible; it has been spoken with regard to them in [our] speeches concerning motion.[98] And it will be clear at the same time [both] concerning the resolution of them [i.e., of these perplexities,] and why the species, [those] of color and of flavor and of tones [of different pitches] and of the other perceptibles, are limited [in number].[99] For of what (pl.) there are extremes, [it is] necessary that what (pl.) [are] within [those extremes] be limited; and the contraries are extremes. And everything that is perceptible has contrariety, for instance, in color the white and the black, in flavor sweet and bitter; and indeed, in all the other [genera of the perceptible] there are [as] extremes the [respective] contraries. Now then what is continuous is cut into infinitely many unequal [parts], but into finitely many equal [ones]; while that which [is] not in itself continuous[, but instead belongs to the continuous as an affec-

98 Cf. *Physics*, Book Six, 231a21–232a25. The expression "speeches concerning motion" most likely refers to Books Five through Eight, or Books Six through Eight, of the *Physics*.

99 Cf. 440b23–25.

tion, is cut] into finitely many species. Since, then, on the one hand, the affections (*pathē*) must be spoken of as species, while, on the other hand, continuity [is] always [present] in them, one must grasp that what is potentially and what is in actuality [are] different; and on account of this, when the grain of millet is seen, 446a
its ten thousandth part escapes notice, even though sight has gone over [it], and the tone within the [interval of] the quarter step escapes notice, even though one hears all [of] the tune, which is continuous.[100] But the interval of what is in between in relation to the extreme [tones of the quarter step] escapes notice. And similarly also with regard to the [parts that are] extremely small in the other perceptibles; for they are visible potentially, but not in actuality, when they have been separated [from the whole].[101] And further, the one-foot [line] is present potentially in the two-foot [line], but [it is] in actuality only when it has been divided [from it]; but increments of such a [small] size, when they are separated, might rea-

100 Aristotle may mean by this a tune, or a part of a tune, that moves stepwise by quarter steps. (For this use of the term "continuous," cf. *Physics* 226b27–30.) But I suspect that he means, in particular, a passage in which the performer produces a sliding sound between the first note of a quarter-step interval and the second. That would make this example a true parallel to the previous one about the grain of millet.

101 I agree with Biehl in reading *hotan khōristhēi* at 446a5–6, in accord with manuscripts L, S, U, W, and X, rather than *hotan mē khōris ēi*, in accord with manuscripts E, M, and Y, and which is also the reading followed in all the other English translations that I know of. This last clause, according to the alternative reading, would be translated, instead of as "when they have been separated [from the whole]," as "when they are not separate [from the whole]." Editors and translators who prefer that other reading do so on the grounds that without it the train of thought leading to what Aristotle goes on to say about the one-foot line is not, in their view, sufficiently intelligible (especially since the words that I translate there as "And further…" would more commonly mean something like "For also…"). But that reading of the sentence contradicts the continuation of Aristotle's argument, and in particular, what he says at 446a14–15 ("and it will be [so] in actuality"). And the comment about the one-foot line makes sense as leading to Aristotle's claim that, in addition to the minute parts of the perceptibles not being perceptible in actuality when separated off, they might well—unlike the one-foot line within the two-foot line—even cease to preserve the character that belonged to them as parts of the wholes.

sonably even disintegrate into their surroundings, just as [does] a minute [amount of] flavor/juice (*khumos*) when it has been poured into the sea. But no matter [whether that would happen to such increments of the perceptibles or not], since the increment of sense perception[102] [is] neither perceptible by itself nor separable (for the increment is present potentially in the [thus] more accurate [sense perception as a whole]), neither will it be possible to perceive in actuality the perceptible of such a [small] size, [if it is] separate, but nevertheless it will be perceptible; for it is [so] potentially already, and it will be [so] in actuality after having been added [to other perceptibles so that together they make up a whole that is perceptible in actuality].[103] So then that some magnitudes and affections (*pathē*) escape notice, and on account of what cause, and how they are perceptible and how not, has been said. And accordingly, whenever [the magnitudes and affections] are already present in such a relation to one another that they are perceptible in actuality, and [this] not only because [they are] in the whole, but also [as] separate, [it is] necessary that colors and flavors and sounds be finite in number. And someone might be perplexed: [do] the perceptibles, or the motions from the perceptibles—in whichever way sense perception comes to be—whenever they are actual/active (*energōsin*), arrive [in all cases] at the middle first, as odor manifestly does, as well as sound? For the one who is near perceives the odor before [one who is far away does], and the sound arrives after the blow. Then [are] what is seen and light also of such a sort, just as in fact Empedocles asserts that the light from the sun arrives at what is in between before [it arrives] at the eye (*tēn opsin*)[104] or as far as the earth?[105] It would seem [to be] reasonable that this happens; for what is in motion is in motion from somewhere to

102 Cf. n. 96 above.

103 This claim that the minute perceptible can be perceived in actuality as part of the whole does not mean, and does not imply, that it is present in actuality in the perceptible object (cf. 446a6–7, a11–12).

104 For this word *opsis*, which more commonly means "sight," cf. 437a22 and n. 10 above.

105 Cf. *De Anima* 418b20–26.

somewhere, so that [it is] necessary that there also be some time in which it is in motion from the one to the other; and every [interval of] time is divisible, so there was [a time] when the [sun's] 446b ray was not yet seen but was still in local motion in what is in between [the sun and the earth]. Even if someone hears and has heard, and in general perceives and has perceived, all at the same time, and there is no coming into being of them [i.e., of hearing and the other kinds of sense perception], but they are, without coming into being,[106] yet none the less [it would seem reasonable that there are such time lags], just as the sound, even though the blow has already been [struck], [is] not yet at the ear (*tēi akoēi*). And also the transformation of letters [i.e., of their spoken sounds,] makes [this] clear [in the case of sound], [indicating] that locomotion comes to be in the [space] in between; for [the hearers] manifestly have not heard [correctly] what was said, on account of the air being transformed while [it is] in local motion. Then are color and light also like that? For [it is] not, indeed, [merely] by [that which sees and that which is seen] being [each] of some sort that the one sees and the other is seen, as equals are [equals merely by their being of such a sort]; for [in that case] there would be no need for each of the two to be somewhere [in particular]; for in the case of things that come to be equal it makes no difference whether they are near or far from one another. Or [is it] concerning sound and odor [that it is] reasonable that this happen; for like air and water, [they are] continuous, and the motion of both [of them] is divided [into parts]. —Wherefore also, in one way, the first [person] and the one [to whom the motion arrives] later hear and smell the same [sound or odor], but in another way, [they do] not. But it seems to some [thinkers] that there is a perplexity even with regard to these [matters]; for some assert [it to be] impossible for one [person] to hear and see and smell the same [thing] as another; for [they assert that] it is not possible that many, who are also separate [from one another], hear and smell [it]; for the one [object] would [then] itself be separate from itself. Or [perhaps],

106 Cf. *Metaphysics* 1048b18–36; *Physics* 258b16–20.

on the one hand, they all perceive that which has first produced the motion, for instance the bell or the frankincense or the fire, [which is] the same and one in number, but on the other hand, [they each also perceive] what is peculiar [to each of them], [which is] different in number, but the same[107] in species; wherefore also many[108] see and smell and hear [the same object] at the same time.[109] And neither are these [perceptibles that are peculiar to each of them] bodies, but an affection (*pathos*) and a sort of motion (for this would not happen [otherwise]), nor yet [are they] without body.—But concerning light [there is] another speech (*logos*);[110] for light is by [dint of] being something (*tōi einai...ti*), but [it is] not [in any sense] a motion.[111] And in general [the case] is not the

---

107 At 446b24, I read *tou autou*, meaning "the same," with all the manuscripts, rather than *tou hautou*, with Biehl, who follows only the earlier Bekker edition. If Biehl's reading is not simply a misprint, this expression would apparently have to be translated, instead of as "but the same in species," as "but in species, what belongs to [each one] himself."

108 Presumably, with smelling and hearing—whatever may be the case with seeing—these "many" include only those at equal distances from whatever it was that first produced the motion.

109 Cf. n. 87 above.

110 This clause is the continuation of the response that Aristotle began to present at 446b13–15 ("Or [is it] concerning sound and odor [that it is] reasonable that this happen").

111 In saying that "light is by [dint of] being something," Aristotle apparently means that it is what he had said it was in *De Anima* (418b9–10), namely, the actuality (*energeia*) of the transparent [medium] as transparent. He also speaks of light as "the completion (*entelekheia*) of the transparent" (*De Anima* 419a11), since it is completely what it is at every moment, and in this important respect it is different from a motion (cf. *Physics* 257b8–9). But though this distinction between light and motion makes good sense, the whole expression (after the semicolon) seems a little awkward. And many modern editors have replaced the reading *tōi einai gar ti phōs estin* at 446b27, which Biehl accepts in accord with almost all the surviving manuscripts, with *tōi eneinai gar ti phōs estin*, a reading that appears in manuscript P as well as in an apparent quotation by Alexander. According to that reading, the second half of this sentence would be translated as "for light is by [dint of] there being something in [the medium], but [it is] not [in any sense] a motion." And Aristotle would be referring to his claim earlier in this treatise that "whenever there is something fiery in a transparent [body, or medium], its presence is

same even as between alteration and local motion; for local motions, reasonably, first arrive at what is in between (and sound seems to be a motion of something in local motion),[112] but with 447a
regard to as many [things] as are altered, [the case] is no longer the same; for it is admissible that they be altered all together, and not the [one] half before [the other], for instance that water freeze all at the same time.[113] Not but that, if there is much of what is being heated or frozen, what is contiguous is acted upon by what [it] is contiguous [to], while what is first [acted upon] changes through the agency of that itself which [first] produces the alteration, and it is not necessary that [the whole] be altered [all] at the same time and all together.[114] And also tasting would be like

---

light" (439a19–20; cf. *De Anima* 418b12–20). And he would conclude the sentence with "but [it is] not [in any sense] a motion," since it could seem that that fiery something, the presence of which is light, must be in motion of a sort (cf. *De Anima* 419b25–33), and he would want to make it clear that light is not in any sense a motion of that (nor indeed of the medium nor of anything else). This reading and this interpretation also make good sense, and they may be correct. But given the weight of the manuscript evidence, I have chosen instead to translate Biehl's text. At all events, what is clear is that Aristotle distinguishes light from sound and odor, on the grounds that while they are motions of a sort, at least secondarily or as peculiar to each perceiver, light is not.

112 Sound could still be a motion of something in local motion, e.g., air, even if it were a motion in which no one portion of the air traveled from the source of the sound to the hearer.

113 Cf. *Physics* 253b23–26.

114 It is not immediately clear why Aristotle even discusses this difference between local motion and (some cases of) alteration, since he has just asserted that light is not a motion, so that it would be neither the one nor the other of these two kinds of motion. But perhaps he is thinking not of light, but of color (cf. 446a25–26, where he speaks of "what is seen," as well as light; 446b9–10, where he speaks of "color," as well as light; and consider the reference to what many "see" at 446b24). And Aristotle teaches that color is seen by its setting in motion the transparent medium, which in turn produces motion in the sense organ (*De Anima* 419a13–15; and cf. 440a15–20 of this treatise). This is his teaching, moreover, even with regard to those colored bodies, such as the sun or a fire, that are also sources of light (440a10–12; cf. *De Anima* 419a22–25). If, then, Aristotle is thinking here of color, and if he is thinking of the kind of motion that it produces in the medium of sight as

odor[115] if we were [i.e., lived,] in water, and [if] we perceived [the flavor of a flavored body] even [from] further away, before coming in contact with it [i.e., with the body itself]. And reasonably, [the parts] of those [bodies] that are in between the sense organ [and the object perceived] are not all acted upon at the same time, except in the case of light, on account of what has been said. And on account of the same [thing, this exception applies] also in the case of seeing; for light produces seeing.[116]

---

alteration (on the grounds, perhaps, that it is not impossible for an extended body to be altered all at once), the result of this inconclusive treatment of alteration would be that we don't know whether or not color is seen, at different distances, all at the same time. But see n. 116 below.

115 Since actual odor and actual smelling are the same (though different in their being), as are actual flavor and actual tasting (cf. *De Anima* 425b26ff.), this claim can be regarded as equivalent to saying that tasting would be like smelling, or that flavor would be like odor, if we lived in water and if we perceived the flavor of a flavored body even before coming in contact with the body itself (cf. *De Anima* 422a11–15). But I don't know why Aristotle didn't say, then, that tasting would be like smelling, or that flavor would be like odor. He might have wanted to use the word "odor," since it is this that permeates the air between the odorous body and ourselves in the gradual way that he has just allowed to be possible in his account of alteration in general. But since his mention of tasting has led us to expect him to say "smelling," rather than "odor," did he also want to suggest, by not using the word "smelling," that if we lived in water, the flavor of distant bodies might gradually permeate it so as to reach our mouths, and we might not even have a sense of smell, as distinct from taste (cf. 444b7–21)? (Although the word *osmē*, which I translate here as "odor," is sometimes used, though only infrequently, to mean the sense of smell, and although some scholars think that even Aristotle sometimes uses it in this way—as for instance at *De Anima* 421a8—I don't agree. Moreover, the sense of smell is at least as much the capacity to smell as it is the act of smelling, and so even if the word *osmē* were being used with that unusual meaning here, it would not be truly parallel to the word for "tasting." Since the term is unexpected, then, with either translation, it seems better to translate it in its usual sense and to ask why Aristotle chose it.)

116 Here Aristotle states unequivocally—what, at the end of n. 114, I said that he would have been unable to assert with any confidence—that all the bodies between the object seen and the organ of seeing are acted upon at the same time. But the reason that he gives for this statement, namely, that light produces seeing, seems inadequate. In *De Anima*, as I observed in that footnote, he teaches that color is what produces seeing (though of course only when there is light), and earlier in this treatise, at 438b3–5, he has said that motion

Chapter 7

There is also a perplexity of a sort, another [one] such [as the preceding one],[117] concerning sense perception, [namely,] whether it is admissible to be able to perceive two [objects] simultaneously in the same indivisible time,[118] or not,[119] if in fact[120] the greater mo-

---

through the medium of sight, whether that medium is light or air, produces seeing. The conclusion seems inescapable, then, that he has some further grounds, beyond what he says here about light— namely, that it is not a motion—for stating that all the bodies between the object seen and the organ of seeing are acted upon at the same time. And let me suggest that these further grounds are the ones he adduced, in response to the question of whether light from the sun takes time to reach us, at *De Anima* 418b20–24, namely, that such an assertion is both contrary to "the lucidity [required] of speech and contrary to the appearances." Indeed, his claim in the sentence before this one that light is an exception to the rule that the parts of those bodies that are in between the sense organ and the object perceived are not all acted upon at the same time, "on account of what has been said," may have been a reference to "what has been said" about light not merely in this passage, but also in that one from *De Anima.* For what he said there applies not only to light, but also to color, even though the transmission of color from the colored object to the eye is a motion. For the colors of very distant and very near objects all appear to us instantaneously as soon as there is light, so that the hypothesis of an imperceptible lapse of time is indeed contrary to the appearances. And if this suggestion of mine is correct, the conclusion of this chapter would be an appropriate place to remind us of that argument from *De Anima*, since the chapter as a whole calls attention, on the one hand, to the fact that what is actually perceived cannot be understood—not with "the lucidity [required] of speech"—as the product of what can never be perceived, and yet, on the other hand, to the possibility of some genuine, if limited, grasp of the world in its entirety through our sense perception itself. Cf. *On the Heaven* 306a16–17.

117 Perhaps Aristotle says "another [one] such [as the preceding one]" because he is asking whether it is possible to perceive two objects at the same time, and the only hypothesis he mentions—if it should not be possible—to account for the apparent fact that we do this, is that we perceive the objects at different times, but that this difference is imperceptibly small (448a19–24ff.); for the perplexity about light and color that he discussed at the end of the previous chapter also involved the claim that there are imperceptibly small intervals of time ("And someone might be perplexed . . . ," 446a20).

118 By "the same indivisible time," Aristotle does not mean a time that is simply indivisible, since he denies that there is any such time (cf. *Physics* 233b15–32), but rather one that cannot be divided into two segments, in the first of

tion always drives out the lesser [one]; wherefore [i.e., because of the greater motion driving out the lesser one, people] don't perceive what comes before their eyes if they happen to be thinking [of] something intently, or to be in a fright, or to be hearing a lot of sound. Let this, then, [i.e., that the greater motion always drives out the lesser one], be supposed, and [also] that it is more possible to perceive each [thing] if it is simple than [if it is] blended, for instance wine unblended [with water] than [if it is] blended, and honey, and color,[121] and the highest-pitched note [of a scale] alone than [if it is] in the octave [i.e., sounded together with the note an octave below], on account of [the two ingredients] obliterating one another [at least to some extent]. And [the things that] do this [are those] from which there comes into being something [that is] one. If, then,[122] the greater drives away the lesser motion, [it is] necessary, if they are simultaneous, for it too to be less perceptible than if it were alone; for the lesser [motion], mixed [in with it], has taken something away, if indeed all simples are more perceptible [than when they are mixed]. If, therefore, [the motions] are equal, while being different, there will be perception of neither; for each will in like manner obliterate the other. And it is not possible to perceive a simple [motion, if there are two at the same time]. So that either there will not be any perception or [there will be] another

---

which there is perception of the one object and in the second of which perception of the other. See 448b19–20.

119 Cf. *De Anima* 426b8–427a16 (and also 431a20–b1).

120 The Greek expression translated here as "if in fact" is *ei dē*, which might also be translated "if really." According to Denniston, this expression, for the most part, though not invariably, indicates skepticism regarding the truth of the condition it introduces. J. D. Denniston, *The Greek Particles*, 2nd ed., rev. K. J. Dover (Oxford: Clarendon Press, 1954), 223.

121 This is a reference to Aristotle's earlier account (440a31–b23) of the colors other than white and black as mixtures of white and black in various ratios.

122 The Greek expression here is *ei dē*, as at 447a14 (cf. n. 120 above); but here the *dē* must be a connective particle, meaning "then" or "accordingly," and so it does not indicate any skepticism regarding the truth of the condition being introduced. Note, however, that this clause, unlike the one at 447a14, doesn't include the word "always."

one [resulting] from both [motions], which very thing seems indeed to come into being from [perceptibles that are] blended, in whatever [whole] they have been mixed[123] [together]. Since, then, from some [perceptibles] something comes into being [as a mixture], but from others [a mixture] does not come into being, and the latter [are] those [that fall each] under a different sense (for [it is] those of which the extremes [i.e., the qualities differing from 447b one another,] are contraries [that] are mixed;[124] whereas it is not possible for a one to come into being from white and high-pitched, except by concomitance,[125] [i.e.,] not as a concord [comes into being] from a high-pitched [note] and a low-pitched [one]); therefore, neither is it admissible to perceive them [i.e., perceptibles that fall each under a different sense] simultaneously. For their motions, if they are equal, will obliterate one another, since one [single motion] doesn't come into being from them; and if [they are] unequal, [only] the stronger [motion] produces perception, since the soul would [be] more [able to] perceive simultaneously, with the one sense, two [perceptibles] of which [there is] one sense, for instance high-pitched and low-pitched; for the motion of the one [sense], [the motion] itself of [the one sense] itself,[126] [is] more to-

---

123 I do not see a significant difference between the two words that I have translated as "blended" and "mixed," either in this sentence or earlier in the chapter. The word translated as "mixed" is the more common one, the one that Aristotle used, for instance, in his account of the mixing of colors in Chapter 3; the word translated as "blended," both here and at 447a18–19, often refers in particular to the mixing of liquids. Cf. *Topics* 122b26.

124 Cf. *On Coming into Being and Perishing* 328a31–33 and context.

125 At *Metaphysics* 1015b16–22, Aristotle says that a single person might be both just and musical, but that "the just" and "the musical" are one only by concomitance, namely, by each being a concomitant of one and the same being. Here, however, he is speaking of the coming into being of something one from different kinds of perceptible qualities, rather than of qualities of a being that is assumed to underlie them all, and so he probably means that these qualities are concomitant (i.e., go together) with one another, without their undergoing any blending or mixture.

126 At 447b8, I read *hē kinēsis tēs mias autē autēs*, with manuscripts L, U, and H[a], rather than *hē kinēsis tēs mias tautēs*, with Biehl, who follows manuscripts E, M, and Y (and who doesn't even record the other reading in his apparatus).

gether [i.e., more one with itself,][127] than [the motions] of the two [senses], for instance sight and hearing. But with the one [sense] it is impossible to perceive two [perceptibles] simultaneously if they are not mixed; for the mixture wishes/tends[128] to be one, and of the one [perceptible] there is one perception, and the one [perception] is simultaneous with itself.[129] So that from necessity [one] perceives simultaneously the [perceptibles that are] mixed, because one perceives [them] with one perception in actuality [i.e., with one act of perception]; for of one [perceptible] in number the [perception] in actuality [is] one, but [of perceptibles that are one] in species, the [perception] as a potentiality [is] one. And if, then, the perception in actuality [is] one, it will say [that] those [perceptibles are] one. It is necessary, therefore, for them to have been mixed. Whenever, therefore, they are not mixed, there will be two perceptions in actuality.[130] But [it is] necessary for the actuality in ac-

---

According to Biehl's text, the beginning of this clause would be translated, instead of as "for the motion of the one [sense], [the motion] itself of [the one sense] itself," as "for the motion of this one [sense]." Now "this one [sense]" would presumably be the sense of hearing, to which Aristotle has just alluded in his example of high-pitched and low-pitched sounds. But it seems to me that he is speaking here not only of hearing, or of any one particular sense, but of them all.

127 The Greek word translated here as "together" is *hama*, which primarily means, and which I have usually been translating as, "simultaneous" (or "at the same time"); but with that translation, this clause would be practically repeating the previous one ("since the soul . . ."), rather than attempting to give support for it, as the initial word "for" suggests that it will do.

128 Cf. n. 46 above.

129 Although the second part of his sentence, beginning after the semicolon with the word "for," presents itself as giving evidence for the claim with which the sentence begins, it does not do so, since the fact that if two perceptibles are mixed, they can be simultaneously perceived, implies only that if they cannot be simultaneously perceived, they are not mixed, which is the converse of the claim that if they are not mixed, they cannot be simultaneously perceived.

130 This conclusion follows from what was said three sentences before (447b13–14) only on the premise that the perception of perceptibles that are one (merely) in species is one *merely* as a potentiality, and never also in actuality. But all that Aristotle's argument has established is that the perception of what

sponding way, but [each] in another genus, are still more distant from each other and differ [more] than those spoken of in the same genus (for instance, the sweet and the white [are in a sense the same], but [only] as corresponding [to one another],[134] whereas they are different in genus), and [if] the sweet differs still more from the black, by [dint of] its species (*tōi eidei*),[135] than from the white, it would be still less admissible to perceive them [i.e., sweet and black, or even sweet and white,] simultaneously than those [that are] the same in genus. So that if [it is] not [admissible to perceive] these [simultaneously], neither [is it admissible to perceive] those.[136]

---

134 This parenthetical expression, according to Biehl's text, which follows manuscripts E, M, and Y, is *hoion to gluku kai to leukon all' hōs sustoikha*, and I have had to expand my literal translation with some speculative bracketed material in order to make sense of it. Now manuscripts L, S, U, and P, which most of the other editors follow, have the reading *hoion to gluku kai to leukon kalō sustoikha*, which can be easily translated as "for instance, I call the sweet and the white corresponding [perceptibles]." Although I am not certain that Biehl's text is correct, it is easier to interpret the other reading as some scribe's attempt to improve upon it than to see how Biehl's version would have crept into the manuscript tradition, and therefore I have accepted it.

135 Although Biehl prints the words *tōi eidei*, which I have translated as "by [dint of] its species," in his text, he encloses them in square brackets, since he thinks they were not in fact written by Aristotle. And if one were to translate these words as "in species" (i.e., "and [if] the sweet differs still more in species from the black than from the white"), they would indeed appear out of place, since it is only things belonging to the same genus that are said to differ in species (and since it seems unlikely that the word *eidos* is being used here in its broader sense to mean not "species," but merely "kind"). But the thought of difference in species can also be expressed by the word *eidei* alone, without the definite article *tōi* (just as the thought of difference "in genus" was expressed in the previous line by the word *genei* alone). And since there is a definite article, the words seem to me to be a reasonable way of saying that the sweet, since it is a positive quality, differs more from the black, which is a privative one, than it does from the white, which is itself another positive quality, since positive qualities are species of the same sort as one another, and of a different sort from the privative ones.

136 It is not clear, at least not to me, why the greater distance between perceptibles belonging to different genera should make them less perceptible simultaneously than contraries belonging to the same genus. A perceptible body, at any rate, cannot be white and black at the same time in the same indivisible part of itself, but it might be both white and hot, or white and cold. And so

And as for what some of those [who speak] about concords say, that the sounds [of the different notes] don't arrive simultaneously, though they appear [to], and [that this] escapes notice whenever the [difference in] time is imperceptible, is this said correctly or not? For perhaps someone would assert also now that, in consequence of this, one [merely] seems to see and hear [different perceptibles] simultaneously, because the times in between [the different acts of perception] escape notice. Or [is] this not true, and is it not admissible for there to be an unperceived time or for any [time] to escape notice, but it is admissible [i.e., possible,] rather to perceive [it] all. For if, when someone himself perceives [either] himself or [something] other in a continuous time, it is not admissible [i.e., not possible,] for it then to escape his notice that he is [i.e., exists], but there is in the continuous [time] a certain [shorter time] and [one] so small that it is wholly imperceptible, [it is] clear that then [i.e., during that shorter time,] it would escape his notice whether he is and whether he sees and perceives;
448b and if he still does perceive, there would not be either [any] time or any thing (*pragma*) which he perceives or in which [he perceives], except in this way, that he sees in some [part] of this [time] or that [he sees] some [part] of this [thing], if indeed there is some magnitude both of the time and of the thing [that is] wholly imperceptible on account of [its] smallness; for if one sees the whole [line][137] and perceives [it] during [what is] continuously the same

---

what about the motions that these different qualities produce in the perceptive part of the soul (cf. 448a2–3)? It might have been partly in recognition of this difficulty that the translator Beare proposed moving this sentence, together with the one before it, to 448a1, just before the beginning of the argument in terms of contraries. But Beare had no manuscript support for his suggestion, and it has rightly been rejected by other translators and editors. *De Sensu et Sensibili*, trans. J. I. Beare, in *The Works of Aristotle*, vol. 3, ed. W. D. Ross (Oxford: Clarendon Press, 1931), n. 3 at 448a2.

137 I supply the word "line" in brackets, since the adjective translated here as "whole" is feminine, and the most plausible feminine noun for it to agree with is *grammē*, or "line." Aristotle appears to use one and the same line to represent indifferently both the magnitude of what is perceived and the time during which it is perceived.

time, [it is] not by [doing so in] one of these nows [i.e., in one of the instants that fall within that time interval].[138] Let the [line] CB [i.e., BC], in which one was not perceiving, have been taken away [from the whole line ABC]. Then [one perceives] in a certain [part] of this [line, understood as representing the time,] or [one perceives] a certain [part] of this [line, understood as representing the thing], just as one sees the earth as a whole, because [one sees] this [part] of it, and one walks in the year, because [one walks] in this part of it. But again, in the [time] BC one perceives nothing. Therefore, by perceiving in a certain [part] of this [whole time], [namely,] AB, one is said to perceive the whole [thing] and for the whole [line, i.e., for the whole time]. But the same speech (*logos*) [applies] also to the [line] AC; for [one perceives] always in a certain [part of the time] and [one perceives] a certain [part of the thing], but it is not possible to perceive the whole [thing]. [But this

---

138 In saying that one does not perceive a whole line by doing so in an instant, Aristotle is relying on what he had said in *De Anima* (425a16–18), that one perceives magnitude by [dint of] motion (if only the motion, or change, with respect to which part of the magnitude one attends to as one surveys it in its entirety); for motion cannot happen in an instant, but it takes time. And the word "for" introducing the if-clause after the semicolon at 448b4 makes sense, since Aristotle's assertion here serves to explain what would otherwise be a puzzling feature of the earlier part of the sentence (beginning at 448a30), where he said that if there is an imperceptible interval of time within the whole time during which one perceives something, not only does one perceive during only part of the time, but one perceives only part of the thing. (It serves to explain this, at any rate, on what seems to me to be a reasonable assumption, namely, that the statement at 448a30–b1, that "there would not be... [any] time... in which [he perceives]," applies in particular, and most importantly, to the least time required for perceiving the whole magnitude of that particular thing.) Now in translating the end of this sentence as "[it is] not by [doing so in] one of these nows," I am following Biehl's text, which reads *ou tōn nun toutōn tini*, in accord with manuscripts M and (for the most part) E. There is, however, a great deal of discrepancy among the manuscripts in this passage, and most of them make no reference to nows, or to perception of a whole line not taking place in any of these. But those other readings allow for no suitable explanation of why Aristotle should say that if one perceives in only part of the time, one perceives only part of the thing. And yet, as appears from the sequel, this premise is at the heart of his argument that there are no imperceptible times.

is absurd.] And so all [things] are perceptible, but they do not appear as big as they are; for one sees the magnitude of the sun and the four-cubit [magnitude] from far away, but it does not[, in either case,] appear as big as [it is], but sometimes [it appears so small as to be] indivisible, though [what] one sees [is] not indivisible. The cause concerning this has been stated in our previous [speeches].[139] And so that there is no imperceptible time [is] manifest from these [considerations]; but concerning the previously mentioned perplexity, [we] must examine whether it is admissible to perceive more [than one object] simultaneously or [whether] it is not admissible.[140] And by "simultaneously" I mean in one indivisible time [for all the objects] in relation to one another.[141] In the first place, then, is it admissible in this way, [namely,] to perceive [them] simultaneously, but [each] by a different [part] of the soul, and not by what is indivisible [simply], but by [something] indivisible in the way that everything that is continuous [is]? Or [must we object], in the first place, with respect to [perceptibles] in accord with the one sense, I mean for instance sight, that if it [i.e., the soul,] will be perceiving one [color] by one part [of itself] and another by another, it will have parts, [namely] these, [that belong to the same genus and are] more [than one] in species?[142] For indeed, it

---

139 Aristotle is presumably referring here to the cause why the object that one sees is not indivisible, but (always) divisible into perceptible parts. Cf. 445b3–20 in the previous chapter. As for his other claim here, namely, that the perceived object does not (always) appear as big as it is, he has not said, at least not so far as I can see, what the cause is; but it seems to me that this is ultimately because size is a relative term, i.e., because a thing is as big or as small as it is, as indeed it is big or small, only in relation to the sizes of other things. Aristotle may have chosen to call attention to this fact about size, which seems only tangentially related to the question of whether there can be imperceptible times, because of its relevance to the larger question of this chapter, namely, whether it is possible to perceive more than one object simultaneously; for it leads us to consider what it means to be one (perceptible) quality or (perceptible) object.

140 Cf. 447a12ff.

141 Cf. 447a13–14 and n.118 above.

142 In this clause, I read *pleiō te merē hexei eidei taũta*, which is the text of Biehl, except for the particle *te*, which I read in accord with all the manuscripts, as

perceives [all colors], again, by the same genus [of sense perception, namely, sight].[143] And if someone were to assert that, as [we have] two eyes, nothing prevents [its being] like this also in the soul, [we would say] that perhaps some one [perceptible object as actually perceived] comes into being from these [i.e., from the two eyes], and their actuality/activity (*energeia*) [as perceivers] is one; but if so, insofar as that [which comes into being] from both [eyes

---

opposed to Biehl's *ge*, a modern emendation first proposed by Bäumker. Biehl also modifies the reading of manuscripts E and M, which he otherwise follows, by reading *eidei* (from manuscripts L, S, U, W, X, and P) instead of *aei*, so that his text reads *pleiō ge merē hexei eidei taûta*, as opposed to the *pleiō te merē hexei aei taûta* of those two manuscripts. The reading *eidei* ("in species") seems to be a clear improvement over *aei* ("always"), especially since the following sentence looks like an explanation of why Aristotle said "more [than one] in species." As for the small difference between *te* and *ge*, it can hardly be captured in translation, but the *te* of the manuscripts makes sense as a way of pairing this clause with the sentence at 448b29, whose translation begins with "furthermore" (*eti* in Greek). This clause and that sentence would thus constitute Aristotle's twofold objection to the proposal that different perceptibles are perceived by different parts of the perceiving soul (with the perceiving soul understood as a continuous magnitude), insofar as his objection concerns perceptibles in accord with a single sense (cf. "in the first place, with respect to [perceptibles] in accord with the one sense," 448b22–23).

143 I translate this sentence in accord with Biehl's text, which reads *kai gar aisthanetai palin tōi autōi genei*. The text of the other chief family of manuscripts, which includes L, S, U, W, and X, is *kai gar ha aisthanetai en tōi autōi genei estin*. According to that other family of manuscripts, the clause preceding this sentence also differs from the reading I have chosen; it reads *pleiō te merē hexei eidei taútá*. The reading of those manuscripts, including that earlier clause, would be translated, instead of my "Or [must we object]... that... it will have parts, [namely] these, [that belong to the same genus and are] more [than one] in species? For indeed, it perceives [all colors], again, by the same genus [of sense perception, namely, sight]," as "Or [must we object] that... it will have more parts [than one that are] the same in species? For indeed, the [perceptibles] that it perceives are in the same genus." Although there are reasons why one might prefer this reading, it is difficult to see why the perception of perceptibles belonging to the same genus, on the assumption that it is by different parts of a single sense, must be by parts that are the same in species; but it does make sense, on this assumption, that the several parts of the same genus of sense perception, i.e., the same sense, each adapted to perceive some particular quality, would be different in species. Cf. 449a16–19.

is] one, that which perceives will be one,[144] whereas if [the perceptible objects are] separate, [the case] will not be similar [to what it is intended to illustrate]. Furthermore, the same senses will [each] be more [than one], just as if someone were to assert [that a science, geometry, for instance, since it studies different species of the same genus of intelligibles, e.g., triangles and squares, is] **449a** different sciences; for neither will there be the actuality [of perceiving each of the different objects of a single sense] without the potentiality pertaining to itself [i.e., distinct from the potentiality for perceiving each of the other objects of that sense], nor without this [i.e., the actuality or actualities just referred to,] will there be a sense. And if one perceives these in one and [an] indivisible [time], [it is] clear that one also [so perceives] the others; for it was more admissible [to perceive] more [than one] of these [latter] simultaneously, [namely,] the ones [that are] different in genus.[145]

---

144 Beginning from 448b28 ("but if so..."), I follow Biehl's text, which accords only with manuscript E (since manuscript M has an ungrammatical *hē* instead of *hēi*), and which reads *ei de, hēi men hen to ex amphoin, hen kai to aisthanomenon estai.* Manuscripts L, S, U, W, and X, however, read *ekei de, ei men hen to ex amphoin, ekeino to aisthanomenon estai*, which would be translated as "but there [i.e., in the soul], if that [which comes into being] from both [parts is] one, that [one, and not the two different parts,] will be what perceives." (And in accord with this, the bracketed "[perceptible object as actually perceived]" in the earlier part of this sentence would have to be replaced with "[sense organ].") But read in this way, the main clause, namely, "that [one, and not the two different parts,] will be what perceives," seems to do little more than repeat the if-clause.

145 I read *tōn tōi genei heterōn* at the end of this clause (449a4–5), following manuscript L, rather than *ē tōn tōi genei heterōn*, with Biehl, who follows all the other manuscripts (and doesn't even record the reading of L in his apparatus). According to Biehl's text, instead of "for it was more admissible [to perceive] more [than one] of these [latter] simultaneously, [namely,] the ones [that are] different in genus," the clause after the semicolon would be translated as "for it was more admissible [to perceive] more [than one] of these simultaneously than the ones [that are] different in genus." The difficulty with Biehl's text is that, since the word "these" (in both of its occurrences) would have to refer to the perceptibles that are the same in genus, it makes the entire sentence a non sequitur, in which the clause after the semicolon supports the opposite of the claim that it is apparently intended to support. For this reason, Biehl, along with most editors, proposed to add the word *mē*

But if, then, the soul perceives sweet by one [part] but white by another part, either that [perceptible object in actuality] which [comes into being] from[146] these [parts] is something one or [it is] not one. But [it is] necessary [that it be] one; for the perceptive [part of the soul] is something one.[147] Of what one [object], then, is that [one something, which perceives both sweet and white, perceptive]? For [there is] nothing one [resulting] from these [i.e., from sweet and white].[148] [It is] necessary, therefore, that there be

---

(i.e., "not") to the first part of the sentence so that it would be translated as "And if one does not perceive these in one and [an] indivisible [time], [it is] clear that one also [does not so perceive] the others. . . ." This proposed emendation, however, would be a major change, and one that has no manuscript support; moreover, it doesn't seem to me to offer as clear a train of thought between this and the following sentence as does the version I have translated. On the other hand, the difficulty with the reading I have chosen from manuscript L is that it contradicts the earlier part of the chapter, where Aristotle had said, for instance, "But again, if [it is] impossible [to perceive] simultaneously the [perceptibles that fall] under the same sense, if they are two, [it is] clear that it is still less admissible to perceive simultaneously those pertaining to two senses, for instance white and sweet" (447b21–24; cf. 447b6–9, 448a13–19). However, Aristotle's arguments in support of that earlier claim left much to be desired, and in particular they ignored the difficulty involved in perceiving contraries within the same genus at the same time (cf. n.136 above); and so it seems possible that his statement here refers to what an attentive reader would have concluded from that earlier passage, as opposed to its explicit claim. If this is so, the boldness of Aristotle's procedure might help to explain why the true reading (on this view) was preserved in only a single manuscript. Now I am definitely not certain that this reading that I have chosen is the correct one. But if it is, Aristotle's deliberate contradiction of his own earlier claim would be another pointer to the question, which he nowhere in the entire chapter tries explicitly to answer, of how the soul perceives contraries within the same genus at the same time (consider, however, 447b24–448a1), a question that would seem to be an important part of the more general question of the character of the "something one" that it perceives.

146 The word *ek*, which I translate as "from," is absent from Biehl's text, through a mere error in printing.

147 Aristotle does not mean by this that the perceptive part of the soul is one in the sense proposed above, namely, a continuum that perceives different objects with different parts of itself. Cf. n.149 below.

148 Aristotle had allowed, however, at 447b1–2, that a sort of one, though only a one by concomitance, might result from such disparate perceptibles.

some one [part] of the soul by which it perceives all [perceptible objects], as has been said before,[149] but [that it perceives] one genus [of perceptibles] through one [sense organ] and another through another. Then insofar as it is undivided in actuality, is that which is perceptive of sweet and white one,[150] but whenever it becomes divided in actuality, [does it become] different [from itself]? Or [rather,] as it is admissible in the case of the things (*pragmatōn*) themselves, [is it] also in the same way in the case of the soul; for the same [thing], one in number,[151] is white and sweet, and [of] many other [qualities], if the affections are not separate from one another, although the being (*to einai*) [is] different for each. Similarly, then, one must set it down also in the case of the soul that what is perceptive of all [perceptibles] is one and the same in number, yet [that] in its being (*tōi einai*) [it is] different, i.e., different in genus [in its perception] of some [groups of perceptibles, namely, those that differ in genus] and [different] in species [in its perception] of others[, namely, those that differ in species]. So that

---

149 This might conceivably be a reference to *De Anima* 426b17–23ff. and 431a20ff., where Aristotle had asserted and argued for this claim that the perceptive part of the soul is one. But when he refers to other works of his own, he typically says explicitly that he is doing so, and therefore it seems more likely that he is referring here to an earlier passage in this same treatise. And in fact he has just said, in speaking of the object of vision, at any rate, that—insofar as a single object of vision may result from the two eyes working together—"that which perceives will be one" (448b28–29). Accordingly, it seems to me that his reference here is to that statement, even though it had applied explicitly only to a single sense.

150 At 449a11, I read *hen esti*, with manuscripts E, M, and Y, rather than *hen ti esti*, with Biehl, who follows the other manuscripts. According to Biehl's text, this clause would be translated, instead of as "is that which is perceptive of sweet and white one," as "is that which is perceptive of sweet and white something one." But I don't think that Aristotle means to suggest here that that which is perceptive of sweet and white must be a "something," as distinct, for instance, from an activity.

151 At 449a14, I read *to gar auto hen arithmōi*, with manuscripts E, M, and Y, rather than *to gar auto kai hen arithmōi*, with Biehl, who follows the other manuscripts. According to Biehl's text, this clause would be translated, instead of as "for the same [thing], one in number, is white and sweet," as "for [what is] the same and one in number is white and sweet."

[the soul] would also perceive [these several perceptibles] simultaneously by [what is] one and the same, though not the same in speech (*logōi*). And that everything perceptible is a magnitude,[152] and [that] it is not possible to perceive an indivisible, [is] clear. For there is [a region], unlimited in its range [i.e., its range of distances from the observer], from where [a visible object] could not be seen, and [a region,] a limited [one,] from where it is seen; and it is similar also for the smellable and audible and as many [perceptible objects] as [people] perceive without touching [them]. And there is some extremity of the range from where [any given object] is not seen, and a first [point] from where it is seen. [It is] necessary, then, that this be indivisible, [that point] where, if [the perceptible] is in the [region] beyond [it], it is not admissible [for it] to be perceived, but [if it is] in the [region] on this side [of it], [it is] necessary that it be perceived. If, then, there is some indivisible perceptible, whenever it is placed at the extremity, [the] last from where it is not perceptible and [the] first [from where it is] perceptible, it will turn out to be visible and invisible simultaneously; but this [is] impossible. And so concerning the sense organs[153] and the percepti- 449b
bles, what manner [of being] they [i.e., the perceptibles,] have, both in common and in accord with each sense organ, it has been said. And of what (pl.) remains, one must examine first concerning memory and remembering.

152 Cf. 445b10–11, where Aristotle had said that "[it is] impossible to see white, but not [to see it as being] so big." This statement is merely a generalization of that one, except for the fact, which seems to me to be important, that here Aristotle uses the noun translated as "magnitude" rather than the adjective translated as "so big." Cf. n. 93 above.

153 This is presumably, in part at any rate, a reference to the discussion of the sense organs in Chapter 2.

On Memory and Recollection

Chapter 1 449b

Concerning memory and remembering one must say what it is, and on account of what cause it comes to be, and to which of the parts of the soul this affection (*pathos*) happens—and [also with regard to] recollecting; for [it is] not the same [people who] are apt at remembering and apt at recollecting, but for the most part those who are slow are more apt at remembering,[1] whereas those who are quick and good at learning are more apt at recollecting. So first, then, one must grasp what sort of [things] are those that can be remembered; for often one is deceived about this. For neither does what is yet to be admit of being remembered—but it can be opined and hoped for/expected (and there might even be some science of that [which is to be] hoped for/expected, as some assert [that] prophecy [is])—nor [can there be memory] of what is present, but [rather] sense perception; for by this we recognize neither what is yet to be nor what has been, but only what is present. But memory is of what has been; no one would assert that he remembers what is present, [namely,] that it is present, for instance this white [thing] here when he sees it, nor [that he remembers] what is contemplated, when in fact he is contemplating and thinking of [it]. But he asserts only that he perceives the one and that he knows the other; but when he has the knowledge and the perception without the activities (*energeiōn*) [of knowing and perceiving], thus [i.e.,

---

1 At 449b7, I read *mnēmonikōteroi*, with the preponderance of the manuscripts, rather than *mnēmonikoi*, with Biehl, who follows manuscript Y and the first hand of manuscript E. According to Biehl's text the translation would read "apt at remembering" instead of "more apt at remembering."

under these conditions,] he remembers[2] the [angles] of the triangle, that they are equal to two right [angles],[3] [remembering] on the one hand that he learned or contemplated it, and on the other hand that he heard or saw it or something of such a sort; for whenever one is active (*energēi*) in remembering, one must speak in this way in one's soul, [saying, namely,] that one heard this, or perceived it or thought/apprehended it, earlier. So memory, then, is

---

2 The word translated here as "remembers" is *memnētai*, a form of the verb *mimnēskein* (whose perfect middle-passive infinitive is *memnēsthai*), rather than of the verb *mnēmoneuein*, which Aristotle has been using so far in this treatise to speak of remembering. This is, in fact, the only occurrence of the verb *mimnēskein/memnēsthai* in Chapter 1, whereas *mnēmoneuein* appears in this chapter a total of twelve times. From what follows later in this sentence, it would appear that the word *memnētai* is being used here as an equivalent to *energei kata to mnēmoneuein*, or "is active in remembering," an interpretation that is supported by a passage in Chapter 2, 452b26–28, where Aristotle seems to identify *to memnēsthai* with "to be active with one's memory" (*energounta... tēi mnēmēi*). And in both of these subsequent passages, "to be active in remembering, or with one's memory" seems to be distinguished from "to remember" in the widest sense of the word at least in part by requiring the present awareness that one remembers. Thus, I take it that Aristotle chooses to use the word *memnētai* here in order to insist on this present awareness. And this would be consistent with the form of the word itself, since the verb *mimnēskein* means "to remind," so that the root meaning of its perfect middle-passive infinitive *memnēsthai* would have been something like "to remind oneself" or "to be reminded," and one must of course become aware of whatever one is reminded of. Now middle-passive forms of the word *mimnēskein/memnēsthai* will be used frequently in Chapter 2, the chapter devoted primarily to recollection, and indeed *anamimnēskesthai*, which means "to recollect" or "to recall [something forgotten] to mind" (and whose active form, *anamimnēskein*, also means "to remind"), is clearly a compound form of the verb *mimnēskein*. Accordingly, in order to indicate the close connection of the word *mimnēskein/memnēsthai* with recollection, and in order to allow the reader to make up his own mind as to whether, in every case where Aristotle uses this word, he intends a genuine distinction between it and the word *mnēmoneuein*, I will translate all subsequent uses of middle-passive forms of *mimnēskein* not as forms of "to remember," but as forms of "to recall."

3 The words translated as "the [angles] of the triangle, that they are equal to two right [angles]" are bracketed by Biehl, who thinks that they should be deleted, even though they appear in all the manuscripts. That the angles of any triangle are equal to two right angles is proved by Euclid in Book One, Proposition 32, of the *Elements.*

neither sense perception nor taking [something] to be the case, but a having (*hexis*)[4] or an affection (*pathos*) of some one of these, when there has come to be time. Of the now in the now there is no memory, as has also been said earlier, but of what is present [there is] sense perception, while of what is yet to be [there is] hope/expectation, and of what has been [there is] memory. Wherefore all memory [is bound up] with time. So that these alone of the animals, as many as perceive time, remember, and [they do so] by means of that by which they perceive [it]. And since it has been spoken earlier concerning imagination (*phantasias*) in the [things said] concerning soul[5] and [since] it is not possible to think/apprehend without an appearance (*phantasmatos*);[6] (for the same **450a** *pathos* happens in thinking/apprehending as in drawing a diagram; for there, even though we do not make any use of [the fact] that the size of the triangle is determinate, we nevertheless draw it determinate in size; and in the same way the one who thinks/appre-

---

4 The word *hexis* is derived from the verb *ekhein*, which means "to have," and its literal translation would be something like "having." Although it is usually translated as "state" (cf. *On Sense Perception and Sense-Perceptibles*, n. 2), the first sense of the word that Aristotle gives in his discussion of it in Book Δ, Chapter 20, of the *Metaphysics* (1022b4–8) is not that; he says, rather, that it is like an activity of that which has something and that which is had, which he describes as being "in between" the one and the other. Thus, for instance, there would be a *hexis* that consists of having (i.e., wearing) clothes, a *hexis* that is "in between" the one who has the clothes and the clothes he has. And if the word is understood in this way, as I think it should be in this passage, the more literal translation "having" seems more appropriate than "state."

5 Imagination (*phantasia*) is discussed thematically and at length in Chapter 3 of Book Three of *De Anima* (427b14–429a9), and it is also treated elsewhere in the work, especially in Book Three.

6 Despite the reference in this sentence to *De Anima*, Aristotle asserts here that "it is not possible to think/apprehend without an appearance" without reminding us of the fact that he had twice made nearly identical assertions there (431a16–17; 432a8–9). Perhaps the reason for his not doing so is this: the assertion here is an unqualified one about thinking as such, whereas those in *De Anima* might seem to be qualified or limited in scope, the first because it occurs in a discussion of the soul's practical thinking, and the second because it is preceded by the somewhat tentative expression "since also there is no separated thing (*pragma*) over and above the magnitudes, as it seems, that are perceptible" (432a3–4).

hends, even if he does not think [of the object of his thought as being] of [any] size, puts before his eyes [something] of [some] size, but does not think [of it] as [being] of [any] size; and if its nature is [such that it is] among those [objects of thought] that are of some size, but not a determinate [size], he puts [before his eyes something] of a determinate size, but he thinks/apprehends it only as of some size); now on account of what cause it is not admissible to think/apprehend anything without a continuous [magnitude], nor the things that are not in time apart from time, [that is] another speech (*logos*); but it is necessary that magnitude and motion be recognized by means of that by which [we] also [recognize] time;[7] and [any] appearance (*to phantasma*) is an affection (*pathos*) of the common sense;[8] so that this is manifest, that the know-

7 The words translated as "time," "magnitude," and "motion" in this passage are all singular forms without a definite article, and I might well have translated them as "a time," "a magnitude," and "a motion." Aristotle is not referring here to the nature of time, that of magnitude, or that of motion, but to particular times, magnitudes, and motions.

8 The "common sense" (*tēs koinēs aisthēseōs*) is mentioned by Aristotle only here and at 686a31–32 of *On the Parts of Animals*. In addition, there is almost certainly another reference to it at 431b5 of *De Anima*, although that passage includes only the feminine adjective for "common," with the noun for "sense" having to be supplied in thought. Now in an earlier passage in *De Anima* Aristotle had spoken of common perceptibles, such as magnitude, figure, and motion, by which he meant objects the perception of which is common to more than one particular sense (*De Anima* 418a8–11, a17–20; cf. 425a27), but he had not spoken of a common sense. But in the later passage, in which he speaks of seeing the motion of an enemy's beacon fire as the work of "the common [sense]," rather than of sight, he seems to have been suggesting that sight as sight sees only color, so that the perceptibles, such as motion, that can be grasped by other senses as well are never properly understood simply as the objects of that one sense. And this reading of that passage is consistent with the fact that here he will go on to say that recognition of the objects of the common sense belongs to "the first perceptive [part]" (450a11–12; cf. a14), by which he seems to mean that the perceptibles such as magnitude and motion are objects not of any particular sense, but of the primary perceptive function of the soul. At all events, we should note that, just as the example of an enemy's beacon fire was presented in *De Anima* in order to illustrate how one is moved whenever one is attending to appearances (*phantasmatōn*), Aristotle says here that when the common sense recognizes its objects, it is their appearance (*to phantasma*) that comes to belong to it as

ledge[9] of these [i.e., of continuity, time, magnitude, and motion,] belongs to the first perceptive [part]; but memory, even that of the intelligibles, is not without an appearance (*phantasmatos*); so that[10] [memory] would be by concomitance of what was thought/apprehended,[11] but in itself [it would be a function] of the first perceptive [part]. Wherefore it also belongs to some others among the animals, and not only to human beings and the [animals] that have opinion or understanding. But if it were some [function] of the thinking/apprehending parts, it would not belong to many of the

---

a *pathos*. Now an "appearance" (*phantasma*) is the work of imagination (*phantasia*; cf. *De Anima* 428a1–2) and something present to imagination. And indeed, this very long sentence began with a somewhat unexpected reference to what Aristotle had said in *De Anima* about imagination. Aristotle seems to be suggesting, then, that the object of the common sense, however we are to understand the common sense, involves the work of imagination, or, in other words, that the work of sense perception is not complete apart from imagination.

9 The word translated here as "knowledge" is *gnōsis*, which has a wide enough range of meanings that Aristotle can speak of it as belonging to all animals, on the grounds that they all have sense perception, which he calls a sort of *gnōsis* (*On the Generation of Animals* 731a31–33). It is closely related to the infinitive *gnōridzein*, which I translated just above (450a10) as "be recognized"; and it is to be distinguished from the noun *epistēmē*, which I translated as "knowledge" at 449b19, and which refers to the knowledge, or science, of intelligible and universal truths (and in particular, in that passage, to the knowledge that the angles of any triangle are equal to two right angles).

10 This would seem to be the beginning of the main clause of the very long sentence that began with "And since it has been spoken earlier..." at 449b30.

11 At 450a13, I read *nooumenou*, with the great preponderance of the manuscripts, rather than *noētikou*, with Biehl, whose reading was suggested by an anonymous Latin translator (though it appears as well in manuscript P, which was unavailable to Biehl). Biehl's text would be translated as "it [i.e., memory,] would be by concomitance [a function] of the thinking [part]" instead of "[memory] would be by concomitance of what was thought/apprehended." In either case, the question arises as to why, even granting all the premises that have been laid out in this long and difficult sentence, memory should be only by concomitance of what was thought (or that it should be only by concomitance a function of the thinking part). And it seems to me that the reading I have chosen points more directly toward a possible answer to this question than does Biehl's.

other animals, and perhaps to none of the mortal ones,[12] since even now [it does] not [belong] to all, on account of their not all having perception of time. For always, as we also said earlier,[13] whenever one's memory is active, [recalling] that one saw this or heard it or learned it, one perceives in addition that [it was] earlier; and the earlier and later are in time. And so it is manifest which of the [parts] of the soul memory is [a function] of, [namely,] that [it is that] which imagination [is] also [a function] of. And able to be remembered in themselves are as many [appearing objects] as are not merely imagined,[14] but [able to be remembered] by concomitance are as many [objects present to the soul] as[, without themselves being objects of imagination,] are not [grasped] without imagination. But someone might be perplexed how, when the affection (*pathos*) is present but the thing (*pragmatos*) is absent, that which is not present is ever remembered. For it is clear that one must think [of] that which comes into being through perception (*dia tēs aisthēseōs*), in the soul and in the part of the body that has it, [namely,] the affection (*pathos*), the having (*hexin*) of which we assert to be memory, as a sort of picture. For the motion as it comes

---

12 At 450a18, I read *thnētōn*, with all the manuscripts, rather than *thēriōn*, with Biehl, who accepts an emendation proposed by Rassow. Biehl's text would be translated as "beasts" instead of "mortal ones."

13 Cf. 449b18–23.

14 At 450a24, I read *osa mē esti phantasta*, with manuscripts E and Y, rather than *osa esti phantasta*, with Biehl, whose reading lacks manuscript support, or *ōn esti phantasia*, which appears in most of the other manuscripts (and also as a marginal note in E). The phrase translated here as "as many [appearing objects] as are not merely imagined" would be translated, if I were to follow Biehl's text, as "as many [things] as appear to the imagination," and according to the third alternative, as "[those things] of which there is imagination." The word *phantasta*, which I translate as "merely imagined," is a very uncommon word, which appears here for the first time in what survives of ancient Greek, and which does not appear elsewhere in Aristotle, nor indeed again for another century. Accordingly, it is difficult to be certain about its meaning. Indeed, Chrysippus, writing a century after Aristotle, seems to mean something quite different by it. But as I translate the text, what Aristotle says here is supported by, and anticipates, what he will say later in the chapter at 451a2–12.

to be stamps a sort of imprint[, consisting] of the percept (*tou aisthēmatos*),[15] like those who make seals with [signet] rings. Where- 450b
fore also memory doesn't come into being for those, on the one hand, [who are] much in motion on account of suffering (*pathos*) or their age, as if the motion and the seal were falling upon running water; and [memory doesn't come into being] for some, on the other hand, on account of their being worn down like old walls, and on account of [the] hardness of that which receives the *pathos*, the imprint doesn't come into being in [them]. Wherefore the extremely young as well as the old are lacking in memory; for the former are in flux on account of their growth, while the latter [are in flux] on account of their decay. And similarly, neither the excessively quick nor the excessively slow appear able to remember; for the former are wetter than what is needed, while the latter are harder; and so for the ones, the appearance (*phantasma*) doesn't remain in their soul, while it doesn't [really] touch the others. But if, then, what happens concerning memory is of such a sort, does one remember this *pathos* or that from which it came into being? For if [it is] this, we would remember nothing of the things that are absent; but if [it is] that, how, in perceiving this, do we remember what is absent, which we do not perceive? And if it is similar to an imprint or a drawing in us, why would the perception of this

15 By adding a comma and the word "consisting" within square brackets after the word "imprint," I am interpreting the genitive *tou aisthēmatos* as a genitive of explanation/appositive genitive (cf. Smyth, *Greek Grammar*, para. 1322). This interpretation is in keeping with a variant reading in manuscript M, which has, instead of the genitive *tou aisthēmatos*, the accusative *to aisthēma*, which is clearly in apposition with the word for "imprint." As I interpret the sentence, the percept is itself already the imprint stamped in us by the motion of perception, rather than something from which the imprint is then stamped. By the form of its ending, the noun *aisthēmatos* (or *aisthēma*), which I translate as "percept," refers to the result of a motion or of an action, as a poem (*poiēma*) is the result of making (*poiein*) and a piece of writing (*gramma*) is the result of writing (*graphein*). Accordingly, the *aisthēma*, or the percept, is a result of perceiving (*aisthanesthai*), i.e., of perception understood as the motion of perceiving, and there is no distinction between this *aisthēma* and the *pathos*, or the sort of picture, that Aristotle has just spoken of as coming into being in us as a result of perception (*dia tēs aisthēseōs*).

itself be a memory of [something] different, but not of this itself? For the one whose memory is active contemplates this *pathos* and perceives this. How then does one remember what is not present? For it would be possible also to see and to hear what is not present. Or is it possible that this is admissible and [that] it happens? For as the figure[16] drawn on the writing tablet is both a figure and a likeness, and this one and the same [thing] is both, yet the being of both is not the same, and it is possible to contemplate [it] both as a figure and as a likeness, so also one must take the appearance (*phantasma*) in us both to be itself in itself an object of contemplation[17] and [to be] an appearance (*phantasma*) of [something] other. And so insofar as [it is] in itself, it is an object of contemplation or an appearance (*phantasma*), but insofar as [it is] of [something] other, [it is] a likeness, as it were, and an object of memory. So that when its motion is active, if the soul perceives it as it is in itself, it appears to come to one as a sort of thought or an appearance (*phantasma*); but if [the soul perceives it] as [being] of [something] other, [it perceives it] just as in the [case of the] drawing one contemplates [the figure] as a likeness, and not having seen Koriskos, as of Koriskos; here the *pathos* of this contemplation is different from when one contemplates [the figure] as a drawn fig-
451a ure, and in the soul as well the [appearance] comes into being, in the one way, only as a thought, while in the other way, as there [i.e., in the case of the drawing, one recognizes] that it is a likeness, [it comes into being here as] an object of memory. And on account of this, sometimes, when such motions come into being in our soul from our having perceived earlier, we don't know if it is happening in accordance with having perceived, and we are in doubt if it is a memory or not; but sometimes it happens that we take thought

---

16 The Greek word for "figure" is *zōon*, which is also, and primarily, the word for "animal."

17 At 450b25, I read *auto kath' auto einai theōrēma*, with manuscripts E and Y, rather than *auto ti kath' auto einai*, with Biehl, whose reading is in accord with manuscripts L, S, and U. According to Biehl's text, instead of "to be itself in itself an object of contemplation," the phrase would be translated as "to be something itself in itself."

and recollect that we heard or saw something earlier. This happens whenever, after contemplating [the appearance] as itself, one changes and contemplates it as of [something] other. And the contrary also comes to be, as happened to Antipheron of Oreus and to others [who were] out of their minds; for they spoke of the appearances (*phantasmata*) [in their souls] as [things] that had been and as [if they were] remembering [these things]. And this comes to be, whenever someone contemplates that which is not a likeness as a likeness. Exercises preserve memory by reminding again [and again]; and this is nothing different from often contemplating [some appearance] as a likeness and not as [it is] in itself. And so what memory is, and to remember, has been said, that it is a having (*hexis*) of an appearance (*phantasmatos*), [taken] as a likeness of that of which [it is] an appearance (*phantasma*), and [it has been said] what part of those in us [it is a function] of, that [it is a function] of the first perceptive [part] and that by which we perceive time.

Chapter 2

It remains to speak about recollecting. And so first we ought to posit as being present [and available] as many [of the statements made] in our tentative speeches as are true.[18] For recollection is neither a getting back (*analēpsis*) of memory nor a getting (*lēpsis*) [of it]; for when one first learns or is affected (*pathēi*), one is neither getting back any memory (for there has been none before) nor

18 The Greek expression translated as "tentative speeches" is *epikheirēmatikois logois*, which can also mean exploratory or (merely) argumentative speeches. An ancient list of Aristotle's works (Diogenes Laertius, 5.1.22–28) contains several that he might be referring to here, but they have not survived, and so the reference remains unclear. It is also unclear, at least to me, what true statements we are being asked to posit as being present. If, as seems likely, it is what he goes on to say here, namely, that recollection is neither a getting back of memory nor a getting of it, he will support these claims with arguments, and so they are not merely being posited. On the other hand, without such arguments, i.e., without fresh insight, it would not have been clear that the statements Aristotle has called true statements are indeed true.

is one getting [one] from the beginning; but when the state (*hexis*) or the affection (*pathos*)[19] has come into being in [one], then there is memory. So that it [i.e., memory,] does not come into being in [someone] together with the affection (*pathous*) as it is coming into being in [him]. Furthermore, the affection, when it has first come into being in the undivided and ultimate [organ of perception],[20] is immediately present in the [organ] that has been affected (*tōi pathonti*), and [so is] the knowledge, if one ought to call the having (*hexin*) or the affection knowledge[21] (and nothing prevents our also

---

19 Aristotle has spoken of memory first as a *pathos* (449b4–5; cf. b24–25), but then later as the having (*hexis*) of a *pathos*, a having, namely, of the appearance that comes into being in the soul as a result of an act of perceiving or thinking (450a27–30, 451a14–16). And though the later formulation would seem to be the more precise one—and Aristotle will soon remind us that he had said that this is what memory is (451b2–4)—he allows here again that memory might be rightly characterized as itself a *pathos*. Perhaps this is because he thought that, in a broader sense of the word, it is one; or perhaps this is an indication that this chapter is not merely an account of recollection, nor merely a sequel to the first chapter, but also a kind of return to the beginning of the treatment of memory.

20 By the "undivided and ultimate [organ of perception]" Aristotle is referring to the organ by which we see appearances (*phantasmata*), the organ that he had called the "first perceptive [part]" in Chapter 1, where he also spoke of it as the seat of memory (450a11–12, 451a14–17; cf. *De Anima* 422b22, 424a24–25, 426b15–16). Aristotle refers to the character of this organ as something one and undivided in Chapter 7 of *On Sense Perception and Sense-Perceptibles*, 449a10–20, a passage that also makes clear that it is not undivided or indivisible in every respect (cf. *De Anima* 427a9–16; *On the Motion of Animals* 702b15–31). Note that Aristotle speaks of an affection having come into being in this bodily organ when one has learned or acquired knowledge, even though the intellect, in his view, does not have a bodily organ (cf. *De Anima* 429a10–b5). Yet what he says here makes sense, since he also holds that one cannot think, i.e., apprehend what is intelligible, without an appearance (449b31–450a1 and n. 6 above), and he regards the ultimate organ of perception as the seat of appearances (cf. 449b30–450a14). Moreover, the knowledge that one acquires is necessarily expressed in words that one must hear or see or at least imagine (cf. 449b18–22; *On Sense Perception and Sense-Perceptibles* 437a11–17), and these words would not appear to one without an affection of that ultimate organ of perception.

21 Aristotle hesitates to use the term "knowledge" for the having (*hexin*, which can also mean "state") or the affection that has come into being in the ulti-

remembering, incidentally, some of the things that we know); yet the remembering, in itself, will not be present before time has passed; for one remembers now what one saw or [the affection one] was affected with before; one does not remember now [the affection] one was affected with [just] now. Furthermore, it is manifest that it is possible to remember without now recollecting, but [remembering, rather,] from the beginning, after perceiving or being affected. But whenever one gets back the knowledge that one had before, or [the] perception or whatever [it is], the having (*hexin*) of which we called memory,[22] this is, and then [there is], recollecting one of the things mentioned. And remembering happens and memory follows.[23] Nor do even these, in fact, without qualification, [constitute recollection] if, having been present before, they come into being in [one] again, but [if they come into being] in one way [they do], while [if they come into being] in another way [they do] not. For it is admissible for the same person to learn and to discover the same thing twice; recollecting, then, must differ from these [cases], and [it must be that] people recollect [only] when a further beginning beyond that from which they learn is present in

---

mate organ of perception when one has learned. But the fact, which he immediately goes on to mention, that we can remember, incidentally, some of the things we know (cf. 450a12–14 and n. 11 above) suggests that one may use it, though only in an attenuated sense of the word "knowledge."

22 At 451a14–16, Aristotle called memory the having (*hexin*) of an appearance, an appearance [taken] as a likeness of that of which it is an appearance.

23 This statement that memory follows [these acts of] remembering helps to explain why Aristotle said at the beginning of the chapter (451a20–21) that recollection is not the getting back of memory. For recollection culminates, not in getting back memory, but in getting back, in an act of remembering, the knowledge that one had before, or [the] perception or whatever it is, the having (*hexin*) of which Aristotle has called memory. And the state (i.e., the "having," *hexis*) that is memory follows this act of remembering, or at least it is likely to do so if one is attentive, just as the memory that had been lost followed the original act of learning or perceiving. (I use the expression "act[s] of remembering" in this footnote, even though Aristotle only says "remembering," because I think it is the activity of remembering, as distinct from remembering in the widest sense of the word, that he is referring to here, and that he then distinguishes from the memory that is said to follow it. Cf. n. 2 above.)

[them]. Now [it is] because this one motion naturally comes to be after this other one [that] recollections happen. If [this sequence is] from necessity, it is clear that when one is moved with that [motion], one will be moved with this one.[24] But if [it is] not from necessity, but by habit, one will be moved [with this motion] for the most part. But it happens that some people are habituated [when they are moved] once, more than others are when they are moved often; wherefore we remember some things after seeing them once, more than others do [after seeing them] often. Accordingly, whenever we recollect, we are moved [at each stage of the process] with a particular one of our previous motions, until we are moved with the one after which that one [i.e., the motion of, or associated with, what we are recollecting,] habitually occurs. Wherefore we also hunt after what comes next in sequence, starting our thinking from [what is happening] now or at some other moment, and from [something] similar or contrary or [from] what is closely connected [to what we seek]. [It is] through this [that] recollection comes to be; for the motions of some of these are the same [as the motion of what we seek], those of others [go] together [with it], and those of others contain a part [of it], so that the remainder through which one was moved after that [part] is small. And so they search in this way, and even when they are not searching, they recollect in this way, whenever that [motion, i.e., the motion associated with what is to be recollected,] comes to be after a different motion. And for the most part, that [different, or penultimate, motion] comes to be after different motions of such a sort as we have [just] mentioned have come to be. And there is no need to examine how we recall[25] those [things] that are distant [from the one we start

---

24 At 451b12–13, I read *hotan ekeinēn kinēthēi, tēnde kinēthēsetai*, with manuscripts S, U, X, and (in part) L, rather than *hotan ekeinē kinēthēi, tēnde tēn kinēsin kinēthēsetai*, with Biehl, who follows manuscripts E, M, and Y (and who does not even record the reading *ekeinēn* as an alternative to his *ekeinē*). Biehl's text would have the translation, instead of my "when one is moved with that [motion], one will be moved with this one," as "when that [motion] is moved, one will be moved with this motion."

25 Cf. n. 2 above.

from], but [only] those that are close [to it]; for it is clear that the manner [of recollection] is the same. (And I mean "what comes next in sequence"[26] without one's having previously sought or [previously] recollected; for the motions follow one another by habit, this one after this one.) And whenever, then, one wishes to recollect, one will do this. One will seek to get hold of a beginning of motion, after which that [motion] will be. Wherefore recollections come to be most quickly and in the finest way from a beginning; 452a for as the things are related to one another in their sequence, so also are the motions. And easily remembered are as many things as have some order, as the mathematical [objects] do; but the inferior things are [remembered] with difficulty. And recollecting differs in this respect from learning again, [namely,] that [in recollecting] one will be able somehow to be moved through one's own agency [so as to come] to that [which follows] after the beginning. But whenever [one is] not [able to do this], but [can be so moved only] through [someone or something] other, one is [in this case] no longer recalling. And often one is unable to recollect at the moment, but after searching, one is able and one finds [what one is seeking]. And this comes about [for someone] when he sets many [things] in motion, until he produces the sort of motion which the thing (*to pragma*) [sought] will follow. For to recall[27] [i.e.,

26 Cf. 451b18.

27 The Greek for "to recall" is *to memnēsthai*. Now in n. 2 above, I suggested that this word was an equivalent for "to be active with one's memory," a suggestion that would also apply to the first of the two previous uses of this verb in the present chapter (451b26, 452a7), since it was referring to the culmination of the process of recollection, and that culmination is indeed remembering in the active sense of the word. But in this passage, Aristotle seems to be using the word not in that sense, or at least not primarily in that sense, but rather as a kind of equivalent for "*to be able* to recall" (in that other sense of the word "recall"). But I don't regard this difference as a reason for rejecting my earlier suggestion, which I still think captures what Aristotle primarily means by the word. For in the present context, he is disregarding the difference between what is active (or actual) and what is merely potential. Thus, for instance, at 452a4ff., he says that recollecting differs from learning again by the fact that (in the former case) one "will be able" to be moved through one's own agency in such a way as to reach that which comes after

to recall in the context of a recollective search,] is for a power, the one that produces [that sort of] motion, to be in one;[28] and this, in such a way that one is moved from [within] oneself and from the motions one has [in one], as has [just] been said. But one must get hold of a beginning. Wherefore [people] are thought (*dokousi*) to recollect sometimes by means of places.[29] And the cause [of this] is that they go quickly from one [thing] to another, as from milk to white, from white to air [or mist], and from this to moist, from which one recalls autumn, when one is seeking this season. Now in general, what is in the middle, of all things, is also like a beginning; for if not before, when one comes to this, one will recall, or [one will] no longer [recall] from anywhere else, for instance, if one were to think of [a series of things] labelled A, B, C, D, E, F,

---

the beginning; he does not say that one will be so moved in actuality. And he adds that if one isn't able to be so moved through one's own agency, "one is [in this case] no longer recalling"; he does not say that one is no longer able to recall.

28 At 452a10–11, I read *to eneinai dunamin tēn kinousan*, with manuscripts L, S, and U (and most others), rather than *to eneinai dunamei tēn kinousan*, with Biehl, who follows manuscripts E, M, and Y. According to Biehl's text, this clause would be translated as "For to recall is for the [beginning] that produces [that sort of motion] to be in one potentially." But I prefer the other version, largely because, as I indicated in the previous footnote, n. 27, it seems to me that there is recalling even, and especially, when that which produces the motion in question, i.e., the motion leading up to the thing sought, is present in one in actuality, and not merely potentially.

29 The Greek word translated as "places" is *topōn*, a form of *topos*, and it refers to a mnemonic technique, which was well known in antiquity, that involved the prior memorization of a set of different places (cf. *Topics* 163b28–31). For a discussion of this technique, see Richard Sorabji, *Aristotle on Memory*, 2nd ed. (Chicago: University of Chicago Press, 2006), 22–26, and also Cicero, *De Oratore* 2.353–360 and Quintilian, *Institutio Oratoria* 11.2.17–26. Now the instance of recollection that Aristotle goes to mention here doesn't appear to be an example of this mnemonic technique, since the things he mentions are intelligibly related to one another, whereas the technique is designed to allow one to memorize a set of unrelated items. But Aristotle has said only that people "are thought" to recollect sometimes in this manner, and perhaps they are thought to do this because the speed with which they arrive at the thing sought leads others to believe that this mnemonic technique must have been involved.

G, H; for if he doesn't recall at **, he recalls at **; for from there it is admissible to be moved to both, both to ** and to **. But if he isn't seeking one of these, he will recall after coming to C, if he is seeking ** or **; but if [he is] not, [he will recall after coming] to A, and [so on] always in this way.[30] And the cause of [our] some-

---

30 These two sentences present great difficulties for any modern editor or translator. It seems impossible to make sense of the reading of any one of the manuscripts, or even of a reading that combines several different manuscripts, and so editors and translators have been led to make various emendations. Now the manuscripts are in reasonably good agreement except for the references to single letters, and so rather than attempt a reconstruction of the text myself, I have decided to leave blank spaces where there is no consensus among the manuscripts regarding these letters. There are six places, then, where I have not offered any translation. For the first of them ("if he doesn't recall at **"), the manuscripts have either the Greek equivalent for the letter E or the pair of letters EH; for the second ("he recalls at **"), they have the Greek for the letter H, the letters GH, the letters HE, or, in one case, the letters EH; for the third ("both to **"), they have the Greek either for the letter D or the letter A; for the fourth ("and to **"), they have the Greek either for the letter E or, in one case, the letter H; for the fifth ("if he is seeking **"), they have the Greek either for the letter G or, in one case, the letter D; and in the sixth ("or **"), they have the Greek for the letter F or, in two cases, the letter H or, in one case, the letter B. (In making these claims about the manuscripts, I am relying on the critical apparatus in David Bloch's edition of the text, *Aristotle on Memory and Recollection* [Leiden: Brill, 2007].) Now if I were forced to offer a reading of my own, I would accept one originally proposed by Sorabji (*Aristotle on Memory*, 31–34), since it makes the best sense to me of any of the alternatives I am aware of. Here is a translation of these two sentences according to Sorabji's suggestion: "Now in general, what is in the middle, of all things, is also like a beginning; for if not before, when one comes to this, one will recall, or [one will] no longer [recall] from anywhere else, for instance, if one were to think of [a series of things] labelled A, B, C, D, E, F, G, H; for if he doesn't recall at H, he recalls at F; for from there it is admissible to be moved to both, both to G and to E. But if he isn't seeking one of these, he will recall after coming to C, if he is seeking D or B; but if [he is] not, [he will recall after coming] to A, and [so on] always in this way." The chief feature of this interpretation, as opposed to other possible ones, is that the term "what is in the middle" refers to the middle of each of several triplets, e.g., EFG, BCD. And in favor of this interpretation is the fact that Aristotle's claim at 452a18–19 that "when one comes to this" [i.e., to what is in the middle], "one will recall, or [one will] no longer [recall] from anywhere else" makes the best, or at least the most obvious, sense if the middle that he has in mind is adjacent to whatever is being sought; and in Sorabji's interpretation this is the case. On the other hand, there

times recalling, but sometimes not, [when starting] from the same [item] is that it is admissible to be moved beyond [the item one is seeking, as well as to it,] from the same beginning, for instance from C [one can be moved] to F or to D. Indeed, if [one is seeking to recollect through items] through which one hasn't been moved for a long time, one is moved to what is more habitual. For habit is then like nature. Wherefore we recollect quickly those things which we are often thinking about,[31] for just as this comes after

---

remains what is for me a decisive difficulty with this suggestion, and with this argument for it in particular, namely, that at 452a25–26, Aristotle will say that "it is admissible to be moved beyond [the item one is seeking, as well as to it,] from the same beginning, for instance from C [one can be moved] to F or to D." And if one can be moved from C, not to its neighbor D, which one was seeking, but to the more distant F, which one was not, why could one not be moved to the item one was seeking from one that is not adjacent to it? At all events, the emendations required by Sorabji's reading of the text are the following: at 452a20, where it reads "if he doesn't recall at H, he recalls at F," the letters H (according to Bloch) and F occur in none of the manuscripts; and at the end of that sentence, where it reads "both to G and to E," the letter G likewise appears in none of the manuscripts. In addition, at 452a23, where it reads "if he is seeking D or B," the letters D and B occur only in manuscript X, which is not generally considered to be one of the most authoritative manuscripts. Now for the sake of greater completeness, let me include a translation of Biehl's text, which also involves a number of emendations. It would be translated as follows (starting at 452a19): "for instance, if one were to think of [a series of things] labelled A, B, C, D, E, F, G, H; for if he doesn't recall at <H, he recalls at E, if he is seeking G or F>; for from there it is admissible to be moved in both directions, both towards D and towards <F>. But if he wasn't seeking one of these, he will recall after coming to C; but if not, [he will recall after coming] to A, and [so on] always in this way." (I have placed angular brackets around the letters or phrases for which Biehl has no manuscript support. Also, Biehl has chosen to omit an if-clause, "if he is seeking ** or **," after the words "he will recall after coming to C" at 452a22–23.) Among the other modern editors and translators, Mugnier follows Biehl's text; Beare, G. R.T. Ross, and David Ross have each proposed readings of their own; Hett accepts still another suggestion by David Ross (as reported in G. R.T. Ross' edition); Siwek (independently and before the fact) reads a variant of Sorabji's proposal; and Bloch accepts Sorabji's proposal. Let me say in conclusion that I am afraid the problem of discovering what Aristotle actually wrote in these two sentences is one that may well never be solved.

31 At 452a28, I read *dio ha pollakis ennooumen*, with manuscripts L, S, and U, rather than *dio pollakis ha ennooumen*, with Biehl, who follows manuscripts

that by nature, so [it] also [does] in actuality [even when not by nature]; and the [fact of its happening] often makes [it] nature. And since among the [things that are] by nature there come to be 452b
[occurrences] that are also contrary to nature and from chance, still more so [does this happen] among the [things] from habit, to which nature does not belong in the same way; so that one is sometimes moved not only there [i.e., to what one was seeking,] but also elsewhere, especially when [something] drags one from there to some other place. And also on account of this, when there is a need to remember a name, [we are dragged to] a similar one, and we make a verbal mistake with regard to that [proper one]. So then recollecting happens in this manner. But the most important [thing is that] one must recognize the time,[32] either by a measure or indeterminately. Now let there be something by which one judges the more and less [of time]; it is reasonable [that one judges these] as [one judges] magnitudes; for one thinks [i.e., apprehends,][33] the big and distant ones not by stretching out one's intellect [to them] there, as some assert [that one stretches out] sight[34] (for one will think [i.e., apprehend, them] in the same way even though they are not [present]), but by proportional motion

---

E and Y. According to Biehl's text, instead of "wherefore we recollect quickly those things which we are often thinking about," this sentence would be translated as "wherefore often we recollect quickly those things which we are thinking about."

32 As becomes clear from the sequel (452b23–24), the discussion here concerns not merely recollecting, but more generally being active with one's memory (i.e., "recalling"), which is indeed the culmination of the process of recollection (cf. n. 23 above), but which can also occur apart from it.

33 The Greek word translated as "thinks" is *noei*, a form of *noein*, which means "to think." But the Greek word differs from the English "think," which can refer to thinking erroneously as easily as it does to thinking correctly, since it refers primarily to genuine apprehension of what is true. Accordingly, I have sometimes translated it, as I did for instance at 449b31–450a1, as "thinks/apprehends." And in translating passages, like this one, where it seems to me that the notion of intellectual apprehension is especially prominent, I will write "thinks [i.e., apprehends,]" as I do here.

34 Cf. *On Sense Perception and Sense-Perceptibles* 437b10–438a5.

[of thought]; for similar figures[35] and motions are within them;[36] in what way[37] will it differ, then, when one thinks [i.e., apprehends,] the bigger [figures], that one is thinking [i.e., apprehending,] those or the smaller ones?[38] For all the inner ones are smaller

---

35 Similar rectilinear figures are defined as those with equal angles and proportional sides (Euclid, *Elements*, Book Six, Definition One; cf. *Posterior Analytics* 99a11–14). Now proportionality is the sameness of two ratios, so that having proportional sides means that the ratio between the sides around any one angle in the first figure is the same as that between the sides around the corresponding angle in the other. Hence the proportional motion that Aristotle has just spoken of in the previous clause would be motion or motions through, or represented by, the corresponding sides of each of the similar figures.

36 At 452b12, I read *autois*, with manuscripts E, M, and Y, rather than *autēi*, with Biehl, who follows manuscripts L, S, and U. Biehl's text would be translated, instead of "similar figures and motions are within them," as "similar figures and motions are within it [i.e., within one's intellect]." But Aristotle is concerned here with the relative sizes of different *external* magnitudes, which would correspond to the relative lengths of different times, not with the relation between something external and something within the intellect or soul. As for the referent of the word "them," it presumably refers to other figures, and to interpret Aristotle's claim here, I suggest that one begin by considering the example that he is about to give (cf. n. 43 below). This example uses two similar triangles that share a common vertex and a common angle at that vertex, and with parallel sides opposite to that common angle. Thus, the smaller triangle is wholly contained within the larger one. The parallel sides of these triangles can represent the magnitudes of what is thought or apprehended (i.e., the nearby thing whose magnitude is apprehended directly and the more distant thing whose magnitude one seeks to judge), while one of the other sides can represent one's distance away from those things.

37 At 452b13, I read *tini* instead of Biehl's *tina*, which is merely a typographical error.

38 At 452b13–14, I read *noēi, hoti ekeina noēi ē ta elattō*, with manuscripts E, M (for the most part), and Y, rather than *noēi, ē hotan ekeina noēi ta elattō*, with Biehl, who follows a modern conjecture by Freudenthal. Biehl's text would be translated, instead of "in what way will it differ, then, when one thinks [i.e., apprehends,] the bigger [figures], that one is thinking [i.e., apprehending,] those or the smaller ones?", as "in what way will it differ, then, when one thinks [i.e., apprehends,] the bigger [figures] or when one thinks [i.e., apprehends,] those smaller ones?" But the manuscripts that I am relying on here seem quite intelligible, and so I see no need for emendation. Furthermore, the word translated as "thinks," in the clause "when one thinks the bigger [figures]," could also have been correctly translated as "tries to think"

and[39] proportional to the outer ones. And as with the forms[40] it is possible to grasp another [that is] proportional [to it] within it [i.e., within each of the bigger ones], so [is it] also equally [possible] with the distances.[41] Accordingly, just as, if one is moved [with] the [motion] AB, BE, one makes the [line] CD, for the [motion, or line,][42] AC and the [motion, or line,] CD are proportional [i.e., AC to AB and CD to BE are proportional],[43] [so does the one who recollects proceed in trying to apprehend an event that is distant in time]. Why, then, does one make the [line] CD rather than the

---

or "wants to think" (cf. 452b21–22), which would make the manuscript reading that I have chosen still easier to understand.

39 At 452b14 I read *kai*, with manuscripts L, M, S, and U, rather than *hōsper*, with Biehl, who follows manuscripts E and Y. Biehl's text might perhaps be translated, instead of as "all the inner ones are smaller and proportional to the outer ones," as "all the inner ones, [though] smaller, [are] as it were proportional to the outer ones." But I see no need to qualify the word "proportional" in this way; the text that I have chosen has the natural meaning that the sides of the inner figures are proportional to those of the outer ones. Cf. n. 35 above.

40 By the word "forms" Aristotle means in this context "perceptible forms," each of which has some particular magnitude; hence the word can be used as an equivalent for "figures." Cf. *De Anima* 424a17–26, 432a3–6.

41 Since proportionality, as the sameness of two ratios, requires four terms, Aristotle must mean here that the ratio of the two distances will be the same as some other ratio. Thus, for instance, the ratio of two lines that represent distances, whether spatial or temporal, can be the same as that of the corresponding sides of two similar triangles.

42 Throughout this passage, the letters or pairs of letters are preceded by a feminine definite article, which could be understood to stand either for the noun "motion" or the noun "line," since both are feminine. And since Aristotle is apparently thinking of the motion of thought as it surveys a particular line, it doesn't seem to make much difference which of these two nouns one supplies.

43 Imagine a triangle ABE, with side AB stretching away from you from point A to point B and with side BE at right angles to it and side AE at some acute angle to side AB (so that AB can be regarded as the distance away from you of the line BE). Then extend side AB to any point C, and from C draw a line parallel to BE and intersecting the extension of side AE at point D, so as to make a bigger triangle ACD that is similar to the enclosed triangle ABE (cf. Euclid, *Elements*, Book One, Propositions 29 and 32, together with Book Six, Proposition 4). Thus AC is to CD as AB is to BE (cf. n. 35 above), so that, alternately, AC is to AB as CD is to BE (cf. Euclid, *Elements*, Book Five, Proposition 16), which is what Aristotle says here.

[line] FG? Or [perhaps the situation is that,] as the [line] AC[44] is to the [line] AB, so is the [line] H to the [line] I.[45] Thus, one is moved [with] these [motions, one] together [with the other].[46] But if one wishes to think [i.e., apprehend,] the [line] FG,[47] he similarly thinks the [line] BE, but instead of the [lines] H [and] I, he thinks the [lines] K [and] L; for these are [to one another] as FA to BA. Accordingly, whenever the motion of the thing and that of the time [i.e., the thought that apprehends the thing and the thought that apprehends the time,] come into being together, then one is active with one's memory. But if one supposes [that he is thinking them both] although he is not doing it, he [merely] supposes that he remembers; for nothing prevents someone from being deceived, and thinking (*dokein*) that he remembers, although

44 I read AC here, with all the manuscripts, rather than AF, with Biehl, who accepts a modern conjecture by Freudenthal.

45 I read "I" here, with manuscripts E, M, and Y, rather than "M," with Biehl, who reports that he is following manuscripts S and U, but whose reading, according to Bloch, agrees only with manuscript b (a reading that Biehl was unaware of). However, manuscripts L, S, and U, among others, do report the letter "M," though with a neuter rather than a feminine definite article. At all events (if we apply the example to recollection of past events, rather than to the apprehension of magnitudes at a distance), the lines referred to by these single letters would stand for lengths of time extending from the present into the past, with one of the lines perhaps being a measure and the other some multiple of it. And Aristotle would be assuming that one has some prior knowledge of the ratio between the time represented by the greater line H and that represented by the smaller line I (according to the text that I have chosen); it is this knowledge, together with the proportion given here, that allows one to find the determinate length AC along the extension of side AB, so that one can construct the determinate triangle ACD with side CD parallel to BE, where CD stands for some quantity (perhaps its duration) associated with the event or thing that one recalls.

46 In other words, one's thought moves over the line AB (or one might also say, in the light of the next sentence, the line BE) as it would over the line I, so that one can understand that it would move over the line AC (or the line CD) as it would over the line H.

47 Think of FG as a line parallel to CD and BE, but originating from some point F along the extension of AB and meeting the extension of AE at the point G. Thus, FG forms the third side of triangle AFG, which is similar to triangles ABE and ACD.

he does not remember.[48] But when someone is active with his memory, it isn't possible [for him] not to suppose [that he is], but to be unaware that he is recalling;[49] for this was recalling itself.[50] But if the [motion, i.e., the thought,] of the thing comes to be apart from that of the time, or this [latter] one apart from that [former] one, he does not recall. But the [motion, i.e., the thought,] of the time is of two sorts; for sometimes one doesn't recall it [i.e., the thing,] with a measure [of the time], as for instance that one did 453a
something or other two days ago, but sometimes [one recalls it] also with a measure [of the time]; yet one recalls even if not also with [such] a measure. And people are accustomed to say that they recall [that something happened], but that they don't know when, whenever they don't recognize the quantity of "the when" with a measure. Now that [it is] not the same ones [who are] apt at remembering and apt at recollection, is among the things said earlier.[51] And recollecting differs from remembering not only with

48 Cf. 451a2–12.

49 Aristotle appears again to be using the word "recalling" here as an equivalent to "being active with one's memory" (cf. nn. 2 and 27 above). And his use of the word "recalling," rather than "remembering," as in the previous sentence, suggests the thought that it may be possible to remember, in the broadest sense of the word, without being aware, or without paying attention to the fact, that one remembers.

50 Aristotle is presumably not making the paradoxical claim that recalling itself is being aware that one is recalling. What he means, rather, I think, is that recalling itself is being aware that one remembers. (As I indicated in n. 2 above, "remembers" would also be an acceptable translation of the word that I have translated as "recalling" just before the semicolon in this sentence.) Aristotle has said in Chapter 1 that whenever one is active with one's memory, i.e., recalling, one necessarily says in one's soul that one has previously perceived the object, the perception or knowledge of which one has in one (as an appearance) without any longer actively perceiving or knowing it (449b18–23; cf. 450a19–21). In other words, one necessarily says in one's soul that one remembers it. And one must of course be aware of what one says in one's soul. And the present statement, which points back to those earlier ones, seems to me to extend them so as to say that this awareness of one's remembering is precisely what recalling, or being active with one's memory, is.

51 Cf. 449b6–8.

respect to time,[52] but [in the fact] that many of the other animals also share in remembering, but not one, so to speak, of the animals that we are acquainted with, except for man, [shares] in recollecting. And the cause [is] that recollecting is like a sort of reasoning (*sullogismos*); for the one who is recollecting reasons [to the "conclusion"] that he saw or heard [something] or was affected with some such [affection] before, and it is like a sort of search.[53] And this is found by nature only in those [animals] to which the deliberative [faculty] also belongs; for deliberating is also a sort of reasoning. A sign that the *pathos*[54] is bodily and that recollection is a search for an appearance in something of that sort [i.e., in something bodily,] is that it causes some people much annoyance when they are unable to recollect, even after directing their thought very much [toward doing so], and when they are no longer attempting [to], they recollect none the less; and [this is] especially [the case with] those who are melancholic; for appearances move these [people] most of all.[55] And the cause of the recollecting not being up to them is that, just as for those who throw [something], stopping [it] is no longer up to them, so also the one who is recollecting and hunting sets in motion something bodily in which the *pathos* [that he is searching for is present]. And those in whom moisture happens to be present around the place [in their body] that is involved in perception are especially annoyed; for it [i.e., the moisture,] does

52 Cf. 451b2–5.

53 Aristotle is speaking here of recollection in the full sense of the word. He has already said that there can be recollecting—or "being reminded," as we might translate the words *to anamimnēskesthai* in such cases—without a search (451b22–24; cf. 452a7–8; cf. *Nicomachean Ethics* 1166b13–17), and indeed if there weren't this natural basis for it, it is hard to see how recollection as a search would even be possible.

54 By "the *pathos*," here and at 453a23, Aristotle is referring to memory, or more precisely, to that appearance, the having of which he has called memory (see 450a27–30, together with 451a14–16) and that one seeks to get back again in recollection (451b2–5), rather than to recollection itself.

55 Those with a melancholic temperament, attributed in antiquity to a preponderance of black bile, were thought to be impulsive, high-strung, and especially sensitive to external influences, as well as being melancholic in our sense.

not easily cease being moved until what is sought comes back and the motion proceeds directly [to it]. Wherefore also angers and fears, when they have caused something to move, since these [things that they have moved] set up counter motions against them, do not subside, but they set up counter motions [of their own in reaction to those counter motions], toward the same [end as they were originally aiming at]. And the *pathos* [we are describing] is also like names and tunes and phrases (*logois*), whenever one of them has been very much on [people's] lips; for when they have stopped and don't wish to, it comes over them to sing or say [it] again. Also, those whose upper [parts] are larger, and the dwarfish, are worse at remembering than those of the opposite sort, on account of their having a lot of weight on the perceptive [part] and [because, as a result,] neither are their motions [i.e., those having to do with perception,] able to remain, but are dispersed, nor do they easily proceed directly [to their goal] in recollecting. And those who are extremely young and [those who are] very old are without memory (*amnēmones*) because of the motion [in them]; for these are in decay, while those are in [a state of] much growth; furthermore, small children are also dwarfish until a considerable advance in age. And so concerning memory and remembering, what their nature is and by which of the [parts] of the soul animals remember, and concerning recollecting, what it is and how it comes to be and on account of what causes, has been said.[56]

56 Compare with this concluding sentence the beginning and the end of Chapter 1, 449b4–6 and 451a14–17.

ON SLEEP AND AWAKENESS

Chapter 1 453b

Concerning sleep and awakeness[1] one must examine what they in fact are, as well as whether they are peculiar to the soul or to the body or common [to both], and if they are common, to what part of the soul or of the body [they belong]; and [one must examine] on account of what cause they belong to animals; and whether all [animals] have a share in both, or some do in the one but others only in the other, or some in neither and others in both. And in addition to these [things, one must examine] what a dream is and on account of what cause those who are asleep sometimes dream but sometimes don't dream; or [else] it always happens to those who are asleep that they dream, but they don't [always] remember; and if this comes about, [one must examine] on account of what cause it comes about; and [one must examine] whether it is admissible [i.e., possible] to foresee what is yet to be, or whether it is not admissible, and in what manner, if it is admissible; and whether [it is possible to foresee] only the things yet to be done by man, or also those of which the daemonic (*to daimonion*) has the cause [i.e., for which it is responsible,] and [which] come to be by nature or from chance. Now in the first place this, at any rate, is manifest, that awakeness and sleep belong to the same [part] of the animal; for they are opposed [to each other], and sleep appears as a certain privation[2] of

---

1 I translate the Greek word *egrēgorsis* by the somewhat awkward English word "awakeness" in order to make it clear that it is a noun, and thus parallel to the noun *hupnos*, which means sleep. I will use the English expression "being awake" only as a translation of the infinitive form *egrēgorenai*.

2 Cf. *Metaphysics* 1018a20–21, where Aristotle lists privation and possession, i.e., lacking something and having it, as being among the kinds of opposites.

awakeness; for always, both in the case of the other [things] and in the natural ones, contraries manifestly come into being in the same receptive [substrate] and are manifestly affections (*pathē*) of the same [substrate], I mean, for instance, health and sickness, beauty and ugliness, strength and weakness, sight and blindness, hearing
454a and deafness. And [this] is clear also from the following. For that by which we recognize the one who is awake is that by which [we] also [recognize] the one who is asleep; for [it is] the one who is perceiving [whom] we hold to be awake, and [we hold that] everyone who is awake perceives something, either among the external [things] or among the motions within himself. If, then, being awake lies in nothing else than perceiving, it is clear that [the part] by which [animals] perceive is the one by which those that are awake are awake and those that are asleep are asleep. And since perceiving is peculiar neither to the soul nor to the body (for that of which the potentiality [is a potentiality] is also that of which the actuality [is an actuality]; and what is called sense perception, as an actuality, is a certain motion, [coming] through the body, of the soul), it is manifest that neither is the affection (*pathos*)[3] peculiar to the soul nor is a body that lacks soul capable of perceiving.[4] And since distinctions have been made previously in other [writings][5] concerning what are spoken of as parts of the soul, and since the nutritive [part] is separated from the other [parts] in bodies that have life, but none of the other [parts is present] without this, it is clear, for as many among the living beings as have a share only in growth and decay, that neither sleep nor awakeness belongs to these, for instance to plants; for they don't have the perceptive part, whether it is separable or not separable [from the nutritive part]; for in its potentiality and in its being (*tōi einai*)[6] it is separable. And [it is] likewise [clear]

3 Aristotle is probably referring here to the affection, or *pathos*, that is sleep. Cf. the following footnote, n. 4.

4 Cf. 454b11–12, where Aristotle says that everything that is asleep *is* capable of perceiving.

5 Cf. *De Anima*, Book Two, Chapters 2 and 3, 413a21–415a13.

6 Cf. *On Sense Perception and Sense-Perceptibles* 449a16–20, where distinctness in being (*tōi einai*) is identified with distinctness in speech (*logōi*).

also that there is nothing that is always awake or always asleep, but [that] both of these *pathē* belong to the same ones among the animals. For it is not admissible, if there is some animal that does not[7] have sense perception, that this one be either asleep or awake; for both of these are *pathē*, having to do with sense perception, of the first perceptive [part]. And it is also not admissible that either of these always be present to the same [animal], for instance, that some genus of animals be always asleep or that some [genus] be always awake, because for as many [things] as according to nature have some work (*ergon*), when they go beyond the time in which they are capable of doing something, it is necessary that they [then] be incapable, for instance, that the eyes, from [a period of] seeing, also cease doing this, and likewise also a hand and everything else that has some work. If, then, perceiving is the work of something, and [if] this exceeds the extent of time for which it was capable of perceiving continuously, it will be incapable and it will no longer do this. Then if being awake is defined by this, by sense perception 454b
having been released [from incapacity], and [if] it is necessary that, of some contraries, one of them always be present, but of others not,[8] and [if] being awake is contrary to being asleep, and [if] it is

7 At 454a21–22, I read *ei ti esti zōon mē ekhon aisthēsin*, following a modern emendation proposed by Beare, rather than *ei ti esti zōon ekhon aisthēsin*, with Mugnier and all the manuscripts. The manuscript reading would be translated, instead of "if there is some animal that does not have sense perception," as "if there is some animal which has sense perception" (perhaps with a comma before the word "which"). It would not be acceptable Greek, insofar as I understand it, to translate the passage, following the manuscript reading, as "For it is not admissible, if there is some animal which has sense perception, that this one be neither asleep nor awake" (see Smyth, *Greek Grammar*, para. 2761), although if I had chosen the manuscript reading, that is how I would, reluctantly, have translated it.

8 At 454b1–2, I read *tōn d'enantiōn tōn men anangkē thateron aei pareinai tōn d'ou*, with Mugnier, who follows manuscripts L, S, and U, rather than *tōn d'enantiōn to men anangkē pareinai to d'ou* with manuscripts E, M, and Y. With the alternative reading, the clause would be translated, instead of as "and [if] it is necessary that, of some contraries, one of them always be present, but of others not," as "and [if] it is necessary that, of contraries, one be present and the other not." Most modern editors and translators prefer the version that I have chosen, because the claim made in the alternative version contradicts

necessary for one of them to belong to every [animal], it would be necessary [for every animal, i.e., for every animal that lives to a normal lifespan,] to sleep. If, then, such a *pathos* is sleep, and this is an incapacity on account of an excess of being awake, and [if] the excess of being awake [is] sometimes connected with sickness but sometimes comes to be without sickness, so that the incapacity and the cessation[9] will also be like that [i.e., sometimes connected with sickness and sometimes not], [it would be] necessary that everything that is awake admit of sleeping; for [it is] impossible that it be always active/actual (*aei energein*). And likewise, neither is it admissible that anything always be asleep; for sleep is a certain *pathos* of the perceptive part, like a fetter and a certain lack of motion, so that it is necessary that everything that sleeps have the perceptive part. And "perceptive" is that which is capable of perceiving in actuality (*kat' energeian*); and it is impossible [for anything] to be engaged (*energein*) in sense perception, in the sovereign and unqualified sense, while at the same time sleeping; wherefore it is necessary that all sleep be subject to awakening. Indeed, nearly all the other [animals] clearly share in sleep, those that swim, those that fly, and those that go by land; for all the kinds of fish and also of

---

the well-known Aristotelian teaching that it is *not* necessary, for all contraries, that one or the other of them must be present in the substrates in which they may be present (cf. *Categories* 12b27–34). On the other hand, this very fact makes it seem at least possible that the version I have chosen is not what Aristotle wrote, but rather an ancient "correction." On either manuscript reading, this sentence presents a highly questionable argument for its conclusion that it is necessary for every animal that lives to a normal lifespan to sleep. But the alternative reading, by its inclusion of what Aristotle clearly knew to be a false premise, would emphasize the inadequacy of this argument somewhat more.

9 The Greek word translated as "cessation" is *dialusin*, a word formed from the same root as *lelusthai*, which I translated just above, at 454a32–b1, as "having been released [from constraint]." The verb *luein*, which means primarily "to unbind" or "to unfasten," can mean both "to unbind [and hence set free from constraint]" and "to unbind [and hence to separate a whole into its parts, and thus bring it to an end or destroy it]." In the sequel, at 454b10 and again at 454b26, Aristotle will speak of sleep as being like a fetter of the perceptive part or of sense perception, and at 454b27 he will speak of awakeness as the release (*lusin*) of sense perception, usages that are all in keeping with his use of *lelusthai* at 454a32–b1.

the cephalopods have been seen sleeping, and all the other [kinds of animals] that have eyes; for even those that have hard eyes, and the insects, are [sometimes] manifestly in repose; but all such [animals] sleep for short periods; wherefore it might, indeed, often escape someone's notice whether they participate in sleeping or not. But as for the testaceans, it has not yet become manifest to sense perception whether they sleep; but if the speech that has been spoken is persuasive to anyone, he will be persuaded of this. So, then, that all animals share in sleep is manifest from these [things]; for animal is defined by having sense perception, and we assert that sleep is, in a certain manner, the lack of motion and as it were a fetter of sense perception, and that its release and loosening is awakeness. But none of the plants is able to share in either of these affections (*pathēmatōn*). For without sense perception neither sleep nor awakeness belongs [to any being]; but to those to which sense perception belongs, being pained and being delighted also [belong]; and to those to which these [belong], desire [belongs] also. But none of these belongs to plants. And a sign [that sense perception doesn't belong to plants] is that the nutritive part does its own work when 455a [the animal] is asleep rather more than when it is awake; for it is nourished and grows rather more then, which suggests that it has no need of sense perception for these [ends].

Chapter 2

One must examine on account of what [it is that animals] sleep and are awake, and on account of what sort of sense perception (*aisthēsin*) or what sorts, if [it is] on account of more than one. And since some [animals] have all the senses (*aisthēseis*), but some don't have [them all], for instance sight, whereas they all have touch and taste, except if some [genus] of the animals [is] incomplete (and these have been spoken about in the [things we have said] concerning soul),[10] and [since] it is impossible for a sleeping animal to

10 Cf. *De Anima* 425a9–11, 432b21–23, 433b31–434a2.

perceive, in the unqualified sense [of the word], with respect to any sort of sense perception, [it is] manifest that it is necessary for the same *pathos* to be present to all[11] [the senses] in what is called sleep; for if [it is present] to one, but not to another, [an animal] will perceive by this [other one] while sleeping, but this is impossible. And since[12] there is present, in connection with each sense, something peculiar [to it] and something common [to all], peculiar, as seeing [is] to [the sense of] sight, and hearing to [the sense of] hearing, and in the same manner to each of the other [senses], whereas there is also some common capacity that follows upon them all, by which [one] perceives also that one is seeing and hearing (for surely not by sight, at any rate, does one see that one sees, and surely one judges and is capable of judging that sweet [things] are different from white [things] neither by taste nor by sight nor by both, but by some part [that belongs in] common to all the perceptive [faculties]),[13] for it is one [capacity or actuality], sense per-

---

11 At 455a10, I read *pasais*, with Biehl, rather than *pasin*, with Mugnier, who follows the preponderance of the manuscripts. Biehl regarded his reading as a modern emendation, although in fact, according to Siwek, who also accepts this reading, it occurs in several of the older manuscripts. According to Mugnier's text, instead of "to be present to all [the senses]," the phrase would presumably be translated as "to be present to all [the animals]," but this doesn't make sense to me in the light of the sequel, in which the gender of the words translated as "to one, but not to another" makes it clear that the reference is to one or another of the senses, and not to one or another of the animals.

12 The main clause of this very long sentence begins at 455a25, with the words which I translate as "[it is] then manifest."

13 At 455a20, I read *aisthētikōn* with manuscripts L, S, and U, rather than *aisthētēriōn*, with Mugnier, who, like all the other editors and translators I am aware of, follows manuscripts E, M, and Y. Mugnier's text would be translated, instead of as "common to all the perceptive [faculties]," as "common to all the sense organs." That reading might seem to be supported by *On Youth and Old Age and Life and Death and Breathing* 467b27–29 and 469a11–12, but those two passages do not speak of a part that belongs in common to all the sense organs, let alone of a common part of all the sense organs (as one might also translate those words), but rather of a "common sense organ of the particular sense organs," or "the common sense organ of all the sense organs," by which he means, I think, an organ by which one perceives the particular sense organs, or the particular senses, in their functioning, e.g., an organ by which one sees that one sees, which is what he is speaking about

ception, and the sovereign sense organ is one, but [what it is] to be sense perception is different [for the perception] of each genus, for instance of sound and of color, and this [sovereign sense organ] belongs together with the [faculty] of touch especially; for this [faculty] is separated from the other sense organs [i.e., in those animals that lack them], but the others are inseparable from this; and [we] have spoken about them in our contemplations (*theōrēmasin*) concerning soul;[14] [it is] then manifest that awakeness and sleep are an affection (*pathos*) of this [faculty]. Wherefore also they belong to all the animals; for indeed [the sense of] touch, alone [among the senses], belongs to all. For if sleeping came about by all the senses suffering something, it [would be] strange if, in the case of the [senses] for which it is neither necessary nor in a certain manner possible to be active (*energein*) at the same time, it [were] necessary for them to be inactive (*argein*) and to be motionless at the same time; for the contrary would happen to them more reasonably, [namely,] that they not be at rest at the same time. But according to the way we are speaking now, [what happens] also concerning these is reasonable; for when the sense organ [that is the] sovereign of all the others and to which the others extend has suffered something, it is necessary that all the remaining ones too 455b

---

here as well. As for the claim that Aristotle makes here about this common sense organ, he had asked, in Book Three, Chapter 2 of *De Anima* (425b11–25), whether it is by sight itself or by some other sense that one sees that one sees, a kind of "seeing" that, as he indicates, includes seeing "that which sees," i.e., the organ of sight in its functioning, along with its object, namely, color (425b18–20). And although he went on to indicate how a sense other than sight might be the one that does this, namely, if that other sense (or at least some further sense in a series of such senses) were also perceptive of itself or its own perceiving, he finally claimed that one ought to assume that the sense perceptive of its own perceiving is the first sense, i.e., sight (425b15–17). And so either Aristotle has changed his mind regarding this question since composing *De Anima*, or else, as I suspect, this claim in *De Anima* is meant to be merely preliminary, and to be corrected in light of his subsequent reference there to a previously unmentioned ultimate sense, or sense organ, by which we judge that the white and the sweet are different (*De Anima* 426b12–16, 431b5–6; and compare 455a17–19 of the present treatise).

14 Cf. *De Anima* 413b4–10, 415a3–6, 435a12–14.

suffer together [with it], but when one of those is incapacitated, there is no necessity that this one be incapacitated. And [it is] manifest from many [things] that sleep [does] not [lie] in the senses being inactive and in not using them, nor in not being capable of perceiving. For [something] of this sort happens also in fainting spells; for a fainting spell is an incapacity for sense perception. And also some mental derangements come about [that are] of such a sort. And furthermore, those in whom the blood vessels in the neck are squeezed become insensible. But [it is sleep] whenever the incapacity for use [of the senses] is neither in just any sense organ whatever nor on account of any chance cause, but as has now been said, [when it is] in the first [sense organ], by means of which one perceives all [things]; for whenever this becomes incapacitated, [it is] a necessity also, for all the sense organs, that they be incapable of perceiving; but whenever some one of those [i.e., of the others, becomes incapacitated], there is no necessity for this one [to be incapable of perceiving]. And one must say on account of what cause sleeping happens and of what sort the *pathos* [of sleep] is. And since there are more manners of cause [than one] (for we assert that the for the sake of what, and the from where the beginning of motion [is], and the material, and the [content of the] speech (*logos*) [saying what a thing is] are [each] a cause), first, then, since we say that nature acts for the sake of something, and that this is something good, and that rest is necessary and beneficial for everything of such a nature as to be in motion but not capable of always and continuously being in motion with pleasure, and [since people] assign this metaphor [i.e., the term "rest,"] to sleep, [i.e.,] to the truth itself, in the belief that it is rest, so as for it [i.e., sleep,] to be present[15] for the sake of the preservation of the

---

15 At 455b22, I read *huparkhein*, with Mugnier, who follows manuscripts E, M, and Y, rather than *huparkhei*, with manuscripts L, S, and U. According to this other reading, the phrase translated as "so as for it [i.e., sleep,] to be present for the sake of the preservation of the animals" would be translated instead as "so that [as a result] it [i.e., sleep,] is present for the sake of the preservation of the animals." This reading is certainly easier to interpret than the one that I have chosen. Indeed, as I read the text, the main thought of the whole sentence that began at 455b14 (with "And since there are more

animals; but awakeness is the end; for to perceive and to understand are the end for all those [beings] to which either of them belongs; for these are the best, and the end is [what is] best; so that [it is] necessary that sleep belong to each of the animals. And I mean necessity under a presupposition, [namely,] that if there will be an animal, having its own nature, some [things] must belong to it by necessity, and that if these belong, other [things must necessarily] belong. Further, after these [things], one must say what sort of motion and action [it is, that], when it comes into being in their bodies, being awake as well as sleeping happen to animals. Now then one must take it to be the case that the causes of the *pathos* are the same or analogous for the other animals as for those with blood,[16] and [that they are the same or analogous] for [all] those with blood as for human beings. So that one must consider all [the animals] in the light of these. Now that the beginning (*arkhē*) of sense perception comes to be from the same part in animals [as 456a

---

manners of cause . . .") does not appear until 455b25, with the words "so that [it is] necessary that sleep belong to each of the animals." This thought is that it is necessary (under the presupposition that there will be animals) for sleep to belong to each of them, and not that sleep is present, let alone that it comes to be present, for the sake of their preservation. Now manuscripts L, S, and (perhaps) U, which read *huparkhei* rather than *huparkhein* here, also differ from the reading I have chosen (following Mugnier and manuscripts E, M, and Y) in that later clause; instead of its beginning with *hōste*, they have it beginning with *eti de*, and it is thus a new sentence, which would be translated, not as "so that [it is] necessary that sleep belong to each of the animals," but as "And furthermore, [it is] necessary that sleep belong to each of the animals." In other words, these manuscripts make that clause the beginning of a new thought (a thought, incidentally, that does not include any supporting evidence for what it says), rather than the conclusion of the thought that began at 455b14.

16 At 455b31, I read *enaimois*, in agreement with Mugnier, who follows manuscripts S and X. But manuscripts E, L, M, U, and Y, which together are of considerably greater authority than S and X, read *anaimois*. According to those manuscripts, the words translated as "those with blood" would be translated instead as "those without blood." Now the reading that I have chosen is certainly much easier to interpret than that one is. But I do not think it impossible that Aristotle actually wrote *anaimois*, and that he did so in order to raise doubts about his conclusion that "one must consider all [the animals] in the light of these," i.e., human beings.

that] from which the [beginning] of motion also [comes to be] has been determined previously in other [writings].[17] And this [beginning] is, of three places that have been distinguished,[18] the [one in the] middle between the head and the lower cavity. Now for the [animals] with blood this is the part around the heart; for all the [animals] with blood have a heart, and the beginning (*arkhē*) of motion and of sense perception, [that is,] of the sovereign [sense perception], is from there. And as for motion, [it is] manifest that the beginning (*arkhē*) of the breath, and of cooling in general, is there, and [that it is] with a view to the preservation of the heat in this part [that] nature has made [as it has] the [animals] that breathe as well as those that are cooled by what is wet. [A *logos*] will be spoken about it[, namely, about the preservation, by means of cooling, of the heat around the heart,] by itself later.[19] And for the bloodless [animals] and the insects and [those] that do not take in breath, their naturally inherent breath is manifestly puffed up and [manifestly] subsides in the [place] analogous [to the region around the heart]. This is clear in the case of those that are whole-winged, for instance wasps and bees, and in flies and as many [other animals] as are of such a sort. And since to set something in motion and to act [on it] is impossible without strength, and [since] holding of the breath produces strength, the [holding of the breath] from outside, for the [animals] that draw it in, and the [holding of the] naturally inherent [breath], for those that do not breathe (wherefore also the winged [animals] of the whole-winged [kinds] manifestly buzz whenever they are in motion, because of the rubbing from the breath that strikes against their diaphragm), and [since] every [animal] is set in motion [i.e., self-motion,] on condition that some perception, either internal[20] or external, comes

17 *On the Parts of Animals* 665a10–15.

18 Cf. *On the Parts of Animals* 655b28–37.

19 See *On Youth and Old Age and Life and Death and Breathing*, especially Chapters 14–27 (474a25–480b30).

20 The Greek word translated here as "internal" is *oikeias*, which means more primarily "one's own."

to be in the first sense organ; if, then, sleep and awakeness are affections (*pathē*) of this part, [it is] manifest in what place and in what part sleep and awakeness first come to be. Some [people] are in motion while they are sleeping and they do many [things] characteristic of being awake, not, however, without an appearance (*phantasmatos*) and a sort of perception; for a dream is a percept (*aisthēma*) in a certain manner. And [we] must speak about them later.[21] But as for why [people], upon being awakened, remember their dreams but do not remember their actions characteristic of being awake, [this] has been said in the *Problems*.[22]

Chapter 3

Next after the [things] that have been said is to go through [the question,] under what circumstances[, literally, when what things come to be], and from where, does the beginning of the *pathos*, of being awake as well as of sleeping, come about. Now [it is] manifest—since [it is] necessary for an animal, when it comes to have sense perception, that it, then for the first time,[23] take [in] nourishment and [take on] growth, and [since] for all [animals] the final [form of] nourishment is, for those with blood, the nature of blood, and for those without blood, what is analogous [to it], and [since] the blood vessels are the place of blood and the beginning **456b**
of these is the heart (and what has [just] been said is manifest from the dissections)[24]—that when nourishment from outside enters into the places that can receive it, there comes to be a rising of

21 In *On Dreams*, the essay that follows this one in the *Parva Naturalia*.

22 There is no such discussion in what is extant of Aristotle's *Problems*.

23 Since an animal is defined by the presence of sense perception, any nourishment of the organism, or increase in its size, that precedes the acquisition of sense perception would not yet be nourishment or growth of an animal.

24 This may be a reference to actual dissections (cf. *On the Parts of Animals* 677a9; *On the Generation of Animals* 746a22), although it might also be a reference to a work of Aristotle that has not survived. Cf. *On the History of Animals* 497a32; *On the Generation of Animals* 746a14–15.

vapor into the blood vessels, and [that the vapor], changing there, becomes bloody and proceeds to the beginning [of the blood vessels, i.e., the heart]. It has been spoken about these [things] in the [speeches] concerning nourishment;[25] but now we must recapitulate about them for the sake of this, [namely,] that we may contemplate the beginnings of the motion[26] and [also] what [it is that], when the perceptive part suffers [it], awakeness and sleep result. For sleep is not just any sort of incapacity of the perceptive [part], as has been said. For mental derangement and choking of a certain sort and fainting also produce such an incapacity. And also, to some [people] who have fallen into a severe faint there has even come to be [activity of the] imagination. Indeed, this [phenomenon] contains a certain perplexity; for if it is admissible that the one who has fainted is asleep, it would also be admissible that the appearance [to the imagination] is a dream. And there are many things said by those who have fallen into a deep faint and believed that they were dead; concerning all of which [phenomena] one must take it that there is the same explanation (*logos*).[27] However, as we have said, sleep is not every incapacity of the perceptive [part], but this *pathos* comes to be from the rising of vapor involved in nourishment; for it is necessary that what is vaporized be pushed up to a certain point and then turn back and change [direction] like [the tides in] a narrow strait. And that which is hot in each of

25 This is presumably a reference to a work by Aristotle that has not survived.

26 It is not clear to me what Aristotle means here by "the motion," but perhaps he has in mind the entire process of falling asleep, sleeping, waking up, being awake, and so on. Compare the opening sentence of this chapter, which seems to be suggesting that being awake as well as sleeping are, in some sense at any rate, a single *pathos*.

27 Aristotle is somewhat circumspect here, but as the immediate sequel suggests, the explanation in question seems to be this, that those who have fainted, and even believed that they were dead, have suffered some incapacitation of their perceptive power. Even if, after coming around, they should speak of what they had experienced, in truth they have merely been imagining things, not genuinely perceiving, and in particular not perceiving things inaccessible to our waking perception. And in contrast to what Socrates says about Er in "The Myth of Er" in Plato's *Republic* 614b2–8, they have not really died, and their recovery of consciousness is not a coming back to life.

the animals[28] is naturally in motion upwards. But when it reaches the upper regions[29] [of the body], it turns back again in a mass and moves downward. Wherefore sleep comes about especially in the wake of [taking in] nourishment; for much [vapor], that which is wet as well as that which is like a [solid] body, is moved upward in a mass. And so, coming to a stop, it weighs [one] down and makes [one] drowsy; but when it has inclined downward and, having turned back, has pushed what is hot away [from the upper regions], then sleep comes about and the animal sleeps. And soporifics are a sign of these [things]; for they all produce heaviness of the head, both the drinkable ones and the edible ones, poppy, mandragora, wine, darnel. And when drifting off and drowsy, [people] believe that they are suffering this [i.e., that their head is really heavier], and they are incapable of raising their head and their eyelids. And this sort of sleep [comes] especially after [taking in] food; for [there is] much rising of vapor from food. And furthermore, [this sort of sleep comes] from some states of fatigue; for fatigue is a liquefying [agent], and the liquefied [product], unless it is cold, is like undigested nourishment. And this same [effect] is produced **457a**
by some diseases, as many as [arise] from wet and hot residue, as happens for instance to those who are feverish and in states of lethargy. And furthermore, the first period of life [produces this sort of sleep]; for infants sleep deeply, on account of their nourishment all being moved upward. And a sign [of this is] that the size of the upper parts is excessive, in comparison to the lower [ones], during the first period of life, on account of growth coming about toward these. And on account of this cause they are also prone to epilepsy; for sleep is like an epileptic fit, and in a certain

28 By "that which is hot in each of the animals," Aristotle presumably means to include blood, in the case of animals that have blood, and especially the blood around the heart (cf. *On the Parts of Animals* 649a14–17, b21–30; *On Youth and Old Age and Life and Death and Breathing* 469b6–20). But for whatever reason, he prefers to use this more indefinite expression.

29 The word that I translate as "regions" is a form of *topoi*, which I have been translating as "places." I will continue to translate it by one or the other of these two words.

manner sleep is an epileptic fit. Wherefore also the beginning of this *pathos* happens to some[30] people while they are sleeping, and they have seizures while they are sleeping, but not after they have awakened; for whenever the *pneuma*[31] is moved upward in large quantity, it swells the blood vessels as it goes back down and constricts the passage through which breathing comes about. Wherefore wines are not beneficial for infants, nor for their wet-nurses (for it doesn't make any difference, perhaps, whether they themselves drink [it] or their wet-nurses [do]), but they should drink it diluted with water, and little [of it]; for wine is *pneuma*-producing,[32] and dark [wine] more so [than the other kinds]. And the upper parts in infants are so full of nourishment that for five months they don't even turn their neck; for just as with those who are very drunk, much moisture is moved upward. And it is reasonable that this *pathos* is also the cause of embryos being at rest in the womb at first. And in general, those with inconspicuous blood vessels and those who are dwarfish and those who have large heads are fond of sleep. For the blood vessels of the ones [i.e., those with incon-

---

30 At 457a10, I read *tisi*, with manuscripts E, M, and Y, rather than *pollois*, with Mugnier, who follows manuscripts L, S, and U. Mugnier's text would be translated as "many," rather than as "some."

31 The most common meaning of the word *pneuma* in Aristotle is "breath," referring either to the air that is breathed in or to the naturally inherent breath, which he has recently spoken about as existing in insects (456a12), but which also plays an important role in his account of all animal motion (cf. *On the Motion of Animals* 703a4–25). Here, however, it would seem to refer instead to the vapor that he has been speaking about as rising from nourishment. Now Aristotle has not previously used a noun referring precisely to that vapor, but has spoken instead of *anathumiasis*, which I have translated as "rising of vapor," but whose primary meaning is "steaming up" or "vaporization," and which comes to refer only secondarily to the vapor that is formed and then rises. And if he is indeed referring to that vapor here, it is not clear to me why he uses the word *pneuma* for it. But perhaps he is thinking not so much of its heaviness, which he has been treating as a contributing factor toward sleep, as of its tendency to expand (and contract), which he might be thinking of as leading to the swelling of the blood vessels, and thus to the constriction of the windpipe and to epilepsy. Cf. the account of *pneuma* in *On the Motion of Animals* 703a19–22ff.

32 Cf. the previous footnote, n. 31.

spicuous blood vessels,] are narrow, so that it is not easy for moisture to flow down [through them], while for those who are dwarfish and who have large heads, the upward surge of the rising vapor is great. But those with large blood vessels are not prone to sleep, on account of the easy flow through their blood vessels, unless they have some other counteracting *pathos*. Nor are those who are melancholic [prone to sleep]; for their interior region has been cooled, so that there doesn't come to be much rising of vapor in them. On account of this they are also given to eating, while being thin, for their bodies are in a condition as if they had not benefited at all [from having eaten much]. And black bile,[33] which is by nature cold, also makes the nutritive region cold, and [it also cools] the other parts, wherever residue of such a sort is potentially present. So that [it is] manifest from the [things] that have been said **457b** that sleep is a sort of concentration inward, and a natural compression, of what is hot, on account of the cause that has been stated. Wherefore there is much motion on the part of the one falling asleep. And [the places] from which [the heat] leaves grow cold, and on account of the cooling the eyelids fall. And the upper and the external parts are cooled, but the internal and the lower ones, for instance those around the feet and those in the interior, [become] hot. And yet someone might be perplexed about this, that after [taking in] food there comes to be sleep [of] the deepest [sort], and that wine and other such [things] that contain heat are productive of sleep; [for] it isn't reasonable for sleep to be a cooling, but for the causes of sleeping to be hot. Does this happen because, just as the stomach is hot when it is empty, but filling cools it on account of the motion [involved], so also the passages and regions in the head are cooled as the vapor that is formed is moved upward? Or [is it that] just as a shiver suddenly comes over those who have hot [liquid] poured on them, [so] also in this case, when what is hot rises, what is cold is gathered together and produces

33 The word translated above (457a27) as "melancholic," *melancholikoi*, is formed from the Greek words for "black" and "bile," since melancholy was understood to result from an excess of black bile.

cooling, and it makes what is hot according to nature lose its power and withdraw? And further, when much nourishment comes in, which what is hot [in the body] carries upward, [then] like a fire when logs have been placed upon it, it [i.e., what is hot in the body,] is cooled,[34] until [the nourishment] is digested. For as it has been said,[35] sleep comes to be when the body-like [vapor from nourishment] is moved upward by what is hot [in the body] through the blood vessels toward the head; and when [what is hot] is no longer able [to do this], but that which has been brought up is excessive in amount, [that which has been brought up] pushes back[36] again and flows downward; wherefore human beings fall down when what is hot, which was bringing up [the body-like vapor from nourishment], is withdrawn (for [man] alone of the animals is upright), and as it descends, it produces unconsciousness,[37] and afterwards [activity of the] imagination. Or [rather,] while the solutions that have now been mentioned are admissible [ones] for there coming to be cooling, nevertheless the region around the brain is what is decisive, as it has been said in other [places].[38] For of all the [parts] in the body the brain is the coldest, and for those [animals] that don't have [one, it is] the part analogous to it. And so just as moisture that steams upward by [the ac-

34 At 457b19, I read *katapsukhetai*, with the preponderance of the manuscripts, rather than *katapsukhei*, with Mugnier, who follows manuscript E. According to Mugnier's text, this clause and its sequel would be translated as "it [i.e., the nourishment,] cools [what is hot in the body], until it is digested." Each of these readings is somewhat awkward in the Greek, although the general sense of the sentence seems fairly clear.

35 456b17–28.

36 At 457b23, I read *antapōthei*, with the preponderance of the manuscripts, rather than *antapōtheitai*, with Mugnier, who has the support only of an ancient Latin translation and (according to Siwek) a few of the later manuscripts. According to Mugnier's text, this clause would be translated as "it [i.e., what is hot,] is pushed back again and flows downward."

37 The word translated as "unconsciousness" is *eknoia*(*n*), which I have translated as "mental derangement" earlier in the chapter, since in those places it seems to refer to a condition that leads to unconsciousness (though not to sleep), rather than to unconsciousness (i.e., that of sleep) itself.

38 Cf. *On the Parts of Animals* 652a24–653b8.

tion of] the heat of the sun is cooled, when it comes to the place above, by the coldness there and, condensing, [i.e.,] becoming water again, moves downward, so in the rising of what is hot to- 458a
ward the brain, the residue-like rising vapor collects into phlegm (wherefore also catarrhs manifestly come into being from the head), but the nutritive and wholesome [vapor] condenses, moves downward, and cools what is hot. And the fineness and the narrowness of the blood vessels around the brain contribute toward their being cooled and not easily receiving the rising vapor. So then this is the cause of the cooling, even though the rising vapor has an excess of heat. And one awakens when [the nourishment] has been digested and the heat, which in large quantity has been concentrated from what surrounds it into a small [space], prevails, and the more body-like blood and that which is purest have been separated [from one another]. And the finest and purest blood is that in the head, while that in the lower parts is thickest and most turbid. But the beginning of all the blood, as it has been said both here[39] and in other [writings],[40] is the heart. And of the [cavities] of the heart the middle one opens into each of the two others. And each of those receives [the blood that is still unseparated] from one of the two blood vessels, the great [vessel] and the aorta. And the separation comes about in the middle [cavity]. But to make determinations concerning these [things] is more proper to other *logoi*.[41] And on account of the blood being quite unseparated after the taking in of nourishment, sleep comes to be, until the purest [part] of the blood has been separated off into the upper [parts of the body], while the most turbid [has been separated off] into the lower ones. And when this happens, [animals] wake up, having been released from the heaviness [that comes] from the nourishment. And so it has been said what the cause is of sleeping, that [it is] compression in a mass—by the body-like [portion] of the [vapor rising

39 456b1.

40 *On the Parts of Animals* 647b4–7, 665b9–17.

41 Cf. *On the History of Animals* 496a4–27, 513a16–b17; *On the Parts of Animals* 665b9–667b14.

from nutrition] that was moved upward by the innate heat[42]—against the first sense organ. And [it has been said] what sleep is, that [it is] a seizing of the first sense organ, [thus affecting it] in the direction of its not being able to act, coming about from necessity (for it is not admissible that there be an animal without the [things] that produce it[43] happening), but for the sake of preservation; for rest preserves.

42 This sentence speaks of those things *by* which what is compressed in a mass against the first sense organ is compressed, but it does not say *what* it is that is thus compressed. From 457a31–b2, it could appear that what is compressed is that which is hot in the body, but Aristotle does not say that here.

43 By its gender, which is neuter, the word translated here as "it" must refer to the animal, rather than to sleep. Perhaps Aristotle means to suggest that the necessitating causes that produce an animal (cf. *On Youth and Old Age and Life and Death and Breathing* 477a23–27) necessarily also produce sleep as a concomitant. Cf. 455b25–28.

On Dreams

Chapter 1 458a

After these things we must investigate concerning [the] dream,
and [ask] in the first place to which of the [parts] of the soul it 458b
appears, i.e., whether this is an affection (*pathos*) of the thinking
[part] (*tou noētikou*) or of the perceiving [part]; for [it is] by these
[parts] alone of those in us [that] we recognize anything. Now if
the employment of sight is seeing and of hearing, to hear, and of
sense perception in general, to perceive, and [if] common to the
[several] senses are, for instance, shape and size and motion and
the other [perceptibles] of this sort, while peculiar [to one partic-
ular sense] are, for instance, color, sound, [and] flavor, and [if] all
[animals] are unable to see when their eyes are closed and they are
sleeping, and similarly also with the remaining [senses], so that,
clearly, we don't perceive anything in sleep; then we do not, indeed,
perceive a dream by sense perception. But neither [do we perceive[1]
it] by thought (*doxēi*);[2] for we assert not only that what is ap-
proaching is a human being or a horse, but also [that it is] white

---

1 I supply the verb *aisthanometha*, which is the verb that Aristotle has just used in the last clause of the previous sentence. This verb can often mean "perceive" in a wider sense than "perceive through the senses," even though Aristotle usually uses it with the narrower meaning. Alternately, one might supply the verb "recognize" from 458b3, although it seems less likely to me that it is what Aristotle had in mind.

2 At 458b10, I translate *doxa* by "thought," rather than by, e.g., "opinion" or "belief," since I think that Aristotle is here taking up the alternative mentioned in the opening sentence of whether the dream is "an affection (*pathos*) of the thinking [part] (*tou noētikou*)." I don't think that he is here concerned with the difference between thinking and opining, but only with the difference between the activities of thought, on the one hand, and that of sense perception, on the other.

or beautiful; none of which [things] does thought (*doxa*) declare,[3] neither truly nor falsely, without sense perception. But it happens in sleep that the soul does this; for just as we think we see that the one who is approaching is a human being, [so] also [we think we see] that he is white. Furthermore, over and above the dream we have something other in mind (*ennooumen allo ti*), just as [we do] when perceiving something while we are awake; for often we are also considering (*dianooumetha*) something about what we are perceiving. So also in sleep we sometimes have in mind (*ennooumen*) other [things] over and above the appearances (*ta phantasmata*). And this would become apparent to someone if one were to direct one's attention and try to remember [one's dream] upon arising. And some people have indeed seen such dreams, for instance those who think[, while dreaming,] that they are putting the [things] presented to them [into their places] according to the mnemonic rule;[4] for something else often happens to them, above and beyond the dream, [namely,] putting an appearance (*phantasma*) into its place before their eyes.[5] So that [it is] clear that what appears (*to phan-*

---

3 At 458b12, I read *apophainetai*, with manuscripts E and Y, rather than *an phēseien*, with Mugnier, who follows manuscripts S and U. According to Mugnier's text, the phrase that I translate as "does thought (*doxa*) declare" would be translated as "could thought (*doxa*) assert."

4 The mnemonic rule that Aristotle apparently has in mind here is the so-called "place" system, which Richard Sorabji has called the most famous among those developed in ancient Greece (so that it might well be referred to as "the" mnemonic rule). According to Sorabji, this technique consisted of memorizing in advance a set of places, such as houses on a familiar street, and then superimposing in one's thought some token of each object to be remembered upon one particular place within the set of those that have been previously memorized. Sorabji, *Aristotle on Memory*, 22–31. Cf. *On Memory and Recollection*, n. 29.

5 Because of its word order, and in particular the placement of the word *phantasma* at the end, this clause is quite difficult to interpret and even to translate. But it might be significant that the word I have translated here as "dream" (*enupnion*) is adjectival in its form; indeed, its first recorded use is in a Homeric verse where it modifies a different noun for "dream" (*oneiros*) and means "in sleep" (*theios moi enupnion ēlthen oneiros*, i.e., "a divine dream came to me in my sleep," *Iliad* 2.56; *Odyssey* 14.495). And though such a use of the word would be highly unusual in Classical Greek prose, one might never-

tasma) in sleep is not all of [the] dream,[6] as well as that what we have in mind[, while dreaming,] we think by virtue of thought (*tēi doxēi doxazomen*). And concerning all these [matters] this much, at any rate, is clear, that the same [part] by which we are deceived even while we are awake during illnesses, that this very same [part] also produces the *pathos* [i.e., the dream,] in sleep. And even to those who are healthy and know [better], the sun nevertheless seems to be a foot across.[7] But whether, indeed, the imaginative

---

theless, in light of this possibility, translate the clause as "for something else often happens to them, above and beyond that which appears in sleep (*to enupnion...phantasma*), [namely,] putting [it] into its place before their eyes." This interpretation would allow, and even suggest, the thought that the dream includes more than the object or objects that appear in sleep. And in this regard, one might note that whereas Aristotle says at 458b15 that [in sleep] we have something other in mind "over and above the dream," he reformulates this assertion at 458b17–18 as an assertion that in sleep we sometimes have in mind other things "over and above the appearances."

6 I translate this clause in the way I do, even though the Greek might more naturally be translated as "So that [it is] clear that not all of what appears (*to phantasma*) in sleep is a dream." And indeed, the difficult clause at the end of the previous sentence might have been translated, in keeping with this alternative translation, as "for it often happens to them that they are putting some other appearance (*phantasma*), above and beyond the dream, into its place before their eyes." But I rejected that translation because I can't see what appearance, above and beyond the dream, Aristotle could have been referring to. As for the clause before us here, my translation of it is supported, and even confirmed, I think, by a feature of the text that might seem at first to contradict it. For near the end of the treatise (462a15–28) Aristotle will state unambiguously that not all of what appears in sleep is itself a dream [or part of a dream]; but he will support that claim with very different examples from the one he mentions here, and he will not give the slightest indication that he had already made the same assertion earlier in the treatise. In that later passage, moreover, he will go on to say that true thoughts (*alētheis ennoiai*, 462a28–29) that come about in sleep, above and beyond the appearances, do not belong to the dream. But that very claim makes one wonder about false thoughts.

7 Cf. *De Anima* 428b2–4, where Aristotle makes (basically) the same claim. In that passage, however, he uses the verb *phainetai*, or "appears," whereas here he uses the verb *dokei*, which I have translated as "seems," but which I might well have translated, in keeping with my translations of other forms related to *doxa*, as "is thought." Contrast 460b18, where Aristotle will make this claim again, but will use instead the verb *phainetai*, as he had done in *De Anima*.

[part] of the soul is the same as or different from the perceptive [part], nonetheless [the deceptive appearance] does not come into being without [one's] seeing and perceiving something. For seeing wrongly and hearing wrongly [are *pathē*] of one who sees and hears something true, although not what one believes [that one sees and hears]. But we have assumed that in sleep one neither sees nor
459a hears nor in general perceives anything. [Is it] true, then, that [one] doesn't see anything [in sleep], but not true that [one's] sense perception doesn't suffer anything? Is it admissible, rather, that both sight and the other senses suffer something, and that each of these [i.e., of the things suffered,] somehow impinges on sense perception, as when one is awake, but not in the same way as when one is awake; and [that] sometimes thought (*doxa*) says that what is seen is false, as [it sometimes says] to [people] who are awake, whereas sometimes it is taken over and follows [the lead of] the appearance? And so [it is] manifest that this affection (*pathos*) that we call dreaming is not [a *pathos*] of that which thinks (*tou doxazontos*) or of that which considers (*tou dianooumenou*). But neither is it [a *pathos*] in the unqualified sense of that which perceives; for [if it were, dreaming] would be seeing and hearing in the unqualified sense. But we must examine how, then, and in what manner [it is a *pathos* of that which perceives]. And let it be assumed—what is manifest—that the *pathos* belongs to the perceptive [part], if indeed sleep does; for sleep doesn't come to be present to some one [part] of animals and dreaming to another, but [both] to the same one.[8] And since it has been spoken about imagination in the things [we have said] concerning soul,[9] and [since] the imaginative [part] is the same as the perceptive [part],[10] although to be imaginative

8 Cf. *On Sleep and Awakeness* 454a4–7, a22–24, b9–10.

9 This is a reference to *De Anima*, and especially to Chapter 3 of Book Three (427a17–429a9), where Aristotle gives a thematic treatment of imagination.

10 Aristotle did not say in *De Anima* that the imaginative part is the same as the perceptive part. However, he did say, in connection with the work's only use of the expression "*to phantastikon*," i.e., "the imaginative [part]," that there is much perplexity as to whether the imaginative part, while being different in its being from all the other parts, might not nevertheless be the same as

and to be perceptive are different, and imagination (*phantasia*) is that motion which comes into being by virtue of sense perception in [its] actuality/activity (*kat' energeian*),[11] and [since] a dream appears to be some appearance (*phantasma*)—for an appearance in sleep [is what] we call a dream, whether [an appearance] simply or [only] if it comes into being in a certain manner[12]—[it is] manifest that dreaming is [a *pathos*] of the perceptive [part], but of this insofar as it is imaginative.

Chapter 2

What the dream is and how it comes into being, we would best contemplate from the [things] that happen in connection with sleep. For the perceptibles corresponding to each sense organ produce sense perception in us, and the *pathos* that comes into being through their agency is present in the sense organs not only while the senses are active, but also after they have gone away.[13] For it

---

some other one (in a list that includes the perceptive part), on the assumption that there are separate parts of the soul (*De Anima* 432a31–b3). And beyond that, his claim here is prepared by the opening sentence of this treatise, 458b2–3. Cf. also 458b29–30.

11 Cf. *De Anima* 428b25–429a2 (accepting the manuscript reading at 428b26 and reading *hē phantasia* at 428b30–429a1 with manuscript E).

12 Cf. 462a15–28, as well as n. 6 above.

13 Aristotle is not speaking here, as he will do at 460a32–b3, of the persistence in the sense organs of the *pathos* produced by the perceptible external objects (or, as he puts it there, that of the percepts produced by them) after those objects have gone away. Nor is he speaking, as he will do at 461b21–23, of the persistence of a residue of an original percept after that percept has gone away. And although the singular form of the word that I have translated as "the senses," in the phrase "not only while the senses are active, but also after they have gone away," was used with the meaning of "sense perception" earlier in the sentence, neither is he speaking of the persistence of this *pathos* after "the sense perceptions" (or "the perceptions") have gone away; for it is not the (plural) perceptions, e.g., the seeing of this red ball, that can be active (and hence also merely capable of activity), but rather the senses. To understand what Aristotle does mean, it helps to note that he is presenting this observation as an explanation of his initial statement that we would best contemplate what a dream is and how it comes into being on the basis of what

looks as if the *pathos* is similar in these cases and in the case of [bodies] in local motion. For also in the case of [bodies] in local motion, they are [still] in motion when that which has set [them] in motion is no longer in contact with [them]; for that which set [them] in motion set a certain [portion of] air in motion, and this in turn, being in motion, [set] a different [portion of air in motion].[14] And so in this manner, until they come to a stop, they produce their
459b [own] motion,[15] both in air and in liquids. And similarly, one should take this to be the case also with alteration; for that which has been heated by what is hot heats what is near it, and this passes [the heat]

---

happens in connection with sleep. And it indeed makes sense to speak of the senses having "gone away" during sleep, i.e., of their having ceased to be active, not by becoming merely capable of activity (which in the fullest sense they are not), but rather by leaving their normal position of relatedness to the external world.

14 Compare *Physics* 266b27–267a20, where, however, Aristotle says that each of the successive portions of the medium continues to set the next portion in motion even after its own motion has ceased.

15 The Greek expression I have translated as "they produce their [own] motion" is *poieitai tēn kinēsin*, quite an unusual expression for Aristotle. To be sure, it is acceptable Greek, and I might even have translated it simply as "they are in motion." But by his use of the middle voice form *poeitai* with the word for motion as its object, Aristotle seems to be suggesting the additional thought that the bodies in local motion through air and liquids are not merely acted upon by the initial and subsequent movers, but that they somehow contribute to the continuation of their own motion. And the suggestion that a body in local motion contributes to the continuation of its own motion, or that its motion cannot be fully accounted for by the action of any external moving cause or causes, would make good sense. For Aristotle's attempt to explain the continuation of its motion by the action of successive portions of the medium through which it moves must presuppose that these portions of the medium contribute to the continuation of *their* own motion, since they must continue their motion for a time, even after their external moving cause is no longer in motion (or at least is no longer in contact with them). And finally, the suggestion that a moving body contributes to the continuation of its own motion, even after it is no longer in contact with any external moving cause, is directly relevant to what Aristotle is trying to show by this analogy, namely, that the *pathos* produced in the sense organ by the perceptible object persists even after the sense is no longer active. Indeed, without this suggestion, it is hard to see how the two analogies presented here would suggest anything more than that perception of an object at a distance is possible.

on until [it reaches] the beginning.[16] So that also in that [organ] in which [there is] perceiving, since sense perception in [its] actuality is a sort of alteration, it is necessary that this happen. Wherefore the *pathos* is not only in the sense organs while they are perceiving, but also in [them] after they have ceased [perceiving], both deep inside [the body] and on the surface. And [this] is manifest (*phaneron*) whenever we perceive something continuously; for when we shift our perception, for instance from the sunlight into darkness, the *pathos* [associated with the earlier perception] follows; for [what] happens [is] that we don't see anything, on account of the motion, [which was produced] by the light, still subsisting in our eyes. And if we look at one color for a long time, either white or green, whatever we turn our sight toward appears (*phainetai*) like it. And if, after looking at the sun or some other bright [object], we close our eyes, if we [then] observe carefully, it appears straight ahead, in whatever direction our sight happens to be looking, at first

16 It is difficult to see what Aristotle means here by "until [it reaches] the beginning." But let me suggest that by the word "beginning" (or "principle," *archēs*), he is referring to sense perception, and in particular to that organ, common to all the perceptive faculties, that he has called the sovereign sense organ, and which he has also spoken of as the first sense organ (*On Sleep and Awakeness* 455a19–23, 456a21, 458a28–29; cf. *De Anima* 422b22, 424a24–25; and compare Aristotle's use of this same word, *archē*, in the next chapter of this treatise on dreams, at 461a31 and 461b4). As for the significance of such a reference to sense perception, I note that early in the *Meteorologica*, a work in which Aristotle speaks frequently of heat as a cause of various effects through interactions that sometimes involve only inanimate bodies, he says, "Concerning the heat that comes into being, [the heat] that the sun provides, it is more fitting to speak [of it], in itself and precisely, in the [speeches or writings] concerning sense perception (for the hot is a certain *pathos* of sense perception)." Consider also *Meteorologica* 385a1–11 and then 388a10–13, where Aristotle first makes, and then retracts, the suggestion that there are *pathē* of bodies that are independent of the sense of touch and of the other senses. And it makes sense that Aristotle should remind us here that sense perception is the beginning or principle of heat, in the full or precise sense of the word "heat," and that it is difficult to speak with any clarity about heat apart from sense perception. For he is using the transmission of heat as an analogy for unperceived changes in the media through which we perceive objects at a distance, as well as for unperceived *pathē*, remaining in the sense organs, that we have to suppose as being factors in the production of dreams.

of such a sort [as it was] in color, [and] then it changes to crimson and then to purple, until it comes to the color black and disappears. And also the [motions] [persist in our eyes] when we turn away from [things] in motion, for instance from rivers, and especially from those that are flowing most quickly; for the [things] at rest appear in motion. And from loud sounds [people] become poor at hearing, and from strong odors poor at smelling, and [likewise] in the similar [cases]. Manifestly (*phanerōs*), these things happen in the way we say [they do]. And a sign that the sense organs quickly perceive even a small difference is what comes about with mirrors, [a subject] which, even in its own right, someone might stop to examine and raise perplexities about. And at the same time, it is clear from them [i.e., from mirrors,] that just as sight is acted upon, so also it produces some [effect]. For with mirrors that are extremely clean, whenever women who are menstruating look into the mirror, what is on the surface of the mirror comes to be like a blood-red cloud; and if the mirror is new, it is not easy to wipe off that sort of stain, but if it is old, [it is] easier.[17] And the cause [is], as we have said,
460a that not only is sight acted upon by the air, but it also produces some [effect] and causes motion, as bright [objects] also [do]; and indeed sight[18] is among the bright [objects] and those that have color. Now the eyes [during menstruation] are in a [particular] condition, just like any other part of the body[, as one] reasonably [assumes]; and indeed by nature they happen to be full of blood vessels. Wherefore when menstruation comes about, the difference in the eyes, on account of the disturbance and bloody inflammation, while it is unclear to us, is [nevertheless] present (for the same

---

17 In addition to raising questions about the relevance of this section to Aristotle's overall argument, scholars have been amazed at his apparent acceptance of these superstitious beliefs about menstruating women and mirrors. But what is most important, I think, is not the question of whether Aristotle shared these obviously false beliefs, but rather the fact that he presents the alleged phenomena as having wholly natural causes.

18 Here Aristotle is using the word normally translated as "sight" to refer to the organ of sight, i.e., the eye. Presumably, then, his use of this same word earlier in the sentence (460a1), as well as two sentences earlier (459b27), was also intended to refer to the eye.

nature [is constitutive] of semen and menses), and the air is set in motion by them, and it makes the air on [the surface of] the mirrors, which is continuous [with it], of a certain quality, namely, of the quality with which it is affected itself; and this [air does the same] to the surface of the mirror. And as with garments, those that are cleanest are most quickly stained;[19] for what is clean makes clear precisely whatever it receives, and what is most [clean makes clear] the smallest motions. And bronze, on account of its being smooth, best perceives[20] any sort of contact (and one should be aware that the contact of the air is as it were a rubbing and like a wiping and a washing), and on account of its cleanness, [the contact] becomes conspicuous no matter how much [or how little] it is. And the cause of [the stain] not going away quickly from new mirrors is that [a new mirror] is clean and smooth; for [the stain] penetrates, on account of such [qualities], both deep inside and all over, deep inside on account of its [being] clean, and all over on account of its [being] smooth. But in old [mirrors] it does not remain, because the stain doesn't penetrate as much, but is more superficial. So then it is manifest from these [things] that a motion comes about as a result of small differences, that perception (*hē aisthēsis*) is quick, and furthermore that the sense organ for colors is not only acted upon but also acts in return. And what happens concerning wines and the preparation of perfumes bears witness to the things [we have] said. For both oil that has been made ready and wine quickly take on the odors of the [things] that are near them; for they take on the odors not only of what is thrown in or mixed in, but also of what is placed

19 This clause might have been translated as "those that are most pure are most easily defiled," since the Greek word Aristotle uses for "clean" throughout this discussion of mirrors also means "pure," and the word he uses for "stain/stained" also means "defilement/defiled."

20 The Greek verb that I have translated as "perceives" is *aisthanetai*, which indeed almost always means "perceives." But since its subject in this sentence is a bronze mirror, here it must mean instead something like "registers." And indeed, since this example has been introduced to show that the sense organs quickly perceive (*aisthanetai*) even a small difference (459b23–24; cf. 460a23–24), it seems possible that even in making that statement Aristotle was using the verb *aisthanetai* in this unusual sense.

near their containers or has grown there. Now with respect to our
460b inquiry from the beginning, let one [thing] be assumed, which is manifest from the things [we have] said, that even when the external perceptible [object] has gone away, the percepts (*aisthēmata*) remain and are perceptible; and in addition to these things, [let it be assumed] that we are easily deceived with regard to our perceptions (*aisthēseis*)[21] when we are in passionate states (*pathesi*)—different ones [of us] in different [states]—for instance the coward in [a state of] fear, and the erotic [man] in love, so that on the basis of a slight similarity the one thinks he sees his enemies, while the other one [thinks he sees] the [boy] he is in love with; and the more passionately one is affected, the slighter the similarity on the basis of which these [things can] appear (*phainetai*). And in the same manner also in anger (pl.) and in all desire (pl.) all [people] become easily deceived, and more so the more they are in passionate states. Wherefore also, to those who are feverish, animals sometimes appear on the walls on the basis of a slight similarity with the lines [on the walls] when put together. And this [false appearance] is sometimes strengthened along with their passionate [or feverish] states in such a way that if they are not excessively afflicted, it doesn't escape their notice that it is false, but if the *pathos* is greater, they even move in relation to them [i.e., the false appearances]. And [the] cause of these things happening is that [it is] not owing to the same capacity [that] what is authoritative judges and [that] the appearances come to be. And a sign of this is that the sun appears (*phainetai*) a foot across, but something different often speaks against the imagination (*tēn phantasian*). And by crossing our fingers, the one [thing that we touch with them] appears two, but we nevertheless do not assert [that there are] two; for sight is more authoritative than touch.[22] But if there were only touch, we would judge the one [thing to be] two. And [a] cause of our being deceived is that not

21 Again, perhaps the word *aisthēseis* is being used here in the unusual sense of "what is registered by our sense organs," as distinct from anything that we actually perceive.

22 Cf. 461b2–5. Aristotle indicates, however, at 461b31–462a2 that he does not regard sight as being more authoritative than touch in all circumstances.

only do [appearances] of whatever sort appear when the perceptible [object] is set in motion [so as then to produce those appearances], but also when the sense by itself [i.e., apart from any action upon it by the perceptible object,] is set in motion, if it is set in motion in the same way as [it would have been] by the perceptible [object]; I mean, for instance, [that] to those who are sailing, the land seems (*dokei*)[23] to be in motion, although sight[24] is being set in motion by [something] other.

Chapter 3

From these [things], then, it is manifest that the motions that come into being from our percepts—the [percepts] that are present in [us][25] from outside as well as those from the body [by itself][26]— appear not only when [we are] awake, but also when this affection

23 Cf. n. 7 above.

24 Here again Aristotle seems to be using the word that he normally uses for the sense of sight to refer to the organ of sight. Cf. n. 18 above.

25 If the manuscript tradition, which overwhelmingly favors the reading *enuparkhousōn* (or *huparkhousōn*) at 430b30, is correct, the word translated as "that are present in [us]" is a feminine participle modifying the word that was translated as "percepts," even though that word is neuter and not feminine. However, the Greek word for "motions" is feminine, and Aristotle may be implicitly substituting it for the word for percepts, and doing so in order to call attention to the fact—i.e., to what must be a fact—that percepts are themselves motions (of the body), just as the motions that Aristotle is discussing here are also percepts, at least to the extent that they appear to us. At all events, this is how I interpret the sentence. Regarding this construction, compare the (admittedly less harsh) anacoluthon at 460a5, where Aristotle used the masculine adjective *phlebōdeis* to characterize the eyes as being by nature "full of blood vessels," as if he has just referred to the eyes with the masculine word *ophthalmoi*, rather than, as he did in fact, with the neuter *ommata*. And as further evidence for the suggestion that Aristotle seems to be making here, compare 461a18–19 and 461b21–23, where Aristotle speaks of the motions that result from our percepts as being "residue" from them and as being "left over" motions.

26 By the percepts that are present in us "from the body [by itself]" Aristotle seems to be referring, at least in part, to those deceptive appearances that arise on the basis of our own passionate states.

(*pathos*), which is called sleep, comes about, and [they appear] more
461a then; for during the day they are driven out, with the senses and the intellect (*dianoias*) working together, and they are obscured, like a smaller fire next to a large one and small pains and pleasures next to great ones, although when these have ceased, even the small [things] come to the surface. But at night, on account of [the] idleness of the partial [i.e., particular,] senses and [their] incapacity to be active, [which results] on account of there coming to be the reflux of what is hot from the external [parts] to the interior [part],[27] they [i.e., these motions,] are carried in to the beginning [point] of sense perception and they become manifest as the disturbance subsides. And one must take it to be the case that, like the small eddies that come into being in rivers, so each motion is coming into being continuously, often in a uniform way, but often breaking up into other shapes on account of the striking against [it by other motions]. Wherefore also dreams don't come about after [the taking in of] nourishment, nor to those who are very young, such as young children; for [in these cases] there is much motion on account of the heat from the nourishment. So that, just as in a liquid, if someone sets it in motion vehemently, sometimes no [reflected] likeness appears, while sometimes one appears, but [is] altogether distorted, so that [the reflected object] appears different from the way it is, although when [the liquid] has come to rest [the likenesses] are pure and manifest; so also in sleeping, the appearances and the leftover motions that result from our percepts are sometimes altogether obscured by the motion that has been spoken about [i.e., the motion on account of the heat from nourishment,] [when it is] too great, while sometimes the apparitions[28] [arising from these motions] appear disturbed and monstrous,[29] and the dreams [are] unhealthy, as in the case of those who are melancholy, feverish, or drunk; for

27 Cf. *On Sleep and Awakeness* 457a33–b2, 458a25–28.

28 The Greek word translated as "apparitions" is *opseis*, the plural of the word for the sense of sight. In a different context it might have been translated as "sights."

29 The Greek word translated as "monstrous" can also mean "portentous."

all such *pathē*, since they are full of *pneuma*,[30] produce much motion and disturbance. But as the blood, in the animals with blood, quiets down and is separated off [into its purer and less pure parts], the motion of the percepts from each of the sense organs, being preserved [in its original form], makes the dreams [that we have] healthy, as well as [making] something appear and [making] us think (*dokein*), on account of the [percepts] that are being brought in from sight (*apo tēs opseōs*),[31] [that we] are seeing, and on account of those from hearing (*apo tēs akoēs*), [that we] are hearing. And in a like manner [this happens] also [with the motion of the percepts] from the other sense organs; for by means of motion coming from there [i.e., from the particular sense organs,] to the beginning [point of sense perception], even when one is awake, one thinks (*dokei*) that one is seeing and hearing and perceiving, and because **461b** of sight sometimes being thought (*dokein*) to be moved when it is not being moved, we assert (*phamen*) [falsely] that we are seeing,[32] and by [the sense of] touch reporting two motions, the one [object] is thought (*dokei*) to be two.[33] For in general, the beginning[, or principle, of sense perception] affirms (*phēsin*) what [comes] from each sense, if a different, more authoritative, [sense][34] doesn't contradict [it]. So then [something] appears in every case, but that

30 Cf. *On Sleep and Awakeness*, n. 31.

31 The Greek word translated here as "sight" seems to be used as an equivalent for "the eyes," just as the word translated as "hearing" later in the sentence seems to be used as an equivalent for "the ears." Cf. nn. 18 and 24 above.

32 Aristotle seems to be referring here to visual hallucinations. From his account it is not clear whether, in the cases he has in mind, the sense of sight was ever moved in just such a way as would have produced the appearances in question.

33 Cf. 460b20–22.

34 I have supplied the word *aisthēsis*, or "sense," as the feminine noun that is needed here, since this is the most natural way to read the sentence. However, one might have chosen instead the word *dunamis*, which means "capacity," and which would include not only the senses but also, for instance, the intellect (*dianoia*). For there might well be cases where one rejects an apparent perception as unreal on the grounds of its intrinsic absurdity, rather than because of contradictory evidence from a different sense. On the other hand, since this sentence speaks only about what happens "in general," the translation that I have given seems appropriate.

which appears is not thought [to be as it appears] in every case; but [it is so thought] if that which judges is taken over [by the appearance] or doesn't move with its proper motion. And as we have said that different people are easily deceived, [each] on account of a different *pathos*, so the one who is sleeping [is easily deceived] on account of his sleep and his sense organs being moved and the other things that happen in connection with sense perception,[35] so that that which has a slight resemblance [to something] appears [as] that. For when [one] is sleeping, as most of the blood sinks inward to the beginning [point of sense perception], the motions that are in it, some [only] as a potentiality [for some appearance], but others as actuality (*energeiāi*), go along with it. And they are so disposed that if something moves the blood, one motion will rise to the surface from it, but if this one is destroyed, another one [will]. And [these motions] are related to each other like the artificial frogs that rise up in water as the salt [that someone has put in it] dissolves. In this way they are in [the blood] as potentiality, but when that which hinders them has been relaxed, they are active (*energousin*); and as they are set free in the small amount of blood that is left in the sense organs, they begin to move [as appearances], bearing a resemblance [to this or that], just as the [shapes] in the clouds do, which, as they quickly change, [people] liken to human beings and to centaurs. And each of these is, as it has been said,[36] a residue of the percept [that was present] in the actuality (*tēi energeiāi*) [of sense perception]; and it is in us after the percept, the true (*tou alēthous*) [one], has gone away, and it is true to say that it is like Koriskos, but not [that it is] Koriskos. And when one was perceiving, that [part in us] which is authoritative, i.e., that [part in us] which judges, did not say [of the percept that it was] Koriskos, but on account of this [it said that] that one, the one who is truly (*ton alēthinon*) [Koriskos], [is] Koriskos, perceiving whom, indeed, it also says [that][37]—[but

35 Cf., e.g., 460b3–18.

36 459a23–28; cf. 461a17–19.

37 In addition to the changes that I indicate in the following two footnotes, I have changed some of Mugnier's punctuation in the remainder of this sen-

in sleep] this [authoritative part], if it is not completely held down by the blood [so that nothing appears to it even as a dream], just as if it were perceiving,[38] this is set in motion by the motions in the sense organs, and it is thought (*dokei*) that what is like [some being] is itself the true (*to alēthes*) [being].[39] And the power of sleep is so great as to make this escape one's notice. Accordingly, just as if it were to escape someone's notice that his finger was pressing under his eye, not only will the one [object] appear [as two] but it will also 462a
be thought (*doxei*) to be two, whereas if this doesn't escape his notice, it will appear, but will not be thought, [to be two], so also in

---

tence. Mugnier's text of the beginning of this clause, which I follow, reads *hou dē kai aisthanomenon*, in accord with manuscripts S and U. Manuscripts E and Y, however, read *hōi dē kai aisthanomenos*. That reading would lead to putting a period after "[is] Koriskos" and then beginning a new sentence. The beginning of that sentence would be translated, "[That part], indeed, by means of which one perceives and also says this, if it is not completely held down by the blood . . . ," and the sentence would continue in the same way as I have translated it. That reading has the advantage of being grammatically more regular, so as not to require the dash, followed by the words "[but in sleep]," that I have added for the sake of clarity. However, it would require an abrupt shift in sense, from referring at the beginning of the sentence to a person as the one who perceives, to referring later in the sentence to the authoritative part within him as being that which perceives. And more importantly, by not making explicit what the object of the perception is, it would not bring out the fact that in genuine perception we do not perceive a percept, e.g., the percept on account of which we say that the man who is truly Koriskos is Koriskos, but rather, on account of that percept, we perceive Koriskos himself. And this objection is also a reason for not accepting the suggestion of those modern editors and translators who try to simplify the grammar by replacing the initial genitive masculine pronoun *hou* with the nominative neuter pronoun *ho*, leading again to a new sentence after "[is] Koriskos" and the translation, "[That part], indeed, which as it perceives also says this, if it is not completely held down by the blood . . . ."

38 At 461b27–28, I read *hōsper aisthanomenon*, with the preponderance of the manuscripts, rather than *hōsper mē aithanomenon*, with Mugnier, who follows manuscript L. According to Mugnier's text, the phrase translated here as "just as if it were perceiving" would be translated as "just as if it were not perceiving."

39 At 461b29, I read *to alēthes*, with manuscripts L, M, S, and U, rather than *alēthes*, with Mugnier, who follows manuscripts E and Y. According to Mugnier's text, these last words would be translated as "true" rather than "the true [being]."

sleep, if [someone] perceives that he is sleeping, i.e., [if he is aware] of the sleeping *pathos* in which the perception[40] [occurs], [it] appears, but something in him says that it appears [as] Koriskos, but it is not Koriskos (for often when one is sleeping, something in one's soul says that what appears is a dream); but if it escapes his notice that he is sleeping, nothing will contradict the appearance (*tēi phantasiāi*). And that [the things] we are saying [are] true, and [that] in the sense organs there are motions capable of being appearances (*kinēseis phantastikai*),[41] [becomes] clear if someone should try attentively to remember how we are affected when we are dropping off [to sleep] as well as when we are waking up; for sometimes, as one is waking up, one will detect that the likenesses that appear to him while he is sleeping are motions in the sense organs; and indeed to some of the younger ones [i.e., children], even when their eyes are wide open, there appear many moving likenesses, if there is darkness, so that they often cover their heads in fear. From all these [considerations], then, one must conclude that the dream is a sort of appearance and [that it occurs] in sleep; for the likenesses that we just now spoke of are not dreams, nor [is] anything else if it appears after the senses have been set free; and neither is every appearance in sleep [a dream]. For in the first place, it happens to some [sleepers] that they perceive, in a way, sounds and light and flavor and touch,[42] but weakly and as from afar; for [it is known to have] in fact [happened to some people that] with

---

40 For this use of the word "perception" (*aisthēsis*), compare 459a25, as well as n. 21 above.

41 The Greek words that I translate here as "motions capable of being appearances" might also have been correctly translated as "motions that can produce appearances," a translation in keeping with Plato's use of the word *phantastikē* in the *Sophist* (236c3–4). But the continuation of this sentence, along with the passages at 461b11–21 and 460b28–32 (cf. n. 25 above), lead me to prefer the translation that I have given.

42 The Greek word translated as "touch" is *haphēs*, which is Aristotle's usual word for the sense of touch, but which seems here to mean something more like "contact," i.e., contact with the objects of the sense of touch. Perhaps Aristotle uses this word on account of the difficulty, which he had noted in *De Anima* (Book Two, Chapter 11, 422b17–33), of identifying a single underlying class to which all the various objects of touch belong.

their eyes partly open in their sleep, what they faintly saw [as] a light of the lamp, as they supposed, while they were sleeping,[43] they then immediately recognized upon awakening as [truly] being the [light] of the lamp, and faintly hearing [the] sound [characteristic] of cocks and [that] of dogs, they recognized [these] with certainty upon awakening. And some [sleepers] even reply when questioned; for it is admissible in the case of being awake and sleeping that, when one [of them] is present in the unqualified sense, the other be present in a way. None of these [appearances just referred to] should be asserted to be a dream. Neither, indeed, [should] as many true thoughts as come to be in sleep over and above the appearances. But the appearance that [originates] from the motion of our percepts, whenever it is [present] in [the state of] sleeping, insofar as one is sleeping, this is a dream. And it has in fact happened to some [people] that they did not see a single dream throughout their **462b** life, while [it has happened] to others that they saw [dreams] after they were rather far advanced in age, although they had not seen [any] before. And the cause of [dreams] not coming into being [in these cases] appears similar to that in the case of small children and after [our taking in] nourishment. For with all those whose nature is so constituted as to have much vapor rising to the upper region [of the body], which [vapor] in coming back down makes a great deal of motion, [it happens] reasonably [that] no appearance appears to them. But as they advance in age [it is] not at all strange for a dream to appear; for when some change comes about either in accord with age or in accord with [some] *pathos*, it is necessary for this opposite condition to result.

---

43 I have placed the phrase translated as "as they supposed" after the words translated as "a light of the lamp," since this seems to be the most plausible understanding of the sentence. In the Greek, however, that phrase follows directly after the words translated as "while they were sleeping," and if one were to place it there in the translation, the clause beginning with "what they faintly saw" would describe sleepers who thought that the light that they faintly saw was a dream appearance, and who thus supposed that they were sleeping. The ambiguity regarding the expression that this phrase is meant to qualify may well be intentional on Aristotle's part, in keeping with the ambiguous character of this sort of experience.

ON PROPHECY FROM SLEEP

Chapter 1 462b

Concerning prophecy[1] that comes into being in sleep and that is said to result from dreams, it isn't easy either to despise [it] or to be convinced [of it]. For [the fact] that all or many people take it to be the case that dreams have something of the character of signs lends credence (*pistin*) [to reports of prophetic dreams], as being spoken from experience, and it is not incredible (*apiston*) that there is [genuine] prophecy in dreams concerning some things; for [this claim] makes some sense (*logon*); wherefore someone might also suppose the same about the other dreams. But [the fact] that one sees no cause that makes sense (*eulogon*) through which [such prophecy] would come to be, this makes one distrust (*diapistein*); and indeed, as for a god being the one who sends [prophetic dreams], in addition to the rest of its unreasonableness (*alogiai*), it is also strange that

1 The Greek expression translated as "prophecy," both here and in the title of the treatise, is the definite article plus the adjective *mantikē*, meaning "prophetic," with the noun that the adjective would modify left unexpressed (similarly at 462b16-17 below, and earlier at 449b12-13). That unexpressed noun might be understood to be *epistēmē*, which means "knowledge" or "science," or *technē*, which means "skill" or "art"; but it might also be understood to be *dunamis*, which means "power" or "capacity." In the former two senses, there would be a strong presumption that prophecy is a genuine kind of knowledge or skill, but in the other sense, it might be either a genuine gift for seeing into the future or a spurious capacity that leads its possessors to be deceived and to deceive others. Also, the preposition in the title of the treatise that I have translated as "from" has the primary meaning of "down from," as in "down from a high place to a lower one"; and it might suggest that if this kind of prophecy is genuine, the prophet's waking pronouncements have their origin from visions in sleep, with sleep being thought of as occupying a "higher place" than the waking world.

he should send [them], not to those who are best and most intelligent, but to ordinary people.[2] But if causation from the god is set aside, none of the other [conceivable causes] appears to make sense (*eulogon*); for it seems to be beyond our intelligence to discover the principle why some people should have foresight concerning the [things that happen] at the Pillars of Heracles[3] or on the Borysthenes.[4] But be that as it may, it is necessary that dreams are either causes or signs of the things that come to be, or incidental concomitants, either all or some [i.e., two,] of these or one only. By "cause," I mean for instance that the moon [is a cause] of the sun being eclipsed and fatigue [is a cause] of fever; by "sign," that the star coming into view [is a sign] of the eclipse, and that roughness of the tongue [is a sign] of being feverish; and by "incidental concomitant," that the sun is eclipsed while someone is walking; for this is
463a neither a sign nor a cause of its being eclipsed, nor is the eclipse [a sign or a cause] of his walking. Wherefore none of the incidental concomitants comes to be [as such] either always or for the most part. Then are some dreams causes and signs,[5] as for instance of

2 The Greek expression translated as "ordinary people" is *tois tukhousi*, from the verb *tugkhanō*, and it could also be translated, more in accord with the root meaning of this verb, as "people that one just happens upon," or "any chance people." But since one might happen upon one of the most intelligent people by chance, and since Aristotle has just denied that a god sends prophetic dreams to such people, the translation given in the text seems better. What Aristotle will say about *tous tukhontas* in Chapter 2, at 464a22–24, confirms, I think, the superiority of this translation.

3 The present-day Strait of Gibraltar.

4 The present-day Dnieper River.

5 At 463a3–4, I read *ta men aitia kai sēmeia*, following manuscripts L, M, S, P, and U (and most others), rather than *ta men aitia, ta de sēmeia*, with Mugnier, who follows manuscripts E and Y (although manuscript E has the word *estin*, and manuscript Y the word *einai*, after *aitia*). Mugnier's textual apparatus doesn't even include the reading that I have chosen, though it is acknowledged in the editions of Ross and Siwek. According to Mugnier's reading, which is also the reading of all the other editions I am aware of, the beginning of this sentence would be translated as "Then are some dreams causes, and others signs. . . ." Now neither my textual reading nor my translation excludes the possibility that this is what the Greek expression means, just as the expression "either all or some of these or one only" at 462b28 might mean that

the things that happen with regard to the body? Even the higher class[6] among the doctors, at any rate, say that one must pay extremely close attention to dreams; and to take this to be the case is sensible (*eulogon*) also for those who are not skilled in the craft, but who are examining something and philosophizing. For the motions that come into being [from within the body] in the course of the day, if they are not extremely great and strong, escape notice in comparison with the motions [from outside] that are characteristic of being awake, which are greater. But in sleeping the opposite [happens]; for even those [motions] that are small seem to be great. And [this is] clear in cases [such as the following] that happen often during sleep; for [sleepers] suppose that they are being struck by thunderbolts and thunderclaps when small noises are coming into being in their ears, and that they are enjoying honey and sweet flavors when a drop of phlegm is running down [their throats], and that they are walking through fire and becoming extremely hot when a slight heating is taking place around certain parts [of the body]. But as they wake up, these [happenings become] manifest [as] having this character. So that since the beginnings[7] of all [things] are small,

perhaps there are these three different kinds of dreams, or perhaps only two of them, or perhaps only one. But my reading allows also for the possibility that Aristotle is asking whether some dreams are both causes and signs. One difficulty with the reading I have chosen is that the word *men* at 463a3 would not be answered, as it usually is, by a corresponding *de* (cf. Smyth, *Greek Grammar*, para. 2896). But on the other hand, the grammatical irregularity makes it less likely that this reading stems from an ancient scribe's attempt to improve the text, and it is hard to see another reason why the false reading, whichever one it is, arose.

6 The Greek word translated as "higher class" is *kharientes*, which might be translated more literally as "graceful," "cultivated," or "refined." It seems to refer to those doctors who show respectful consideration for each particular patient, approaching him or her as a whole being and trying to learn what's really wrong, rather than merely treating the most obviously visible symptoms in the quickest and easiest way. Cf. *Nicomachean Ethics* 1102a21–23 and also Plato, *Laws* 720b5–e2.

7 The Greek word translated as "beginnings" is *arkhai*, which also means "principles" (cf. 462b26), and which Aristotle often uses as a near equivalent for the word *aitiai*, or "causes." Cf. *Metaphysics* 1013a16–17.

it is clear that [the beginnings are small] both of diseases and of the other affections (*pathēmatōn*) that are about to[8] come into being in bodies. It is manifest, then, that [it is] necessary for these [i.e., the beginnings,] to be more apparent in sleep than in [one's] being awake. But indeed, it is also not unreasonable that some, at any rate, of the appearances during sleep are causes, for each [individual], of his own actions; for just as when we are about to act and when we are [engaged] in the actions or have completed them, we are often [involved] with these [things] and perform [these actions] in a direct dream[9] (and the cause [is] that the motion [that appears as the dream] in fact had the way paved for it from its beginnings in the course of the day), so it is also necessary, conversely, that the motions during sleep are often beginnings of our actions in the course of the day, through the thought of these [actions] also having had the way for it paved, in the other direction, in the appearances [that come] at night. In this way, then, it is admissible for some dreams to be both[10] signs and causes. But most [dreams] look to be

8 The Greek word translated here, and in the next sentence, as "about to" is the present participle of the verb *mellō*, which I translated at 453b21–22 as "yet to be" and "yet to." This word does not necessarily refer to the imminent, as distinct from the more distant, future, although in this sentence, and especially in the next, it seems clear that this is what Aristotle has in mind.

9 The Greek word translated as "a direct dream" is *euthuoneiria*, which comes from the prefix *euthu*, meaning "straight" or "direct," and a form of the word *oneiros*, which means "dream." This word does not appear in any extant Greek before Aristotle, who uses it only in this treatise. And although it is usually translated as "a vivid dream," its etymology would suggest the translation I have given. What it seems to mean is a dream that represents, without distortion (and on the basis of some genuine causal connection), some real actions or events, whether these are past, present, or future. Thus Aristotle can say, for instance, at 464b7, that it takes no particular skill to judge or interpret these dreams. Forms of the word *euthuoneiria* appear also at 464a27, 464b7, and 464b16.

10 At 463a31, I read *enia kai sēmeia* with manuscripts L, S, and U, rather than *enia sēmeia*, with Mugnier, who follows manuscripts E, M, and Y. Mugnier's text would be translated without the word "both." I prefer the reading I have chosen in part because it strengthens a suggestion that I think Aristotle may well have intended, namely, that this last-mentioned kind of dream includes some that, by presenting actions that one recalls upon waking and then

incidental concomitants, and especially[11] all those that are extraordinary as well as those of which the beginning [i.e., the beginning of the actions or events dreamed about,] is not in [the dreamers] themselves, but [which] are about a naval battle and things that are happening far away; for with regard to these, it is likely that [the situation] is of the same sort as when someone finds that this [very thing] that he has mentioned in fact comes about; for what prevents [one's anticipating some real event] in this way also in sleep? Rather, it is likely that many such things occur. Then just as one's mentioning this person is neither a sign nor a cause of his approaching, so in that case the dream is neither a sign, to the one who sees it, nor a cause of its turning out [to be true], but an incidental concomitant. Wherefore also many dreams do not turn out [to be true]; for the incidental concomitant comes to be [as such] neither always nor for the most part. 463b

Chapter 2

And in general, since some of the other animals also dream, dreams would not be sent by the gods, nor have they come into being for the sake of this [i.e., to foretell future events]; [they are,] however, daemonic; for nature is daemonic,[12] but not divine. And

---

chooses to perform, are a kind of cause of one's performing them, but that are also signs of these same actions, the immanifest causes of which would have led one to perform them even if one had not recalled the dreams. Cf. n. 5 above.

11 At 463b1, I read *malista de* with manuscripts L, S, and U, rather than *malista hoion*, with Mugnier, who follows manuscripts E, M, and Y. The beginning of this phrase in Mugnier's text would be translated as "especially, for instance," rather than as "and especially."

12 The adjective translated as "daemonic" is *daimonia*. Compare 453b23, where the word *daimonion* seemed to characterize the kind of power responsible for whatever comes to be by nature or else from chance, as distinct from the actions brought about by human beings. (The phrase that I translated there as "and [which] come to be by nature or from chance" might well have been translated instead as "i.e., [which] come to be by nature or from chance.")

[here is] a sign; for quite paltry human beings are capable of foresight and have direct dreams, as [one would expect] if [it is] not a god sending [them], but [if it is rather the case that] all those whose nature is prattling, as it were, and melancholic[13] see all sorts of apparitions; for because of their being moved many [times] and in all sorts of ways, they hit upon visions[14] [that are] similar [to real events], hitting the mark[15] in these just as [do] some who play odds and evens;[16] for as it is said, "if you make many throws, you will throw differently at different times," this happens also in the case of these [people]. And that many dreams don't turn out [to be true] is not at all strange; for also [many] of the signs in bodies[17] and [many] of the heavenly [signs], for instance those of [impending]

In that passage, then, the word seemed to mean little, if anything, more than "superhuman" in that sense. Here, however, in speaking of nature as daemonic, Aristotle is apparently attributing to our human or even animal nature a capacity for sensing, in dreams and perhaps also in other ways, indications of future events, some of whose causes are daemonic in that other sense. Consider Socrates' account of his own daemonic voice (or sign). Plato, *Apology of Socrates* 31c4–e1 and *Theages* 128d1–130e4.

13 Cf. *On Memory and Recollection* 453a19 and its n. 55, as well as *On Sleep and Awakeness* 457a27ff. and its n. 33.

14 The Greek word translated here as "visions" is *theōrēmasin.* Cf. 450b25ff., where I translated the word *theōrēma* as "object of contemplation," but where the context made it clear that it referred to visions in the soul, as opposed to the things remembered, which those visions resembled. Similarly here, the word *theōrēmasin* refers to visions in the soul, as distinct from the events in the external world that they resemble.

15 The Greek words translated here as "they hit upon" (*epitugkhanousin*) and "hitting the mark" (*epitukheis*) are etymologically related to the noun *tukhē*, which means "chance."

16 The Greek words translated here as "who play odds and evens" are *artia meridzontes*, which would literally be translated as "who divide up evens," an expression that doesn't seem to make sense. Some of the manuscripts have a different reading, which also doesn't seem to make sense, and so Schneider, a modern scholar, proposed to emend the text to read *artiadzontes*, which means "who play odds and evens" ("odds and evens" being a game that involved using knucklebones as dice). For want of a plausible alternative, I translate the text in accord with Schneider's proposed emendation. Johann Gottlob Schneider *ad* 463b20, in Ross, *Aristotle* Parva Naturalia, 282.

17 Cf. 463a17–21 (and perhaps also a22–27).

rains and winds, do not; for if another motion should occur, more decisive than this one from which, when it was about [to occur], the sign came into being,[18] it [i.e., the impending motion,] does not come to be. And many, among the [deeds] that should have been done, that were finely planned have been put an end to [i.e., left undone,] because of other, more decisive beginnings. For in general not everything that was about to be[19] (*to mellēsan*) comes to be, nor is it the same, that which will be and that which is about to be (*to mellon*); but nevertheless one must say that there are indeed some beginnings[20] from which [the normal consequences] do not come to completion; and these are by nature signs of some [things] that do not come to be. Now concerning dreams that don't have beginnings of such a sort as we have spoken of,[21] but [ones that are] remote [from the dreamer], either because of the times or the places or the magnitudes, or [regarding which, while the beginnings are remote] in none of these [ways], yet those who see the dream don't have the beginnings in themselves, if the foreseeing doesn't come about by incidental concomitance, it would be of the following sort more [reasonably] than as Democritus says, when he adduces images and effluences as causes.[22] For just as, when something[23] sets water or air in motion, this [water or air] sets a

18 Aristotle does not mean here that the event we regard as a sign came into being from, or as a consequence of, a motion that was yet to occur, but rather that it came into being *as* a sign, i.e., that it derived its significance, from that impending motion, which would have followed it, and would perhaps even have followed from it, in the normal course of things.

19 Cf. n. 8 above.

20 Cf. n. 7 above.

21 The beginnings that have been spoken of are motions in the body of the dreamer, thoughts of actions that he was about to perform, and (in a different sense of the expression "have beginnings") appearances contained in the dream itself, insofar as they prompt him to action. Cf. 463a17–30.

22 Cf. Sextus Empiricus, *Against the Mathematicians* 9.19.

23 At 464a7, I read *ti to hudōr*, with manuscripts L, S, U, and M, rather than *tis to hudōr*, with Mugnier, who follows manuscripts E and Y. According to Mugnier's text, the translation here would have the word "someone" instead of "something."

different [portion of the water or air] in motion, and after that [initially moved portion] has come to a stop, it [still] happens that such motion proceeds up to a certain point, even though what caused the motion is not present, so nothing prevents a sort of motion and perception (*aisthēsin*) from coming to souls that are dreaming, [coming] from the [objects] that Democritus represents his images and his effluences [as coming from]; and however it happens that [the motions] arrive, [nothing prevents them] from being more perceptible at night because of their being dissipated more when they are moved during the day (for the air at night is less disturbed on account of the nights' being freer of winds), and from producing perception (*aisthēsin*)[24] in the body because of sleep, because of [our] perceiving (*aisthanesthai*)[25] even small internal motions more while sleeping than when awake. And these motions produce appearances, from which they foresee what (pl.) is about to be also[26] with regard to such things.[27] And because of these [things] this *pathos* happens to ordinary people and not to those who are most intelligent. For it would have come to be during the day, and

24 See *On Dreams*, n. 21. Perception "in the body" is presumably the incoming motions as registered by the primary sense organ, rather than perception in the normal or full sense of the word.

25 Cf. *On Dreams*, n. 20.

26 The word translated here as "also" is *kai*, which I read in accordance with manuscripts E and Y, although Mugnier, who follows the preponderance of the manuscripts, chooses not to include it.

27 By "such things," Aristotle is referring to the kinds of things mentioned at 463b31–464a4. Aristotle doesn't spell out here how, on the basis of appearances originating from present events, the dreamers (or perhaps others to whom they tell their dreams) come to foresee future ones. But especially since he says in the next sentence that this *pathos* happens only to ordinary people, whose intellect is as it were empty of all things, and not to those who are most intelligent, I am inclined to think that in his view the predictions of future events, even when they happen to be correct, are illegitimate interpretations of what appears to the dreamers in their dreams, and hence not genuine foresight. (As for Aristotle's use of the word "foresee," compare 464a4–5, where he alludes to a different class of dreams in which there is also what he calls "foreseeing," but merely from incidental concomitance.) And I would contrast such interpretations of dream appearances with the direct dreams that Aristotle goes on to speak of at 464a27. On direct dreams, cf. n. 9 above.

to the wise, if a god were the one sending [it]; but [if it originates] in this way [that we have stated,] it is a likelihood that ordinary people should foresee. For the intellect of such people is not given to thinking, but is as it were deserted and empty of all [things], and when it has been set in motion, it is led in accord with what moves it. And the cause of some of those who are unstable having foresight is that their own proper (*hai oikeiai*) motions do not disturb [others], but are driven away; and so they especially perceive [motions that are] foreign [to them]. But that certain people have direct dreams, and in particular that familiar [friends][28] especially have foresight [in dreams] regarding their familiar [friends], [this] happens because familiar [friends], especially, give thought to one another; for just as they[29] especially recognize (*gnōridzousi*) and perceive [one another] from far away, so also [they especially recognize and perceive] the motions that come [from one another]; for the [motions] of familiar [friends] are more familiar [i.e., recognizable].[30] And those who are melancholic, because of their [being] vehement, as if [they were shooting], have good aim from far away.
And because of their being changeable, what is coming next be- **464b**
comes apparent to them quickly; for just as even crazy people re-

28 The Greek word translated here as "familiar [friends]" is "*gnōrimous*," which implies more in the way of familiarity than of friendship. Though such people are closer than mere acquaintances, they are, as such, not as close as real friends.

29 At 464a30–31, I read *aisthanontai, houtō*, with manuscripts L, S, and U, rather than *aisthanontai hoi sunētheis, houtō*, with Mugnier, who follows manuscripts E and M. Mugnier's text would be translated here as "those who are accustomed [to one another]," rather than as "they."

30 This account of dreams in which familiar friends have foresight regarding one another does not assert that the motions coming from one another that they, especially, recognize and perceive must come to them while they are sleeping. In other words, it is compatible with their first coming to recognize, while they are awake, indications of what is impending for one another, and for this recognition to be subsequently reflected in dreams of those impending events (cf. 463a23–27). Similarly, Aristotle says nothing in this context that would exclude the possibility that the foresight that he will go on to attribute to the melancholic could have come to them, at least initially, whether or not they were fully aware of it at the time, while they were awake.

cite and go through in their minds[31] the poems of Philaigides[32] [with expressions] that fasten upon what is similar, for instance "Aphrodite phrodite,"[33] so also do they [i.e., those who are melancholic,] string [appearances] together into the future. And further, because of their vehemence, their motion [i.e., the motion responsible for the appearance of what is coming next,] is not expelled by a different motion. But the most artful judge of dreams is whoever is able to observe (*theōrein*) likenesses; for it is [within the power] of everyone to judge direct dreams. And by "likenesses," I mean that the appearances [in dreams] resemble images in water, as we said earlier.[34] And in that case, if the motion [of the water] becomes great, the reflection and the images become in no way like the true [beings]. Thus, the one who is quickly able to perceive distinctly and to see together the scattered and distorted [fragments] of the images, [e.g.,] that they are of a man or of a horse or of whatever, would be [the one] skilled at judging the reflections. So also in this case [i.e., that of dreams], this dream[35] has a somewhat similar power [to obscure, and yet point to, something true]; for the motion [within the dreamer] cuts the direct dream into pieces. And so [we have said] what sleep is and what a dream [is], and on account of what cause each of them comes to be, and furthermore, it

---

31 The Greek word translated here as "go through in their minds" is *dianoountai*, which I would normally have translated as "think through."

32 Nothing is known of a poet named Philaigides, nor of one named Philippides, the name that appears here in manuscripts E, M, and Y.

33 At 464b3, I read *Aphroditēn phroditēn*, which appears in manuscripts M, Y, and the first hand of manuscript E, rather than *Aphroditēn*, with Mugnier, who follows manuscripts L, S, and the second hand of E. According to Mugnier's text, instead of the nonsense expression "Aphrodite phrodite," the translation would read "Aphrodite," presumably a reference to an unknown poem of that name.

34 Cf. 461a14ff.

35 At 464b15, I read *to enupnion touto* with the preponderance of the manuscripts, rather than *to enupnion*, with Mugnier, who follows manuscript L. According to Mugnier's text, the words translated here as "this dream"—which I would interpret as a reference to the non-direct or obscured dream—would be translated instead as "the dream."

has been spoken concerning prophecy[36] from dreams,[37] [concerning] all of it.[38] And the motion that is common to animals must be spoken about.[39]

---

36 The word translated here as "prophecy" (*manteias*) is a noun in the Greek as well, not the adjectival form with an unexpressed noun (*mantikē*) that Aristotle had used in the title of the treatise and at the beginning of Chapter 1, and which had suggested that prophecy might be a kind of knowledge or science. Cf. n. 1.

37 Compare this summary statement with the beginning of *On Sleep and Awakeness*, 453b11–24. Note also that Aristotle does not say here that he has given the cause of prophecy from dreams, although he does say that he has said on account of what cause sleep and a dream each come to be.

38 The Greek words translated here as "[concerning] all of it," though they are present in manuscripts E, M, and Y, are absent in manuscripts L, S, and U. I include them largely because it seems unlikely to me that an ancient scribe would have taken the liberty of adding such a striking claim to Aristotle's text.

39 The Greek corresponding to this final sentence is missing in manuscripts S and U, and Mugnier does not include it in his text, omitting it even from his critical apparatus. But it appears in most of the manuscripts, including E, M, Y, and also L, which is a generally superior member of the family of manuscripts to which S and U belong. Now the traditional order of the *Parva Naturalia* includes the treatise *On Long-Livedness and Short-Livedness* immediately after this one, and that traditional order finds some limited support from the beginning of *On Sense Perception and Sense-Perceptibles* (436a5–17), which promises a treatment of youth and old age after that of sleep. However, that very passage also promised a consideration of appetite (*orexis*) after that of memory—even before that of sleep—and the treatise *On the Motion of Animals* is indeed Aristotle's most thorough treatment of appetite. Furthermore, in most of the manuscripts—including even manuscript S—the treatise *On the Motion of Animals* follows immediately after this one. Accordingly, I translate this sentence here, and I will follow my translation of this treatise with a translation of *On the Motion of Animals*. As for the question as to why this sentence comes at the end of the three treatises on sleep, rather than at the end of the one on memory, in keeping with the original promise to consider appetite after memory, I can offer only a very tentative conjecture, namely, that Aristotle's discussion of sleep and dreams, and in particular his account in this treatise of how dreams can lead to actions and of why well planned actions are sometimes left undone, turns out to be an important backdrop for his account of appetite and animal motion.

On the Motion of Animals

Chapter 1

Concerning motion, that of the animals, as many of them as there are, with regard to each kind [of them], and what [their] differentiae [are, insofar as these pertain to their different ways of moving], and what [the] causes [are] of their particular concomitant [attributes], concerning all [these things] it has been examined [by us] in other [speeches].[1] But as a whole, concerning the common cause of [their] being moved[2] with whatever sort of motion (for some of the animals are moved by flying, some by swimming, some by walking, and some in other such manners), it must be examined now. Now then, that what itself moves itself [is the] ruling beginning[3] of 698a

---

1 Aristotle is referring primarily to his treatise *On the Locomotion of Animals* (the title of which is usually translated as *On the Progression of Animals*). But see also *On the History of Animals* 498a3–b10, along with the many passages relevant to the animals' ways of motion in its account of their external parts in Book Four, Chapters 1–7 (523a31–532b28), and also in *On the Parts of Animals*, Book Four, Chapters 6–14 (682a35–697b30).

2 The Greek word translated here as "being moved" is a middle/passive infinitive that can also mean, as a middle form, "being in motion"; and in other treatises I have sometimes translated it, along with the related participle and finite verb, as "being in motion," "is in motion," or "are in motion." But in this treatise on the motion of animals, where the cause of animal motion is the central theme, I will translate these forms consistently as "being moved," "is moved," or "are moved." Also, to avoid ambiguity, I never translate any of these middle/passive forms by the English word "move" (or its variants), but I reserve this translation for the active forms, which are transitive, and which in this treatise I will translate consistently as "move," even when a direct object is not explicitly mentioned, although in other treatises I also use the translations "set in motion" or "produce motion."

3 The word translated as "ruling beginning" is *arkhē*, which I have been translating in the previous treatises as "beginning." But especially in this treatise,

the other motions, while of this[4] what is unmoved [is the ruling beginning], and that the first mover is necessarily unmoved, has been determined before, when [we determined] also concerning everlasting motion, whether it is or not, and if it is, which it is.[5] But we must grasp this not only by means of speech (*logōi*) in general, but also in the particulars and the perceptibles, on account of which we seek general speeches, and with which we suppose that they must accord. For [it is] manifest also in these that [it is] impossible to be moved if nothing is at rest, [at rest] in the first place in the animals themselves. For if any one of their parts is moved, there must be some [part] at rest; and [it is] on account of this [that] the animals have joints. For they use their joints [each] as a center, and the whole part in which the joint [is present] becomes both one and two, and straight and bent, changing potentially and actually on account of the joint. And when [an animal] is bending and being moved, one point of those in its joints is

---

the inadequacy of the English "beginning" for conveying the meaning of this Greek word seems to require this expanded translation. The Greek word *arkhē* can mean, in fact, either "beginning" or "rule," and in its strong sense it means both together, i.e., a beginning that continues to govern the course of what follows from it, as for instance, a seed continues to govern the growth of the animal that comes from it, or as a craftsman continues to govern the production of an artifact that he first brings into being, or as a locomotive continues to govern the motion of a train that it first moves. And since Aristotle seems especially concerned to find the beginning, in this sense, of animal motion, I will continue throughout this treatise to translate *arkhē* as "ruling beginning," or else, if I think that "beginning" (or perhaps "principle") is the more appropriate translation in a particular passage, I will supplement the English translation with a transliteration in parentheses of the Greek.

4 At 698a8, I read *toutou*, together with all the manuscripts that I am aware of, rather than *touto*, with Louis, who mistakenly thought it to be the reading of manuscript S. According to Louis' text, this clause would perhaps be translated, instead of as "while of this what is unmoved [is the ruling beginning]," as "while this [is] what is unmoved." But the self-mover that Aristotle has just spoken of is not unmoved, although it is moved, according to the argument of the *Physics*, by a part of itself that is unmoved (*Physics* 258a5–27), and ultimately by a simply unmoved mover (*Physics* 258b10–260a19).

5 Cf. *Physics*, Book Eight, Chapters 5 and 6 (256a4–260a19) and Chapters 8 and 9 (261b27–266a9).

moved and another remains, as if the [point] A and the [point] D of the diameter were to remain, but the [point] B were to be moved, and the [line] AC were to come into being.[6] But here, the center is thought to be in every way indivisible (and indeed they [merely] fabricate being moved, as they assert,[7] in regard to them [i.e., to points and lines]; for [they assert that] none of the mathematicals is moved), but the [centers] in the joints become, potentially and actually, sometimes one and sometimes divided.[8] But at all events, 698b the beginning (*arkhē*), that against which [animal motion gets its support], is always, [insofar] as [it is] a beginning (*arkhē*), at rest when the part below [it] is moved, for instance, when the forearm is moved, the elbow [remains at rest], while when the whole limb [is moved], the shoulder [does], and when the lower leg [is moved], the knee [remains at rest], while when the whole leg [is moved], the hip [does]. And so [it is] manifest that each [animal] has to have also in itself something at rest, from where the ruling beginning is[9] of what is moved, and supported against which [the animal] will be moved both as a whole altogether and part by part.

Chapter 2

But all the rest in[side] it [is] nevertheless ineffectual unless something outside is simply at rest[10] and unmoved. And [it is] worth

6 This account is accompanied in some manuscripts by the drawing of a circle with center A and diameter D(A)B, along with an additional radius, AC, making an acute angle with the semidiameter AB. Radius AC (taken together with the radius AD) thus shows the state of affairs after the point B, as part of the line AB, has moved to point C on the circumference of the circle.

7 It is not clear to me which mathematicians or philosophers Aristotle is referring to here.

8 Cf. 698a18–21.

9 At 698b6, I read *esti*, with manuscripts E, S, Y, B[e], E[r], and O[d], rather than *estai*, with Louis, who follows most of the other manuscripts. According to Louis' text, the words "will be" would replace the word "is."

10 With the expression "simply at rest," Aristotle is contrasting this necessary outside something with an animal's joint, or what is at rest in it, which never-

stopping to examine concerning what has been said; for it contains [matter for] contemplation, not only insofar as [contemplation] is intent upon the animals, but also [insofar as it has regard] to the motion and local motion of the all. For just as there has to be something unmoved in it if it is going to be moved, so still more does there have to be something unmoved outside the animal, supported against which what is moved is moved. For if it will always give way, for instance to the mice [that burrow] in the earth[11] or to those who try to walk in sand, they will not go forward, and there will neither be walking, unless the earth should remain, nor flying or swimming, unless the air or the sea should provide resisting support.[12]

---

theless undergoes a kind of motion itself, as part of a larger whole, whenever the animal as a whole, or even just the part of it that contains that joint, is moved.

11 Here I follow Louis' text, which is the one given by most of the manuscripts. But most editors and translators have been unhappy with this example, and various emendations have been proposed, one of which is the substitution of the word for certain tortoise-like animals, *emusi*, for the word for mice, *musi*, and another of which is the substitution of the word for mud, *pēlōi*, for the word for earth, *gēi* (while treating the word for mice as referring instead to a type of shellfish, as indeed it could). But to repeat, these are merely conjectural emendations, which should be accepted only as a last resort. Now manuscript E has the word *posi*, or "feet," instead of the word for mice, but this reading of the phrase ("feet in the earth") doesn't seem to me to be persuasive enough to outweigh the evidence of all the other manuscripts. Also, two manuscripts recently collated by Primavesi (B^e and E^r) read *pittēi*, which means "pitch," instead of the word for earth (*gēi*), and Primavesi, who accepts this reading—and who thinks that it was originally also in manuscript E, but then partially erased and overwritten with the word *gēi*—suggests that the phrase ("the mice in the pitch") refers to a kind of mousetrap that was known from an ancient proverb about a greedy mouse. But aside from the fact that pitch makes walking difficult by its stickiness, and so not only by giving way beneath the feet, a reference to a mousetrap (or a proverb about a mousetrap) seems less plausible to me than a reference to a field mouse's burrow, or to the soft earth that has been kicked away and that surrounds its entrance. Moreover, a reminder that earth can be soft and somewhat yielding, as well as hard, seems relevant in the overall context (cf. the next footnote, n. 12). And so again, I prefer the traditional reading that follows most of the manuscripts.

12 Cf. *On the Locomotion of Animals* 705a6–12, where Aristotle makes it more unambiguously explicit than he does here that the outside support for animal motion may give way to some extent, as long as it offers some resistance.

And [it is] necessary that this [resisting support] be different from what is moved, both [that the] whole [be different] from [the] whole, and that what is unmoved in this way be no part of what is moved; otherwise, it will not be moved. And witness to this is what [one] is perplexed about, why ever, if someone pushes the boat from outside, shoving the mast or some other part with his pole, he moves it easily, but if someone while being in the boat itself tries to do this, not even Tityos could move it, nor again Boreas,[13] blowing from inside the boat, if he were in fact blowing in this manner in which the painters represent [him]; for they paint him [as] sending his breath [*to pneuma*] from it[14] [i.e., from inside the boat]. For whether someone throws his breath gently or so forcefully as to 699a
produce the greatest wind, or whether that which is thrown or pushed is something other [than breath], [it is] necessary in the first place that he push while being supported against some one of

---

13 At 698b24–25, I read *oud'...oud'*, with Primavesi, who follows manuscripts B^e and E^r, rather than *out' an...outh'*, with Louis, who follows the great majority of the manuscripts. According to Louis' text, this phrase would be translated as "neither Tityos...nor Boreas," instead of as "not even Tityos...nor again Boreas." I prefer Primavesi's reading, despite its having less manuscript support, because it brings out more clearly than the other one that (the giant) Tityos and (the wind god) Boreas possess two different kinds of strength, and that only Boreas would be attempting to move the boat by blowing.

14 At 698b27, I read *autou*, with the majority of the manuscripts, rather than *hautou*, with Louis, who mistakenly attributed his reading to manuscripts E, Y, S, and P, whereas in fact it appears only in a few manuscripts that Louis did not consult. According to Louis' text, this phrase would be translated, instead of as "sending his breath [*to pneuma*] from it," as "sending the wind [*to pneuma*] from himself." This reading, which might be thought to contrast the picture of Boreas breathing out with an alternative one of him summoning the wind from somewhere else, might be more compelling if Aristotle had not already made it explicit that Boreas is attempting to move the boat by blowing from inside it. It is true, however, that since Aristotle has done this, one would have expected this clause to specify some particular manner of blowing from inside the boat that would make it impossible to move it, and to contrast this at least implicitly with some other manner of blowing from inside it, which might not make it impossible to move it. And in light of this expectation, could Aristotle be hinting at a contrast between Boreas' blowing forward against the sail, as the painters apparently portray him, and his blowing backward into the air? Cf. *On the Generation of Animals* 768b15–20.

the parts of himself that is at rest, and then again that this part, either itself or that of which it is in fact a part, remain planted against something among the [things] outside. But the one pushing the boat, while being himself in the boat and planting himself against the boat, does not move the boat, as is reasonable, on account of its being necessary for that against which he plants himself to remain; but in his case it is the same [thing], what he tries to move and what he plants himself against. But if he pushes or pulls from outside [the boat], he moves [it]; for the earth is no part of the boat.

Chapter 3

But someone might be perplexed as to whether, if something moves the whole heaven, there has to be an unmoved [something][15] and

15 At 699a3, the Greek word (*ti*) for "something," which I supply in brackets, is actually present in manuscripts B^e, E^e, and b, and Primavesi, who collated these manuscripts, includes it in the text of his edition; according to that text, this clause would not be translated as "there has to be an unmoved [something]," but more simply as "there has to be something unmoved." But I choose to follow the great majority of the manuscripts, since the reading that they contain invites an initial misinterpretation of the whole passage that I think Aristotle intended to invite. On that interpretation, this clause would be translated as "it has to be unmoved," and the perplexity referred to would be "whether, if something moves the whole heaven, it has to be unmoved." And Aristotle would be asking whether the mover of the heaven—assuming that there is one—is indeed unmoved, i.e., whether it is the Unmoved Mover that he argued for at the end of the *Physics* and near the end of the *Metaphysics*, an argument that he has reminded us of at the beginning of this treatise (698a7–11). However, the word "this" in the next clause reads quite awkwardly if Aristotle is asking only about something that he has already singled out as the mover of the heaven. And from the following sentence, it is clear that this interpretation of the clause is wrong, and that Aristotle is appealing, at least in part, to the argument of the previous chapter of this treatise, which suggests that there has to be something *bodily* that is unmoved, something that would be touched by the immediate mover, as the earth is touched by the animals that move themselves upon it (contrast *On Coming into Being and Perishing* 323a25–34). Still, Aristotle's reference later in that sentence to the alternative of a mover that is "straightway" unmoved does suggest the Unmoved Mover. And Louis' text, which makes it seem initially that he is asking only about this, makes it clearer than it would otherwise be

this [has] to be no part of the heaven nor in the heaven. For if being itself moved, it moves it, [it is] necessary that it move [it] while touching something unmoved, and that this be no part of the mover; or if straightway the mover is unmoved, [it is] likewise [necessary] that it will be no part of that which is moved. And in this respect, at any rate, they speak correctly who say that since the sphere is moved in circular local motion, no part at all [of it] remains [fixed];[16] for [otherwise,] either it would have to remain [fixed] as a whole or else its continuity [and thus its very being] would be pulled apart. But in that they suppose the poles to have some power, while having no magnitude, but being extremities and points, [they do] not [speak] finely. For in addition to there being no being (*ousian*) that belongs to any of such [things],[17] [it is] also impossible [for the sphere] to be moved in its one motion by two [movers]; but they make the poles two. So then, that there is something related also to the whole nature[18] as the earth is related to the animals and to the [things] that are moved through their agency, someone might from such [considerations] pursue the perplexity [already mentioned regarding this claim]. And those who, by way

---

that, though the detailed discussion in this chapter speaks only of bodies (and their extremities), Aristotle has the doctrine of the (bodiless) Unmoved Mover very much in mind.

16 It is not known who the thinkers are to whom Aristotle is referring here.

17 By "such [things]," Aristotle is apparently referring to things without magnitude. And by saying that no "being (*ousian*)" belongs to any of such things, he doesn't mean that they are not anything at all, but is rather contrasting them with beings in the primary sense of the word (beings that are themselves spoken of as *ousiai*), namely, the things not predicated of, or present in, a substratum (cf. *Metaphysics* 1017b10–26). And Aristotle's observation that things like the poles of the heaven have no *ousian* seems to be a suggestion that only the beings (i.e., *ousiai*) to which *ousia*(*n*) does belong have the power to be movers. (For instance, it is not, strictly speaking, heat that boils water, but rather the fire in which heat is present.)

18 Regarding Aristotle's use of this expression, "the whole nature," instead of "the whole heaven" (as at 699a12), one should note that the Greek *ho ouranos*, which I have been translating as "the heaven," can also mean the world, i.e., the whole of what is enclosed within the outermost circumference of the heaven. Cf. *On the Heaven* 278b9–24.

of myth, make Atlas [as] having his feet on the earth would seem to have spoken the myth on the basis of (discursive) thought, [the thought] that he is like an axis and that he makes the heaven rotate around its poles.[19] And this would happen in accord with reason (*logon*) on account of the earth remaining. However, [it is] necessary for those who say these [things] to assert that it [i.e., the earth,] is no part of the all. And in addition to these [considerations], the force of what moves[20] must be equal [at most] to that of what remains. For there is a certain amount of force and power by which that which remains remains, just as [there] also [is a certain amount] by which that which moves [something] moves [it]; and there is of necessity a certain [quantitative] relation, just as [there is] of the contrary motions, so also of the rests.[21] And those [motions and rests] that are equal [in force] are unaffected by one an-
699b other, but they are overpowered by the excess [of the force of one over that of another]. Therefore, if it is Atlas or something different of such a sort, among the [things] within [the heaven], that moves [it], [the mover] must press against [the earth with] no more [force] than the [force of] rest with which the earth in fact remains; or [else] the earth will be moved from the middle and out of its own place. For as that which pushes pushes, so that which is pushed is pushed, and [in particular] by like force. And that which is at rest [is what] in the first place moves,[22] so that its force of [remaining

19 Atlas was represented in myth as holding the sphere of the heaven upon his shoulders.

20 In other words, "the force of what produces motion," i.e., Atlas. On this translation, see the end of n. 2 above.

21 By "a certain [quantitative] relation . . . of the contrary motions," I think that Aristotle means a relation between the force tending to move a body and its force of remaining at rest, and by such a relation "of the rests," I think he means one between the force of rest of a body that is to be moved and the force of rest of the body that supports the mover.

22 Aristotle has not previously spoken of the external body against which a mover remains fixed while moving itself or something else as itself moving, i.e., being a mover, let alone as being what "in the first place" moves. But this body at rest, in its resistance to downward pressure from that mover, is the beginning (*arkhē*) from where the motion comes, and so there is at least some sense in speaking of it as the first mover. Other translators translate this

at] rest [is] more and greater [than] (or like and equal) [to the force upon it of the mover that moves the heaven directly]. And in the same way [it is] also [greater] than [or equal to] the [force upon it] of that which is moved, but does not move [i.e., that of the heaven].[23] So then the earth will have to have as great a power in its resting as the entire heaven has, and that which moves it. And if this [is] impossible, [it is] impossible also for the heaven to be moved by any such [mover] among the [things] within [it].

Chapter 4

And there is a certain perplexity regarding the motions of the parts of the heaven, which someone might examine as being akin to the [things] that have been said. For if someone should surpass by the power of his motion the [power of] rest of the earth, [it is] clear that he will move it away from the middle. And that the force from which [there is] this power [by which the earth remains in the middle] is not infinite [is] manifest; for neither is the earth infinite, so that neither [is] its weight. And since the impossible is spoken of in more ways [than one] (for we do not assert that it is in the same way impossible for sound to be seen and for those on the moon [to be seen] by us; for in the one [case we mean that it is impossible] from necessity, whereas in the other [we mean that what is] of such

---

clause as "but it creates motion in that which is first at rest" (Forster; cf. Farquharson, Morel, Corcilius) or else as "and that which produces motion starts out by being at rest" (Nussbaum; cf. Louis). But the thought of some prior time when the heaven was at rest and not yet moved is not only implausible in itself, but it would be an unnecessary complication in this discussion of the Atlas myth.

23 At 699b7, I read *tēs*, with manuscripts P, S, and quite a few others, rather than *hē*, with Louis, who follows manuscripts N and Y. According to Louis' text, this sentence would apparently be translated as "And in the same way also the [force] of that which is moved but does not move [is greater than its power of remaining at rest]." Louis' reading makes sense, to the extent that it does, only in keeping with his interpretation of the previous sentence, which I reject (cf. the previous footnote, n. 22).

a nature [as] to be seen will not be seen).[24] And we suppose it to be from necessity that the heaven is indestructible and indissoluble, but according to this speech (*logon*) it turns out [to be the case that it is] not from necessity [that it is indestructible, if indeed it is];[25] for it is natural and admissible for there to be a motion greater [in power than that] from which the earth is at rest and [than that] from which fire and the upper body[26] are moved. And so if there are the surpassing motions, these [bodies] will be dissolved [i.e., separated,] from[27] one another. And if there are not [such motions], but it is admissible [for there] to be [such] (for [a motion] infinite [in power and therefore unsurpassable] is not admissible, on account of its not being admissible for a body to be infinite),[28] it would be admissible that the heaven be dissolved. For what prevents this from happening, if [it is] not impossible? And [it is] not impossible unless its [contradictory] opposite [is] necessary. But regarding this perplexity let there be a different speech (*logos*); but must there be something unmoved and at rest outside of that which is moved, being no part of that, or not? And this [some-

24 This sentence, which began at 699b17 ("And since the impossible..."), lacks a main clause, which one would expect after this parenthesis. Perhaps Aristotle had in mind something like, "it is only the impossible in the former sense that is impossible, strictly speaking," a thought that he might have been hesitant to express here, although it is clearly implied in the continuation of this discussion.

25 Compare Plato, *Timaeus* 41a6–b6, where the Demiurge says to the heavenly gods, i.e., the stars, that although they are dissoluble, since they have come into being, they will never be dissolved, given that his will (to preserve them), i.e., not necessity, is a stronger bond than those with which they were bound when they came into being.

26 By "the upper body," Aristotle is referring to that body from which the heavenly spheres, as well as the stars, are composed, a body that he speaks of elsewhere as differing from earth, air, water, and fire, in part by being indestructible. Cf. *On the Heaven* 269a2–270b25, 289a11–19; *De Anima* 418b7–13.

27 At 699b26, I read the preposition *ap'*, together with manuscript E, rather than *hup'*, with Louis, who follows the other manuscripts, as do all the other editors and translators I am aware of. According to Louis' text, instead of "from one another," this phrase would be translated as "by one another."

28 Cf. *Physics* 266a24–b6.

thing], [is it] necessary also in the case of the all that it be present in such a way? For perhaps it would seem to be strange if the ruling beginning of its motion [were] within [it]. Wherefore it would seem, to those who hold this to be the case, that [the following] was well spoken by Homer:

> But you could not pull from the heaven to the ground
> Zeus, highest of all, not even if you should toil very greatly; **700a**
> Lay hold [of the golden rope], all [you] gods and all [you]
> goddesses.[29]

For what is wholly unmoved does not admit of being moved by anything, whence there is resolved also the perplexity that was spoken earlier,[30] whether it is admissible or is not admissible for the structure of the heaven to be dissolved: [it is resolved, that is,] if [that structure] is fastened [i.e., has its support,] from an unmoved ruling beginning. But in the case of the animals, not only must there be present what is unmoved in this way, but also in the [animals] themselves that are moved with respect to place, as many as themselves move themselves[31] (for one [part] of them[32] must be at

---

29 *Iliad* 8.20–22. In our text of the *Iliad* the verse that Aristotle cites after the other two comes before them (preceded by a reference to the golden rope). And instead of the word *pantōn*, translated as "of all," in the second line, our text of the *Iliad* has the word *mēstōr'*, which means "counselor," so that Zeus is referred to there as the highest counselor, rather than as the highest of all.

30 The Greek word translated here as "earlier" is *palai*, whose more usual meaning is "long ago," though it can also mean "just past." And I translate it as "earlier," rather than as "long ago," since Aristotle is clearly referring to the perplexity that he has just raised at the beginning of this chapter. On the other hand, it seems likely that he also has in mind the meaning "long ago," given that this perplexity, in one form or another, is an ancient one, as is indeed suggested by the passage from Homer, which, as Aristotle says, offers a kind of resolution to it.

31 Aristotle allowed that there are animals, such as sponges and oysters, which are moved, if they are moved, only by something else, in addition to those animals that move themselves. Cf. *On the History of Animals* 487b7–15, 548b5–10.

32 At 700a8, I read *autōn*, with manuscripts X, H^a, L, N, and V^g, rather than *autou*, with Louis, who follows most of the other manuscripts. According to Louis' text, the word translated as "of them" would instead be translated as

rest and another [must be] moved), [there must be something unmoved,] supported against which that which is moved will be moved, for instance, if [an animal] moves one of its parts; for the one [part] is supported against the other as against [something] remaining. But concerning the [beings] that lack soul, as many as are moved, someone might be perplexed whether they all have in themselves both that which is at rest and that which moves,[33] and [whether it is] necessary for these too to be supported against one of the external [beings] that are at rest, or [whether this is] impossible, for instance with respect to fire or earth or some other of the [beings] that lack soul, by which [things, being] first, these are moved.[34] For all the [beings] that lack soul are moved by another,

---

"of it." Some editors who accept Louis' reading would transpose the entire clause within the parentheses, placing it after the phrase that follows it here, namely, "supported against which that which is moved will be moved," even though there is no manuscript support for this transposition.

33 The Greek words at 700a13 that I translate as "that which moves" are *to kinoun*. I read them in accord with Louis' text, which follows all the manuscripts that were known to him, and which agrees with nearly all the others. But manuscripts B^{e}, E^{r}, and b, recently collated by Primavesi, read *to kinoumenon*, which would be translated as "that which is moved," and Primavesi accepts this as the genuine reading. Primavesi doesn't say why he prefers this reading, but perhaps he noticed that Aristotle has not spoken, in his discussion of the motion of animals, of that within them that moves them, but had said only that, with the support of something within them that is at rest, they move themselves (cf. 700a6–11). But that is precisely why, I think, the traditional reading is to be preferred, namely, that it calls attention to the fact that Aristotle had not spoken of what it is within the animals that moves them. In this way, I think, Aristotle calls attention to the difficulty of determining what that is.

34 At 700a15, I follow Louis' text, in particular by reading the word *all'* as having an acute accent on the first syllable, so as to be translated as "other," even though this accentuation appears only in E^{r}, a relatively minor manuscript. (Louis mistakenly believed that this accent was present in manuscripts E, S, and Y.) But since it is believed that accent marks were not invented until after Aristotle's death, I do not regard the absence of this acute accent as sufficient evidence that Aristotle didn't intend for the word to be understood in this way. Without the accent, as the word appears in almost all of our manuscripts, the word means "but," so that the end of this sentence would be translated, instead of as "with respect to fire or earth or some other of the [beings] that lack soul, by which [things, being] first, these are moved," as "with respect

and [the] ruling beginning of all the [beings] that are moved in this way [is] those that themselves move themselves. And among such [beings], [what] concerns the animals has been said; for [it is] a necessity that all the [beings] of this sort have that which is at rest, both in themselves and outside, against which they will be supported. But if there is something [that is] higher and that in the first place moves, [is] unclear, and [there is] another speech (*logos*) concerning the ruling beginning that is of that sort. But the animals, as many as are moved, are all moved while being supported against the [things] outside, even while breathing [in] and while breathing out. For there is no difference at all between throwing a big weight or a small one, which those who spit and cough do, and [also] those who breathe in and breathe out.

Chapter 5

[Is it] only in that which moves itself with respect to place that something has to remain, or [is it] also in that which is altered, itself by itself, and grows? Concerning coming into being, that from [the]

---

to fire or earth or some one of the [beings] that lack soul, but [such external support is necessary only in the case of those beings] by which, [being] first, these are moved." But since Aristotle has already limited his inquiry here to the beings that lack soul, it would be pointless for him to speak of some one of these beings, without further qualification, as an example of them. Moreover, by speaking of "some one of the [beings] that lack soul" as an alternative to fire and earth, this reading suggests the falsehood that fire and earth do not lack soul. And for both these reasons, I cannot accept it. On the other hand, the difficulty with the reading that I do accept is that it suggests that fire and earth have been moved by some other, more primary beings that also lack soul (though they nevertheless, as the next sentence indicates, are not only moved by other things, but also move themselves), and this contradicts well known Aristotelian teachings. But it is quite in keeping with the rest of this chapter, which treats it as a genuine question whether the ordered whole within which we live is impermanent (cf. also 700a20–21), for Aristotle to suggest that the elemental bodies, including fire and earth, have originated from and have been first moved by something other that also lacked soul (while nevertheless having the potential—unlike fire and earth, insofar as they show themselves as fire and earth—to bring about a world that includes beings that do have soul).

beginning (*ex arkhēs*), and perishing, [there is] another speech (*logos*); for if there is the first motion that we assert [there is],[35] this would be responsible for coming into being and perishing, and perhaps for all the other motions. And as in the whole, [so] also in the animal, this [would be the] first motion, when it [i.e., the one or the other,] has come to completion, so that [this motion would be responsible,] both for growth, if ever it [i.e., the animal,] comes to be, itself for itself, responsible [for its growth],[36] and for alteration; but if [there is] not [the first motion that we assert there is], [it is] not necessary[, even after the animal has come to completion, that this motion be responsible for its alteration and growth, nor accordingly that something in the animal remain unmoved while it is being altered and growing]. But the first growths and alterations come into being by the agency of another [being] and through other [motions]; and in no way [is it] possible for anything to be, itself for itself, responsible for coming into being and perishing. For that which moves has to be present before that which is moved [is moved], and that which begets before that which is begotten; but nothing [is] itself prior to itself.

Chapter 6

Now concerning soul, whether it is moved or not, and if it is moved, how it is moved, it has been said before, in the [things] that have been determined [by us] concerning it.[37] And since all the

35 By "the first motion that we assert [there is]," Aristotle is referring to local motion, i.e., motion with respect to place (and ultimately to the circular motion of the heaven). He argues in the *Physics* that motion with respect to place is prior to the other motions, namely, alteration and growth, as well as to coming into being, which in that context he treats as being a kind of motion. *Physics* 260a20–261a26.

36 At 700a33, I do not follow Louis' punctuation. I do not read the comma that he does after the word *ginetai*, but I do read a comma, which he does not, after the word *aition*.

37 *De Anima*, Book One, Chapters 3 and 4 (405b31–409a30, and in particular 406b5–6).

[beings] that lack soul are moved by [something] different [from themselves], and [since] concerning what is first moved and always moved, in what manner it is moved, and how the first mover moves [it], it has been determined before in our [speeches] concerning first philosophy,[38] it remains to contemplate how the soul moves the body, and what the ruling beginning [is] of the motion of the animal. For apart from the motion of the whole, the ensouled [beings are] responsible for the motion of the other [things], as many as are not moved by one another on account of their striking against one another. Wherefore also all their motions have a limit, for those of the ensouled [beings have a limit] also. For all the animals both move [what they move] and are moved for the sake of something, so that of all their motion there is this limit, the for the sake of which. And we see that what (pl.) moves the animal are (discursive) thought (*dianoia*) and imagination and choice and wish and desire. And all these are [i.e., can be,] reduced to thought (*noun*) and appetite. For both imagination and sense perception have the same place as thought, for [these are] all [faculties] of making distinctions, although they differ by virtue of the differences that have been spoken about in other [speeches].[39] And wish and spirit[40] and desire [are] all appetite, while choice is [a product] of (discursive) thought and appetite in common, so that also the [object of] (discursive) thought [is a product of these].[41] But [we

---

38 *Metaphysics*, Book Twelve, Chapter 7 (1072a19–1073a13). See, however, 700a20–21.

39 *De Anima*, Book Three, Chapter 3 (427a17–428a16).

40 The word translated here as "spirit" is *thumos*, which I have translated elsewhere as "spiritedness." But I choose the translation "spirit" here because Aristotle seems to be referring not to a disposition of the soul, a disposition, for instance, to resist threats (to one's life or to the satisfaction of some desire), but to the resistance itself.

41 At 700b23–24, I read *hōste kai to dianoēton*, with manuscripts E, S, Y, and some others, rather than *hōste kinei prōton to orekton kai to dianoēton*, with Louis, whose reading agrees with manuscripts P, B^{e}, E^{r}, and b. According to Louis' text this clause would be translated, instead of as "so that also the [object of] (discursive) thought [is a product of these]," as "so that the [object] of appetite and that of (discursive) thought first moves [the animal]." It seems

are speaking here] not [of] all that is the object of (discursive) thought, but [of] the end [i.e., the goal,] of the [things] to be done [i.e., of actions]. Wherefore what moves is that, of the goods, which is of such a sort, but not all the beautiful; for insofar as another [is] for the sake of this, and insofar as it is [the] end of the [actions] that are for the sake of something other, in this way it moves [what it moves]. And one must presume that also what appears good has [the] place of [the] good—also the pleasant; for it is an appearing/ apparent good. And so [it is] clear that there is a respect in which what is always being moved by what is always moving [it] is moved in the same way as each of the animals, but there is a respect [in which it is moved] in another way, for which reason also the former are always moved, whereas the motion of the animals has a limit. But the eternally beautiful, i.e., that which is truly and in the first place good, and not [good] at one time but at another not, [is] too divine and too high [in rank] (*timiōteron*) to be prior [to anything].[42] And so what is first moves [what it moves] without being moved;

---

to me, however, that this reading is the result of some ancient scribe's attempt to avoid attributing to Aristotle the claim that the object of discursive thought is itself a product of discursive thought in conjunction with appetite, and thus not something that exists independently of our animal appetite. And yet this claim, although perhaps surprising coming from Aristotle, seems to me reasonable on the face of it, at least as regards that kind of discursive thought that Aristotle goes on to discuss, namely, practical thought, or thought about the goals of action.

42 At 700b34–35 I read *hōst' einai proteron*, with the preponderance of the manuscripts, rather than *hōst' einai proteron* <*ti*>, with Louis, who adds the word *ti* that was suggested by the twentieth-century scholar Jaeger, and rather than *hōst' einai pros heteron*, with manuscripts P, B^e, and E^r. According to Jaeger's emendation, this clause would be translated not as "[is] too divine and too high [in rank] (*timiōteron*) to be prior [to anything]," but as "[is] too divine and too high [in rank] for there to be anything prior [to it]." And the reading of manuscripts P, B^e, and E^r would be translated as "[is] too divine and too high [in rank] to be relative to [anything] different." But both of these readings, it seems to me, and especially that of Jaeger and Louis, are attempts to soften the force of Aristotle's claim that "the eternally beautiful" (or "that which is truly and in the first place good"), is not prior, i.e., not related even in that sense, to anything else, a claim that someone might indeed wish to soften, since it makes it difficult to see how such a good should be a moving cause of anything, or even that it should be an object of knowledge.

whereas appetite, i.e., that which is appetitive, moves while being 701a moved. But as for the last of the [things] moved, [it is] not necessary that it move anything. And [it is] manifest from these [things] also that local motion [is], reasonably, the last of the [motions] that come into being in the [beings] that come into being; for the animal is moved, i.e., it goes forward, by appetite or choice, when something has been altered in respect to sense perception or imagination.

Chapter 7

How [is it that] when one thinks [that action is to be taken], sometimes one acts (*prattei*) [in accord with one's thought], but sometimes one doesn't act, and one is moved, but sometimes one is not moved? It looks likely that this [should] happen similarly to [what happens to people] when they think (discursively) concerning the unmoved [intelligibles] and form syllogisms; but there, the end is an object of contemplation (for when one thinks the two premises, one has thought the conclusion, i.e., one has put [the premises] together), but here the conclusion from the two premises becomes the action; for instance, when one thinks that every human being must walk, and [that] one [is] oneself a human being, one walks straightway, and if [one thinks that] no human being should walk now, and [that] one [is] oneself a human being, one straightway remains at rest; and one acts (*prattei*) in both of these ways (unless something [in the one case] prevents [one from walking] or [in the other case] compels [one to walk]. I must make (*poiēteon*) [something] good, and a house [is] good; one makes (*poiei*) a house straightway. I am in want of a covering, and a cloak is a covering; I am in want of a cloak. What I am in want of, I must make; I am in want of a cloak: I must make a cloak. And the conclusion, the "I must make a cloak," is an action. And one acts from a beginning (*ex arkhēs*) [which is in thought]: if there will be a cloak, [it] is necessary that there be this first, and if this, this; and this [last is an action that] one performs straightway. And so, that the action (*praxis*) [is] the conclusion [is] manifest; and the premises that produce [it] (*hai de protaseis hai poiētikai*) come to be through two kinds [of considerations], through [those of] the good and through [those of] the possible.[43] But like some of those who ask questions,[44] so also the (discursive) intellect doesn't stop to examine at all the second premise, the clear one; for instance, if walking is good for a human being, [the premise] that one [is] oneself a human being, it doesn't waste time with. Wherefore also, as many actions as we perform without having reasoned, we perform quickly. For when one is actively directed (*energēsēi*) towards the "for the sake of which" that is the object of [one's] appetite, either through sense perception, or [else] through imagination or thought, one does[45] [it] straightway; for the activity (*energeia*) of appetite comes into being in the place of questioning or thinking. I must drink, says desire; this here [is] drink, said sense perception or imagination or thought; straightway one drinks. And so in this way the animals make a start toward being moved and acting, with the last [i.e., the immediate,] cause of their being moved being appetite, and this [i.e., appetite,] coming into being either through sense perception or through imagination and thinking. And of

43 Cf. *Nicomachean Ethics* 1112b11–28.

44 This is a reference to the practice of dialectics, in which at each stage the questioner asks a question to which his interlocutor must respond in one of two ways, with the responses forming syllogisms whose conclusions the interlocutor, and perhaps for good reason, would not willingly accept. Cf. *Prior Analytics* 24a22–b15; *Topics* 155b3ff.

45 The word translated here as "does" is *poiei*, which I have translated earlier in this chapter as "makes," as distinguished from the word *prattei*, which I have translated as "acts" or "performs an action." Aristotle typically distinguishes these two Greek words on the same basis as we do these English ones, namely, that making, unlike performing an action, is the bringing into being of some product that persists after one's activity has ended. On the other hand, the Greek word *poiei* can also mean "does," in which case it is practically an equivalent to *prattei*, and since Aristotle goes on to illustrate his point here by the example of someone who drinks, I choose to translate it in this way (cf. also the word *poiētikai*, at 701a23–24). On the other hand, Aristotle seems generally attentive in this chapter to the distinction between the activities to which these two words refer, most especially a bit later at 701b1, where he explicitly distinguishes those instances in which animals "make [something]" (*poiousi*) from those in which they "perform an action" (*prattousin*).

those having the appetite to act (*prattein*), some on account of desire or spirit, and others on account of appetite[46] or wish, some 701b
make (*poiein*) and others act (*prattein*). And as automata are moved when there comes to be a small motion, [i.e.,] when the cords are unfastened and [the operators] strike the cords against one another,[47] and [as] the little wagon that a [small child], who is riding

---

46 Here at 701b1, I read *orexin*, which means "appetite," together with Louis and the preponderance of the manuscripts, rather than *prohairesin*, which means "choice," the reading of manuscripts C^{e}, E^{r}, and b. Primavesi, who collated these last three manuscripts, prefers their reading, in the first place on the grounds that Aristotle has said in the previous chapter that desire, spirit, and wish are all subclasses of appetite (700b22), so that a distinction between appetite and wish, as if one could do something on account of one *or* the other of these, would not make sense. And choice is mentioned here, in his view, not as another subclass of appetite—it being, rather, a product of discursive thought and appetite together (cf. 700b23)—but because it selects the actions by which we seek to attain the ends we wish for, and ought therefore to be mentioned among the functions of soul that lead us to act (cf. *Nicomachean Ethics* 1111b26–27). See Primavesi, "Philologische Einleitung," *Aristoteles* De Motu Animalium, ci–cix. On the other hand, it seems to me, when Aristotle speaks of wish as a subclass of appetite, i.e., as rational appetite, he is not treating it, as he does in the *Nicomachean Ethics*, merely as a wish for those ends in pursuit of which we must choose the appropriate means, but rather as appetite determined by reason, which may accordingly encompass choice. Moreover, although he does regard wish, together with desire and spirit, as subclasses of appetite, and indeed as *the* subclasses of appetite (cf. *De Anima* 414b2, *Eudemian Ethics* 1223a26–27), it nevertheless seems to me that he understands there to be a more fundamental appetite than these, namely, the appetite to continue to be, an appetite that becomes conscious in human beings, who know of death, as an appetite to continue to be forever (cf. *De Anima* 415a26–b7). Appetite in this sense is not another subclass of appetite in general, like desire, spirit, and wish, since it is presupposed by them all. But appetite in this sense can nevertheless be presented as a source of action other than wish, and it can even come into conflict with it, as it can also come into conflict with desire and spirit.

47 At 701b3, I read *kai krouontōn pros allēlas tas streblas*, with manuscripts B^{e}, E^{r}, and b, rather than *kai krouontōn allēlas tas streblas*, with Louis, who follows the preponderance of the manuscripts. I am unable to translate Louis' text, though perhaps it means the same as my "and [the operators] strike the cords against one another," though in less standard Greek. This passage has puzzled nearly all editors and translators, and various emendations have been proposed in the attempt to give a clearer picture of the mechanics of these automata. But none of the proposed emendations is sufficiently convincing, it seems to

[it] himself, tries to move straight ahead, and it is contrariwise moved in a circle because of its having wheels [that are] unequal (for the smaller one becomes like a center, as in the case of rollers [i.e., truncated cones]), so also the animals are moved. For they have organs of such a sort, [namely,] the nature of the sinews and that of the bones, these [being] like the pegs and the iron there [i.e., in the automata], and the sinews [being] like the cords, which when they are unfastened and let loose, [the automata] are moved. However, in the automata and the little wagons, there isn't alteration, since if the inner wheels were to become smaller and again bigger [than the outer ones], the same [wagon] would still be moved in a circle, but in the animal, the same [part] is able to become both bigger and smaller [than it was], and to undergo change in its shapes, as the parts get bigger, on account of heat and breath and cooling,[48] and are altered. And imaginations and sense perceptions and thoughts alter [them]. For sense perceptions are straightway, as they are present [in the body], alterations of a sort, while imagination and think-

---

me, to deserve acceptance. Nor, I think, does any of them add anything of real importance to the significance of this example in relation to animal motion.

48 At 701b14–16, I read *auxanomenōn tōn moriōn dia thermotēta kai pneuma kai psuxin*, with manuscripts E, Y, B^e, E^r, and b, and in keeping with the medieval Latin translation by William of Moerbeke, rather than *auxanomenōn tōn moriōn dia thermotēta kai palin sustellomenōn dia psuxin*, with Louis, who follows most of the other manuscripts. Louis' text would be translated, instead of as "as the parts get bigger, on account of heat and breath and cooling," as "as the parts get bigger on account of heat and again contract on account of cooling." Now the reading that I have chosen is admittedly the more difficult one to understand, both because of its unexpected mention of animal breath, which is not discussed thematically until Chapter 10 (703a9ff.), and because of its surprising suggestion that parts of the animal become bigger, not only on account of heat, but on account of cold. Nevertheless, it seems to me that this reading is more illuminating than the smoother alternative accepted by Louis; for as the mention of spirit earlier in this chapter (701a37) may remind us, bodily cooling, which Aristotle presumably thinks of as accompanying fear, does not necessarily lead to flight or to shrinking away from the frightening object, but sometimes to spirited resistance and what at least feels like an enlarged heart. And Aristotle's mention of breath would thus be appropriate here, since even though he has not yet discussed how it contributes to animal self-motion, we are aware of the strength of our breath as an aspect of our spirited resistance to what threatens us.

ing have the power of the things (*tōn pragmatōn*) [that were originally perceived]; for in a certain manner the form that is thought, that of the hot or cold or pleasant or frightening, is in fact of such a sort [in its power] as each of the things (*tōn pragmatōn*), for which reason [people] both shudder and are frightened when [they are] merely thinking. And these are all affections (*pathē*) and alterations. Some [of the parts] in the body, when they are being altered, become bigger and some smaller. And that a small change that comes to be in a ruling beginning produces many and large differences further on is not unclear; for instance, when the rudder is shifted just a little bit, there comes to be a large shift of the prow. Further, when by heat or cooling or by some other such affection, there has come to be an alteration around the heart, and in this, in a part [that is] imperceptible owing to its size, it makes the body very different, with blushings and pallors and shudderings and tremblings and the contraries of these.

Chapter 8

And so the ruling beginning, as has been said,[49] of the motion [is] what, in the [sphere of] what is to be done [i.e., of action], is to be pursued or to be avoided. But of necessity heat and cooling follow upon the thought and the imagination of them. For the painful [is what is][50] to be avoided, and the pleasant [is what is] to be pursued (but this escapes notice when it happens concerning the small

49 Cf. 700b23–26, where, however, Aristotle spoke only of the end or goal of action, and not also of what action seeks to avoid, as he does here.

50 My addition in brackets here, and in the subsequent mention of the pleasant, of the words "is what is," is in keeping with acceptable Greek usage, although this clause would more commonly be translated with the addition in brackets only of the word "is." I choose to translate the clause in this way, as a general statement of what it is that is to be avoided and pursued, despite the apparent implication of 700b25–29, largely because otherwise this sentence does not provide the support it is presented as providing (by beginning with the explanatory clause "For…") for Aristotle's claim that heat and cooling necessarily follow upon the thought and the imagination of what is to be pursued or to be avoided.

702a [pains and pleasures]), and the painful and pleasant (pl.) are pretty much all [bound up] with a sort of cooling and heat. And this [is] clear from the affections. For feelings of confidence and fears and sexual feelings and the other bodily painful and pleasant [affections] are, some of them, [bound up] with heat or cooling in a part, and others [with heat or cooling] throughout the body as a whole; and memories and expectations, using such [affections] as images, are sometimes less and sometimes more responsible for the same [things]. So that the inner [regions], then, and those near the beginnings (*arkhas*) of the organic parts are fashioned reasonably [insofar as they] change from being rigid to fluid and from fluid to being rigid, and to soft and hard from one another. And since these [things] happen in this manner, and furthermore, since that which can be acted upon and that which can act have the sort of nature that we have often said [they have],[51] whenever it happens that that which can act and that which can be acted upon are [present], and each of the two of them lacks nothing of the [determinations] in its definition (*logōi*),[52] straightway the one acts and the other is acted upon. And on account of this, at the same time, so to speak, one thinks that one must walk and one walks, unless something different hinders [this]. For the affections dispose the organic parts suitably, and appetite [so disposes] the affections, and imagination appetite. And this [i.e., imagination,] comes to be either through thought or through sense perception. And [all this occurs] at the same time or quickly, because that which acts and is acted upon is/are in their nature among the [things] related to one another. And [it is] necessary that what first moves the animal be in some ruling beginning. And the joint, that on the one hand,[53] it is a be-

51 Cf. *Metaphysics* 1047b31–1048a24; *Physics* 251b1–7; *On Coming into Being and Perishing* 324a24–b24.

52 Cf., again, *Metaphysics* 1047b35–1048a16.

53 The particle translated here as "on the one hand" (*men*) normally anticipates a parallel, contrasting statement, introduced by a particle that means "on the other hand." But no such statement is present here. Accordingly, some editors and translators reject this reading, though it is present in the preponderance of the manuscripts, in favor of one that appears in manuscripts Y, V,

ginning (*arkhē*) of this and an end of that, has been said.[54] Wherefore nature uses it, on the one hand, as one, and, on the other, as two. For when [the animal] is moved from there, [it is] necessary for one of the extreme points to be at rest and for the other one to be moved; for that that which moves has to be supported against [something] at rest, has been said before.[55] And so the extremity of the forearm is moved and does not move [another], while one [part] of the joint in the elbow is moved, [namely,] that [part] which is in the very whole [i.e., the forearm,] that is moved, but [it is] necessary that there be something also [that is] unmoved, which indeed we assert[56] to be in [its state of] potentiality one point, but to become two in [its] actuality/activity (*energeiāi*); so that if the animal were a forearm, the ruling beginning of [i.e., belonging to,]

B^e, E^r, and b, that lacks the particle *men*. However, *men* can be used in Greek prose without any corresponding particle, in order to suggest that a contrasting statement, which the author chooses not to express, is to be supplied in thought (cf. Smyth, *Greek Grammar*, para. 2896). And though I am not certain that the traditional text here is sound, I have retained it, in order to invite the reader to consider the possibility that Aristotle might have chosen to leave unsaid something that he had in mind regarding the joint.

54 If this is a reference to the present treatise, it must refer to 698a16–b5, although that passage did not say explicitly that a joint must be both a beginning and an end. Aristotle has, however, said this explicitly in *De Anima* 433b21–25.

55 Cf. 698b5–7 and 700a6–11, although neither of these passages has stated that "that which moves" has to be supported against something at rest, but merely that there has to be something at rest, supported against which the animal, or that part of it which is moved, is moved. Neither passage, in fact, made any explicit claim as to what it is that moves the animal, or that part of it—other than that it is the animal—nor is it made clear even in this sentence.

56 Cf. 698a27–b1. All the translators I am aware of, except for Pierre-Marie Morel (Aristote, *Le Mouvement des animaux* suivi de *La Locomotion des animaux* [Paris: Flammarion, 2013]), translate the relative pronoun here, which I translate as "which," with some equivalent of "with respect to which" or "because of which," and they add a direct object that is not present in the Greek, namely, the word "it," after the word "assert." In this way, they make that which "we assert to be in [its state of] potentiality one point, but to become two in [its] actuality/activity" the elbow joint, rather than, as it is in this translation, whatever it is in the elbow joint that is unmoved. Though these other translations are linguistically possible, they are less natural than the one I have chosen.

the soul, the [ruling beginning] that moves [the animal], would be there [i.e., in the elbow joint,] somewhere. And since it is admissible also that one of the [things] that lack soul [should be related] in this way to the hand, for instance if one should move a rod in one's hand, [it is] manifest that the soul would not be in either of the extremities, neither in the extremity of that which is moved [i.e., the extremity of the rod in contact with the hand,] nor in the other beginning (*arkhēi*) [i.e., the extremity of the hand]. For the
702b piece of wood also has both a beginning (*arkhē*) and an end in relation to the hand. So that on account of this, at any rate, if the ruling beginning that moves from the soul is not also in the rod,[57] neither [is it] in the hand; for the tip of the hand is [related] in the same way to the wrist, as also this part [is related] to the elbow.[58] For the [parts that are] naturally attached don't differ at all [in this regard] from those that are not; for the rod becomes like a removable part. [It is] necessary therefore that it [i.e., the ruling beginning that moves from the soul,] not be in any [bodily] beginning (*arkhēi*) that is [the] end of another [part], not even if there is some different [part] further out than that one; for instance, the ruling beginning for the extremity of the rod [is] in the hand, and [that] for this [extremity, i.e., that of the hand, is] in the wrist. And if the

---

57 At 702b2, I read *ei mē kai en tēi baktēriai*, with the preponderance of the manuscripts, rather than *ei mē en tēi baktēriai*, with Louis, who follows manuscript E and a few others. A translation in accord with Louis' text would omit the word "also" here. But it seems to me that this word is an appropriate way of emphasizing Aristotle's reason for saying that "the ruling beginning that moves from the soul" is not in the extremity of the hand, namely, that, on the assumption that the extremity of the hand and that of the rod constituted a joint, this ruling beginning would have to be in the (non-living) rod as well, so that it could hardly be said to move "from the soul."

58 The reason that Aristotle gives in the second half of this sentence for why "the ruling beginning that moves from the soul" is not in the hand differs from the one that he has already indicated in the first half of the sentence ("So that on account of this, at any rate"). And the remainder of the chapter, including in particular the next sentence—"For the [parts that are] naturally attached don't differ at all [in this regard] from those that are not"—is an elaboration only of this second reason. Aristotle leaves it to the reader, then, to consider how these reasons are related to one another.

ruling beginning [that moves from the soul] is not in the hand, because [it is] still higher up, neither is it there [i.e., in the wrist]; for again, while the elbow remains [at rest], all of [the arm] below [it] is moved as a continuum.

Chapter 9

Since [animal motion] is similar, [whether proceeding] from the [parts] on the left or from those on the right, and the[se] contrary [parts] are [i.e., can be,] moved at the same time, so that it is not by the right [side] being at rest that the left [side] is moved, nor again by this [being at rest that] that [is moved], and the ruling beginning is always in that which is higher than both, [it is] a necessity that the ruling beginning of [i.e., belonging to,] the soul that moves be in the middle; for the middle is an extremity of both the outermost [parts, i.e., those on the left and those on the right]. And this [i.e., the middle,] has a similar relation to the[ir] motions, [whether they occur separately or together,] and [also to] those from above and below, for instance those from the head and those[59] from the spine in the [animals] that have a spine. And this has come about with good reason; for the perceptive [part], too, we assert is there, so that when on account of sense perception the place around the ruling beginning is altered and changes, the parts next to it change along with [it], being stretched out as well as drawn together, so that from necessity, on account of these [changes], the animals come to have their motion. The middle part of the body

59 At 702b19, I read *kai tas*, with manuscript N, rather than *pros tas*, with Louis, who follows the majority of the manuscripts. According to Louis' text, the beginning of this sentence would be translated, instead of as "And this [i.e., the middle,] has a similar relation to the[ir] motions, [whether they occur separately or together,] and [also to] those from above and below, for instance those from the head and those from the spine," as "And this [i.e., the middle,] has a similar relation to the[ir] motions, [whether they occur separately or together,] and [also to] those from above and below, for instance, those from the head in relation to those from the spine." Some of the manuscripts have still other readings, which vary only slightly from these two.

[is] one in [its state of] potentiality, but [it is] necessary that it become more [than one] in [its] actuality/activity (*energeiāi*); for [it is the case] both [that] the limbs are moved at the same time from the ruling beginning, and [that] while the one [limb] is at rest, the other is moved. I mean, for instance, in [the broken line] ABC,[60] B is moved and A moves [it]. But yet there must, indeed, be something at rest, if the one is going to be moved and the other [is going] to move [it]. [The vertex] A, then, though it is one in [its state of] potentiality, will be two in [its] actuality/activity (*energeiāi*), so that [it is] a necessity that it not be a point, but some magnitude. But again, it is admissible that C be moved at the same time as B, so that [it is] a necessity that both the ruling beginnings in A move [the lines whose endpoints are C and B] while being moved. There must, then, be something different besides these, that which moves and is not moved. For [otherwise] the extremes, and the ruling beginnings in A, would be supported against one another while [lines AB and AC] are being moved,[61] as if some
703a [people] should move their legs while supporting their backs against [one another]. But [then it is] necessary that the mover be both [i.e., both backs, or what they are meant to illustrate].[62] And

60 In some manuscripts, this passage is accompanied by a diagram of a figure consisting of two lines meeting at the vertex A, with the points B and C being the extremities. And it is clear even without the diagram that when Aristotle speaks of (the broken line) ABC, he means the figure that we would call BAC.

61 The Greek word translated here as "while [lines AB and AC] are being moved" is a genitive absolute participle (*kinoumenōn*), which normally refers to something other than the subject or object of the main clause, and I have translated it accordingly. But it is also possible for it to refer to the subject of the main clause (cf. Smyth, *Greek Grammar*, para. 2073), in which case it would be translated as "while they are being moved." And this translation doesn't seem out of the question to me. Cf. the following sentence (and the footnote to it, n. 62), along with 702a28–31 (and n. 56) and 703b31–33.

62 This sentence might also be translated as "But [it is] necessary that there be that which moves [them] both," and in fact the medieval Latin translation by William of Moerbeke includes the word *unum*, meaning "one," in accord with which the sentence would read in English, "But [it is] necessary for that which moves [them] both to be one." Some editors emend the Greek text in accord with William of Moerbeke's translation, and even those translators who accept

this is the soul, being different from this sort of magnitude, but being in this.

Chapter 10

Now according to the speech that says [what] the cause of motion [is], appetite is the middle that moves while being moved; but in the ensouled bodies there must be some body [that is] of that sort. Now that which is moved, but not of [such] a nature as to move, is capable of being acted upon in accord with another's power; but [it is] necessary for that which moves to have some power and force (*iskhun*) [of its own]. And it is manifest that all the animals both have innate breath and exert force (*iskhuonta*) by means of this. (Now what the preservation of the innate breath [is], has been said [by us] in other speeches.)[63] And it looks as if this [i.e., the innate breath,] is related to the beginning, the soulish[64] [one], in the same way as the point in the joints, that which moves and is moved, [is related] to that [in or of the joint] which is unmoved. And since the ruling beginning for some [animals is] in the heart,[65] while for others [it is] in the analogous [part], it is manifest that, on account of this, the innate breath is there also. Now whether the breath is the same always or [whether it continually] comes into being [and is] always different, let there be another speech

the traditional text all, so far as I know, interpret the word "both" as referring to the objects that are moved, rather than to that which moves them.

63 The reference here is not clear, but perhaps Aristotle is referring to a work of his, *On* (*Growth and*) *Nourishment*, that has not survived. Cf. *On the Generation of Animals* 784b2–3.

64 The Greek word translated as "soulish" here is the adjective *psukhikēn*, which might also be translated as "having to do with soul." But I choose to translate the Greek adjective with an (unusual) English one in order to bring out the fact that Aristotle does not use the noun *psukhē*, or "soul," as he had used it at 702a32 ("the ruling beginning of [i.e., belonging to,] the soul, the [ruling beginning] that moves [the animal]"), at 702b2 ("the ruling beginning that moves from the soul"), and at 702b16 ("the ruling beginning of [i.e., belonging to,] the soul that moves"). Cf. *De Anima* 424a33–34.

65 Cf. *On the Parts of Animals* 665a10–15; *On Sleep and Awakeness* 455b34–456a6.

[about this] (for it is the same [speech] also concerning the other parts); but it is manifest that it [i.e., the breath,] is naturally well suited for being a mover and providing force. The deeds [productive] of motion [are] pushing and pulling, so that the organ [productive of motion] must be capable of expanding as well as contracting. And of such a sort is the nature of the breath; for it does not yield to violence when [it is] contracted, and [it is] able to act with violence and to push on account of the same cause, and it has both weight in comparison with the fiery [bodies] and lightness in comparison with their contraries [i.e., the earthy ones]. And what is going to move [something], not by [causing] alteration, has to be of this sort; for the natural bodies overpower one another by the excess [of the force of one over that of the other], with the light being defeated [and pushed] down by the heavier, and the heavy [being defeated and pushed] up by the lighter. And so by which part, [that part itself] being moved, the soul moves [what it moves], and [also] through what cause [it does so], has been said; but one must take it to be the case that the animal is constituted like a city [that is] well regulated by law. For in the city, when its order has once been established, there is no need for a separated monarch, who has to be present at each of the [deeds] that come to be, but each [person] himself does his own [deeds] as they have been assigned, and this comes to be after that on account of habit; and in the animals this very same [thing] comes to be on account of nature, that is, by each [of the parts] that have been put together in this way having [such] a nature [as] to do its own deed/work, so that there is no need for soul to be in each [part], but with it being in some ruling beginning of the body, the
703b other [parts] live by being naturally attached,[66] while they do their own deed/work because of their nature.

66 Aristotle doesn't specify what the object is (or what the objects are) by their natural attachment to which these other parts live. It might seem at first that it would be the ruling beginning to which he has just referred, but by his silence he invites the thought that the natural attachment by which they live is, rather, one that links all the parts of the body together mutually.

Chapter 11

And so how the animals are moved with their voluntary motions, and because of what causes, has been said; but they are moved, in some of their parts, with some [motions that are] also involuntary, while most [of their motions] are non-voluntary. I mean by involuntary [motions], for instance, that of the heart and that of the genital [part] (for often, when something has appeared, yet without the intellect having bid [them to be moved], they are moved), and [I mean] by non-voluntary [motions], for instance, sleep and awakeness and breathing and as many other [motions] as are of that sort. For neither imagination nor appetite is authoritative, simply [speaking], over any of these; but since [it is] a necessity that animals be altered with natural alteration, and that when the parts are altered, some of them expand and others shrink, so that they are immediately moved and change with the changes whose nature it is to follow upon one another (and the causes of the motions [are] heatings and coolings, those from outside as well as the natural [ones] that are present within), also, indeed, the motions that come to be [that are] contrary to (or in conformity with) reason,[67]

67 The Greek expression that I have translated as "contrary to (or in conformity with) reason" is *para ton logon*. And though its usual meaning is "contrary to reason," it can also mean "in conformity with reason" or "from reason." (For this use of the preposition *para*, compare, for instance, *Rhetoric* 1401a2; *Nicomachean Ethics* 1095a7; *Metaphysics* 1085b23 [according to the manuscripts]; *On Sense Perception and Sense-Perceptibles* 448a23.) And this translation might well also be in accord with what Aristotle is saying here. For when, earlier in the chapter (703b4–8), he first mentioned (what are "also") involuntary motions of the parts in question, he did not say that they were contrary to reason, but only that they occurred without the intellect having bid the parts to be moved in these ways. And at least with respect to the heart, its involuntary motion of resistance to some threat might well be one that reason subsequently approves of and even promotes. Moreover, if he is indeed also speaking of motions "in conformity with" reason, as I think he is, Aristotle may be referring to a wider class than these. He does not speak explicitly here about the motions in question being involuntary, and so he may also be suggesting that even the heart's voluntary motion of resistance to threats, i.e., its motion that follows the bidding of reason, may be ultimately a consequence of the same sorts of causes as those that lead to involuntary and even non-voluntary motions.

of the parts that have been mentioned, come to be when alteration has occurred; for thought and imagination, as has been said before,[68] bring forward the [things] that can produce the affections (*pathēmatōn*); for they bring forward the forms of the [things] that can produce [them]. And among the parts, [the forms of the things that can produce the affections] act upon these [two] especially clearly,[69] on account of each of the two parts being like a separated animal; and [what is] responsible (*aition*) for this [is] that they have vital[70] moisture. Now [as for] the heart, [it is] manifest on account of which cause (*aitian*) [it has such moisture]; for it has the ruling beginnings of the senses. And as for the generative part, that it is of this sort, a sign [is the following]; for, like a sort of animal, the power of the seed comes out from it. And motions come to the ruling beginning from the parts and to the parts from the ruling beginning, reasonably [so], and in this way they reach one another. For one must think [of] A [as] a ruling beginning.[71] Then the motions from each point of those that have been drawn reach the ruling beginning, and from the ruling beginning, when it is moved and changes, since it is potentially many, the ruling beginning for B [is moved] toward B,[72] the [ruling beginning] for C [is moved]

68 701b18–23.

69 Thus, the account given in the previous sentence applies at least to some of the motions of the other parts as well, even though this fact is not so manifest with regard to the other parts as it is with regard to these two.

70 The word translated as "vital" is *zōtikēn*, which I might have translated as "lifish," if it were an English word, on the analogy of "soulish" at 703a12. It means "having to do with life" or "such as to perform, or contribute to, the activities of life."

71 Some of the manuscripts include a diagram here, as in Chapter 9, of a figure consisting of two lines meeting at the vertex A, with the points B and C being the extremities.

72 Though it might seem strange to say that the ruling beginning for B is moved toward B "from the ruling beginning," this follows from the fact that the ruling beginning of the animal, like any of its joints, is partly at rest and partly in motion when it moves anything. Cf. 702a21–32.

toward C, and the [ruling beginning] for both [is moved] toward both. And from B [a motion goes] toward C by going from B to A, as toward a ruling beginning, and from A to C, as from a ruling beginning. And that sometimes, when [people] think these[73] [thoughts], motion in conformity with (or contrary to) reason[74] comes to be in the parts, but sometimes not, [what is] responsible [is] that sometimes the material that can be acted upon is present **704a**
in [them], but sometimes [there is] not so much [material] or such a sort [of material]. And so concerning each of the parts of the animals, and concerning soul, and furthermore, concerning sense perception and sleep and memory and the motion in general [of

---

73 The Greek word for "these" is *ταῦτα*, which appears in the preponderance of the manuscripts, and which was read by modern editors until the twentieth century. Louis, however, has *ταὐτὰ*, a reading proposed by several twentieth-century editors, which differs from the other only in accent and breathing marks (which may well not have been present in Aristotle's manuscript), and which means "the same." And manuscripts P, B^e, E^r, and b read *τὰ αὐτὰ*, which also means "the same." Now these alternative readings do make sense of this sentence, and they are easier to interpret than the reading translated as "these." But I am nevertheless inclined to preserve the traditional reading. If this is indeed correct, "these" thoughts might seem to be a reference to those most recently mentioned (at 703b18–19), thoughts (and imaginations) that bring forward the forms of the things that can produce the affections leading to motions of the heart and of the genitals. However, Aristotle is no longer speaking here only of motions of the heart and of the genitals. Moreover, this sentence appears to be the conclusion of a long section of the treatise that starts at the beginning of Chapter 7 (701a7–8) with the question, which has not yet received an explicit answer, "How [is it that] when one thinks [that action is to be taken], sometimes one acts (*prattei*) [in accord with one's thought], but sometimes one doesn't act, and one is moved, but sometimes one is not moved?" Thus, the true or at least the primary reference of "these" thoughts, it seems to me, would be to the thoughts, regarding action to be taken, that were spoken of there.

74 The Greek expression translated as "in conformity with (or contrary to) reason" is again *para ton logon*. Cf. n. 67 above. And I give pride of place to the translation "in conformity with" reason in this sentence, since I do think that it is the conclusion of a section of the treatise that starts at the beginning of Chapter 7 (cf. the previous footnote, n. 73), and that Aristotle is thinking primarily of why we only sometimes are set in motion in conformity with our rationally expressed intentions.

the animals], we have said [what] the causes[are];[75] but it remains to speak about coming into being.[76]

---

75 This concluding sentence confirms, I think, that this treatise on the motion of animals is meant to belong to the *Parva Naturalia*, and to come after the treatise on sense perception, that on memory and recollection, and those on sleep (cf. n. 39 to *On Prophecy from Sleep*). Also, it is striking that Aristotle states here that he has said what "the causes" are concerning all these things, since, although he ends his treatise *On Sleep and Awakeness* (458a25–26) by saying that he has given the cause of sleeping, he has not said before this that he had given the cause or causes of soul, of sense perception, or of memory. Indeed, in the case of memory, he called attention to the fact that he had not given its cause, and in particular not the cause of its coming to be, by concluding his treatise *On Memory and Recollection* (453b7–10) by saying of memory that he has said what it is and by which part of the soul animals remember, and then going on to say of recollection that he has said what it is and also how and on account of what cause it comes to be. (It is perhaps because some scribe or scribes were aware of this difficulty that manuscripts P, N, X, H[a], and L do not include the words translated here as "the causes.") But perhaps Aristotle speaks here of his having said what the causes are "concerning" even these things in order to indicate that by saying what they are, as he has now finished doing, he has said all that can be said about their causes, except, perhaps, for what can be learned from what he goes on to speak of as the next topic to be considered, namely, the coming into being of the various animals.

76 This is apparently a reference to the treatise *On the Generation of Animals.* Moreover, *On the Generation of Animals* contains a forward reference (at 777b6–8) to the treatise *On Long-Livedness and Short-Livedness*, which comes next in the traditional order of the *Parva Naturalia*, and so it is plausible that Aristotle intended for *On the Generation of Animals* to follow *On the Motion of Animals* and to be followed in turn by *On Long-Livedness and Short-Livedness.* Thus, I might have chosen to translate it next, before turning to that treatise (cf. also Introduction, viii–ix). On the other hand, some of the manuscripts of *On the Parts of Animals* also conclude with a statement that what is to follow is a consideration of how they, i.e., the animals, are generated. And indeed, the beginning of *On the Generation of Animals* reads as a sequel to *On the Parts of Animals* (cf. especially 715a15–18). There is a question, then, about the appropriate place of *On the Generation of Animals*, a question that I am unable to resolve. In addition to this, it is a very long work, whose translation would require a separate volume on its own. And above all for this reason, I have chosen to proceed directly here to a translation of *On Long-Livedness and Short-Livedness* and to conclude this volume with a translation of the final treatise of the *Parva Naturalia*, namely, *On Youth and Old Age and Life and Death and Breathing.*

On Long-Livedness and Short-Livedness

Chapter 1 464b

Concerning some animals being long-lived and others short-lived, and concerning length and shortness of life in general, one must examine the causes (*tas aitias*). And [the] necessary beginning of the examination [is] from at first going through [the] perplexities concerning them. For it is not clear whether [there is] a different cause (*aition*) [in different cases] or the same [one], for all the animals and plants, of some being long-lived and others short-lived; for of the plants too, the life they have lasts, for some, [only] for a year, while for others it lasts for a long time. Furthermore, [it is not clear] whether the same ones, of the [beings] constituted by nature, are long-lived and healthy in their nature, or [whether] being short-lived and being sickly are separate, or [whether] in the case of some diseases the bodies that are sickly in their nature coincide with those that are short-lived, whereas in the case of others nothing prevents there being sickly [human beings][1] who are long-lived.[2]

---

1 I supply the words "human beings" here, rather than "bodies" or "beings constituted by nature," since Aristotle uses a masculine/feminine form of the adjective translated as "sickly," and this agrees neither with the Greek for bodies nor for beings constituted by nature (nor for animals nor plants nor living beings), since these are all neuter forms, but it does agree with the word for human beings.

2 As Mugnier indicates by enclosing the beginning of the chapter up to this point with brackets, he would delete it, even though it appears in all our manuscripts, on the grounds that the rest of the chapter, and in particular the sentence that immediately follows, looks like the beginning of an alternative introduction to the treatise. Ross includes this section in his edition of the text without adding brackets, but he suggests in his notes that it was an unfinished attempt by Aristotle to revise the beginning of the chapter, one that early scribes included along with the older version. Now although I can

Now then sleep and awakeness have been spoken about before, and about life and death [we] must speak later, and likewise also about disease and health, insofar as it pertains to natural philosophy; but
465a now [we] must contemplate concerning the causes of some [living beings] being long-lived and others short-lived, as was said before.[3] And there are whole [genera] that have this difference[4] as against [other] whole genera, and of those [living beings that fall] under one species[5] some [have this difference] as against others. I mean [by] differing according to genus, a human being, for instance, in relation to a horse (for the genus of human beings is longer-lived than that of horses), and [by differing] according to species,[6] a human being

---

see no clear reason why Aristotle would begin the treatise with this apparently double beginning, I don't know that he did not, and so I am simply translating the entire text as it has come down to us.

3 The words translated here as "as was said before" must be a reference to the opening sentence of the chapter (464b19–21), since there has been nothing else to which they could refer. Hence Mugnier would delete them, even though they appear in all the manuscripts, in keeping with his deletion of the earlier part of the chapter. Presumably, he regarded the phrase as a scribe's attempt to justify the inclusion of what seem to be two different opening sentences to the chapter (cf. the previous footnote, n. 2). At all events, one might also note here that the pair long-lived and short-lived is not one of those mentioned at the beginning of *On Sense Perception and Sense-Perceptibles* (436a12–18), in the passage that served as a kind of introduction to the *Parva Naturalia* as a whole. There Aristotle spoke of the pairs awakeness and sleep, youth and old age, breathing in and breathing out, life and death, and also health and disease, as topics needing to be thought about; but he said nothing about length and shortness of life.

4 The word translated here as "difference" can also mean "differentia."

5 Unless Aristotle is following his reference to differences between genera with a reference to differences within a single species, without any mention of differences between the species within a genus—and this seems unlikely—he must be using the word "species" here as an equivalent to the word "genus" (the singular of "genera") above, with each of these words referring in a general way to a class of beings. For a list of passages where Aristotle uses these terms in this way, see Hermann Bonitz, *Index Aristotelicus*, 2nd ed. (Berlin, 1870; repr. Graz, 1955), 151b54–56.

6 Unless the preposition translated here as "according to" is construed as if it meant "within," which it does not, Aristotle is following up his reference, earlier in this sentence, to the human race as a genus with a reference to dif-

in relation to a human being. For there are also [among] human beings some [who are] long-lived and others short-lived, set apart by the ones [dwelling] in some places and the others in others; for those nations [that dwell] in the hot [places] are longer-lived, while those [that dwell] in the cold [places] are shorter-lived. And even of those [human beings] who dwell in the same place, some likewise differ as against one another [in terms of] this difference.

Chapter 2

And one must grasp what, in the beings constituted by nature, [is] that which is easily destroyed and what [is] that which is not easily destroyed. For fire and water and the [others] of the same kind as these, since they don't [all] have the same power (*dunamin*),[7] are in fact responsible for one another's coming into being and perishing,[8] so that [it is] reasonable that also each of the other [things], since

ferent nations within it as different species. This goes against his usual practice, which is to treat the human race as a single species, just as people do today. But especially since the previous sentence used the terms "genus" and "species" interchangeably, it would not be that surprising that in this sentence he should use the word "genus" for what he usually calls a species and the word "species" for a subclass or subclasses within it. And this usage would, if nothing else, warn the reader not to treat the form (*eidos*) of a species (*eidos*), and of the human species in particular, as a cause that adequately explains the length of its members' lives. And whether or not Aristotle intended the apparently double introduction to the treatise, this warning is consistent with his earlier indication (464b22–24) that there might be different causes, i.e., different kinds of causes, for different animals and plants, of some being long-lived and others short-lived.

7 Aristotle is referring to the four so-called elements, earth, water, air, and fire, each of which was said to be characterized by a pair of the contraries hot/cold and wet/dry. Thus, earth was said to be cold and dry, water cold and wet, air hot and wet, and fire hot and dry.

8 The word translated here as "perishing" (*pthoras*) is a form of the word that I translated in the first sentence of the chapter as "easily destroyed" (*euptharton*). In translating forms of this word (the verb *ptheirei* or *ptheiretai*), I will generally prefer some form of the English word "perish," but I will continue to use forms of the word "destroy" (i.e., "cause to perish") when that seems more appropriate.

they are, i.e., are constituted, from these, should share in their nature, [that is,] all those that are not [constituted] from many [parts] by [mere] putting together, for instance a house. Now then concerning the other [things] there is a different account (*logos*); for of many of the things that are (*tōn ontōn*) there are perishings peculiar [to them], for instance of knowledge and of health and of disease; for these perish even when the [underlying beings] that are receptive of them do not perish, but are preserved; for instance recollection and learning [are] a destruction of ignorance, while forgetting and being deceived [are a destruction] of knowledge. But by concomitance, the perishings of the other [things] follow upon [those of] the natural [ones]; for when animals perish, both the knowledge and the health in the animals perish as well. Wherefore someone might draw a conclusion from these [facts] also concerning soul; for if not by nature, but [rather] as knowledge [is] in [a] soul, so also is soul in [a] body, there would also be some other perishing of it, besides the perishing that it perishes [i.e., undergoes,] when the body perishes. So that, since it [i.e., soul,] is not manifest [as] being of such a sort [as to perish even apart from the perishing of the body], it would be related to the community of the body in a different way [than knowledge is related to the soul in which it is present].

Chapter 3

465b And someone might reasonably perhaps be perplexed [as to] whether there is [a place] where the perishable will be imperishable, for instance fire up above, where its contrary is not [present]. For [it is] what (pl.) belongs to the contraries [that can] perish by concomitance, by dint of those [i.e., the contraries,] perishing; for the contraries are destroyed by one another; but none of the contraries in the beings (*en tais ousiais*) [as constituents of them] perishes by concomitance, on account of the fact that being (*tēn ousian*) is not predicated of anything underlying [it].[9] So that it would be impos-

9 The word *ousia*, here translated as "being," means primarily an independent being, one that stands on its own, and of which other things are predicated,

sible for that which has no contrary[10] or [is in a place] where it has no [contrary] to be destroyed; for what will it be that will destroy it, if indeed it is the case that [things] are destroyed by [their] contraries alone, and this [i.e., a contrary,] is not present [to it], either not at all or[11] [not] there? Or [is] this true in one way, but in another way not; for [it is] impossible for contrariety not to belong somehow to that which has material. For it is admissible for heat and straightness to be in [it] everywhere, but [it is] impossible [for it] to be entirely [i.e., nothing but,] hot or straight or white; for [if that were the case] the affections (*pathē*) will have been separated [from anything underlying them]. If, then, whenever that which acts and that which is acted upon are together, always the one acts and the other is acted upon, [it is] impossible [for them] not to change.[12] Further-

---

rather than being predicated of something else—a dog, for instance, as distinct from its color or its size. And though Aristotle begins this chapter by asking about fire, he did not regard fire and the other such elements as beings (*ousiai*), since they are not genuine unities, but only as the potential from which beings can come (cf. *Metaphysics* 1040b5–10). Later in the chapter, however, he no longer speaks of fire, but rather of flames, and though a flame may not be a being (*ousia*), it is at least like one in being something particular that maintains its shape through its own activity. And by saying that the contraries in the beings do not perish by concomitance, he would mean, in the case of a flame, that its heat, for instance, since is not predicated of something other, but is rather a constituent of the flame itself, does not perish by mere concomitance. And in the case of living beings, he would mean above all that neither of the elemental contraries that belong to their essential nature, namely heat and wetness (cf. 466a18–20), perishes by mere concomitance.

10 Aristotle teaches elsewhere that a being (*ousia*) has no contrary, since there is nothing contrary to a horse, for instance, or a human being. (Cf. *Metaphysics* 1068a10–11, *Categories* 3b24-32.) But consider the previous sentence, including the bracketed "as constituents of them," together with the previous footnote, n. 9.

11 The word translated here as "or" is missing in Mugnier's text, because of a mere error in printing.

12 Regarding the necessity for change in that which acts—i.e., in "that which acts" in the most authoritative sense of the term, namely, that which is in immediate contact with what is acted upon—as well as change in that which is acted upon, whenever the former acts upon the latter, see *On Coming into Being and Perishing* 324a24–34, and compare in particular 324a33–34 with 324b27, along with 322b26–29.

more also, if [it is] necessary [for something] to produce residue, and residue is a contrary, [it is impossible for it not to change]; for change is always from a contrary, and the residue is a remnant of the former [contrary]. But if [something] drives away entirely that which is contrary in actuality, it would be imperishable even here. Or [is that] not [so], but [rather] it is destroyed by what surrounds [it]. Then if [it is indeed so destroyed], from the [things] that have been said [the conclusion is] sufficiently [established that what is perishable must indeed perish]; but if [it is] not [destroyed by its surroundings], one must suppose that there is something in [it that is] actually contrary [to it], and [that] there comes to be residue.[13] Wherefore the smaller flame is burned up by the large one, by concomitance, because the nourishment that it uses up in a long time, [namely,] the smoke,[14] this the large flame [uses up] quickly.[15] Wherefore all [things] are always in motion, and they are coming into being or perishing. And what surrounds [them] either works with or works against [them]. And on account of this, when [things] change their place, they come to be longer-lasting and shorter-lasting than [their] nature, but nowhere everlasting, as many as have contraries; for material immediately has contrariety, so that if [it is contrariety] of the where, they change in respect to place, while if [it is contrariety] of quantity, [they change] in respect to growth and decay, and if [it is contrariety] of affection (*pathous*), they alter.

13 Whether or not this supposition is true for all things, it is manifestly true for animals, since they must nourish themselves and since they produce residue from their nourishment, which was to begin with a sort of contrary. And it is also true of the flame that he will go on to discuss here. For a burning flame contains within itself the fuel from which it is fed, and this fuel is a kind of contrary from which it produces ash as a residue.

14 On smoke being the nourishment of flame, and on its contrariety with it, cf. *On Coming into Being and Perishing* 331b25–26: "this [i.e., flame,] is burning smoke, and smoke is from air and earth." Compare also *Meteorologica* 388a3.

15 This sort of perishing by concomitance is a different sort of perishing by concomitance than the one that Aristotle had said was impossible for the contraries in the beings (*en tais ousiais*, 465b5–6).

Chapter 4

Neither are the biggest [living beings] more imperishable (for a 466a horse is shorter-lived than a human being), nor the small [ones] (for most insects last [only] for a year), nor [are] plants altogether [more imperishable] than animals (for some plants last [only] for a year), nor [are] the [animals] with blood [more imperishable than the others] (for a bee is longer-lasting than some [animals] with blood), nor [are] the bloodless (for cephalopods[16] last [only] for a year, though they are bloodless), nor those on land (for there are both [terrestrial] plants and land animals that last [only] for a year), nor those in the sea (for there too both the shell-skinned[17] [animals] and the cephalopods are short-lived). But in general, the longest-lived are [found] among the plants, for instance the date palm. [The] next [longest-lived] are [found] among the animals with blood more than among the bloodless, and among land [animals more] than among those [that live] in water. So then also if [these] two [characteristics are] coupled: the longest-lived of the animals [are found] among those with blood and [that are also] land [animals], for instance human being and elephant. And in particular, the bigger [ones], speaking for the most part, are longer-lived than the smaller [ones]; for [large] size goes together also with the other [ones] that are longest-lived, as [it does] with those that have been mentioned.

16 The Greek word translated as "cephalopods" is *malakia*, which might be translated literally as "softies." Included among these are such soft-bodied animals as octopuses, cuttlefish, and squid.

17 On the "shell-skinned" animals, cf. *On Sense Perception and Sense-Perceptibles*, n. 64.

Chapter 5

Someone might contemplate the cause[18] concerning all these [things] from the following. For one must grasp that an animal is by nature wet and hot, and [that] living is of such a sort, whereas old age [is] dry and cold, and [so is] that which is dead; for this is manifest. And these, the hot and the cold and the dry and the wet, are the material, for the animals,[19] of their bodies. It is necessary, then, [for an animal] to become dry as it becomes old. Wherefore its wetness ought not to be easily dried. And on account of this the [animals that are] oily[20] are not prone to rot. And [the] cause [of this is] that [they are constituted] of air;[21] and air, in relation to the other [elements], is fire [i.e., it is hot]; and fire does not become rotten. Moreover, the wetness ought not to be little [in quantity]; for also that [wetness] which is little [is] easily dried. Wherefore, to speak generally, also the big [ones], both animals and plants, are longer-lived, as was said before;[22] for [it is] reasonable that the bigger ones have more [of the] wet. But not only on account of this

---

18 It is noteworthy that Aristotle should speak here of the cause, in the singular, of all these things, especially after his having raised the question in Chapter 1 (464b22–24)—at least if that portion of Chapter 1 is truly part of this treatise—of whether there is in fact a single cause, for all animals and plants, of some being long-lived and others short-lived. And even apart from that question in Chapter 1, it is not easy to see how what follows in this chapter presents a single cause. See also n. 23 below.

19 At 466a21, I read *tois zōiois*, with manuscripts M and Z, rather than *tois ousi*, with Mugnier, who follows manuscripts L, P, S, and X. Mugnier's text would be translated, instead of as "are the material, for the animals, of their bodies," as "are the material, for [all] the things that are, of their bodies." But since it is only animals (and plants) that have bodies, as distinct from being mere bodies themselves, and since Aristotle's focus in this chapter is on animals, and not plants, the text as I have translated it seems more likely to be the correct one.

20 The Greek word translated as "oily" is *lipara*, which can also be translated as "fatty." I use "oily" only so as to preserve a single translation for this word.

21 In *On the Parts of Animals* 651a24ff., Aristotle says that the oily (or fatty) ingredient in substances that are wet is constituted of air and fire in common.

22 466a13–16.

[are some] longer-lived; for the causes are two: [there is] quantity and well as quality, so that not only ought there to be a large amount of [what is] wet, but this [ought] also [to be] hot,[23] so that it [will] neither be easily frozen nor easily dried. And on account of this a human being is a more long-lived [animal] than some bigger [ones]; for those [animals] that fall short in the amount of their wetness are longer-lived [than others] if [their wetness] exceeds [that of the others] by a greater ratio (*logōi*) in terms of quality than it falls short in terms of quantity. And for some [animals] what is hot [in them] is the oily, which makes at the same time [for their being] not easily dried as well as not easily frozen; but for some, [what is hot in them] has another flavor.[24] Furthermore, that which is going to be not easily destroyed ought not to be productive of residue. For what is of that sort [i.e., residue,] destroys, either by disease or by nature; for the power of residue is contrary and destructive, sometimes of the nature [of the animal] and sometimes of a part [of it]. Wherefore also the [animals that are] prone to copulation and have much seed become old quickly; for seed is a residue, and furthermore, it dries [the body] by leaving [it]. And on account of this [a] mule is longer-lived than both [a] horse and [an] ass, from which it came into being, and females [are longer-lived] than males, if the males are prone to copulation; wherefore male sparrows are shorter-lived than females. Furthermore, as many males as are subject to toil also [are shorter-lived], and on account of their toil they become old more [quickly]; for toil dries [them], and old age is dry. But by nature, and speaking overall, males are longer-lived than females; and [the] cause [is] that the

23 Aristotle's claim here that there are two causes of an animal's being longer-lived calls attention to the difficulty of the suggestion with which this chapter begins, namely, that it might provide evidence for there being a single cause "concerning all these things" (cf. n. 18 above). Perhaps, however, Aristotle thinks of these two causes, the quantity and quality of an animal's wetness, i.e., its wetness and its heat, as two aspects of a kind of unity. Compare what he says about flame and its nourishment at 465b23–25 and 466b28–33.

24 Aristotle regarded oiliness, along with sweetness and sourness and the like, as a flavor. Cf. *De Anima* 422b10–12; *On Sense Perception and Sense-Perceptibles* 442a17.

male is a hotter animal than the female. And the same [animals] are longer-lived in warm than in cold places, on account of the same cause [as that] on account of which [they are] also bigger. And especially clear [is] the [greater] size [there] of the animals that are cold in their nature. Wherefore snakes and lizards and scaly [animals are] big in hot places, and [so are] the shell-skinned [animals] in the Red Sea; for the hot wetness is responsible for their growth as well as their life. But in cold places the wet that is in animals is more watery; wherefore it is easily frozen, so that some of the animals that have little blood or [are] bloodless do not come into being at all in the northerly places, neither the land [animals] on land nor the water [animals] in the sea, while some [of them] do come into being, but [they are] smaller and shorter-lived; for the frost takes away from their growth. Both plants and animals perish if they don't take in nourishment; for they consume themselves; for just as a large flame burns up and destroys a small [one] by using up its nourishment, so the [living being's] natural heat, that which in the first place produces digestion, uses up the material in which it is. And water [animals] are less long-lived than land
467a [animals], not because they are wet simply, but because they are watery; and that sort of wetness is easily destroyed, because [it is] cold and easily frozen. And a bloodless [animal is easily destroyed] on account of the same [thing], unless it is protected by its size; for it has neither oil nor [what is] sweet. For the oily in an animal [is] sweet; wherefore bees are longer-lived than other, larger animals.

Chapter 6

The most long-lived [beings] are [found] among the plants, i.e., more than among the animals, in the first place because [they are] less watery, so that [they are] not easily frozen; next, they have oiliness and stickiness, wherefore, even though they are dry and earthy, nevertheless the wetness they [do] have [is] not easily dried. And concerning the nature of trees being long-lasting, one must grasp the cause; for they have [a nature that is] peculiar [to them], as against animals, except for the insects. For plants are ever becoming new; wherefore [they are] long-lasting. For their shoots [are] ever different [i.e., new ones keep emerging], while the others are becoming old. And their roots likewise. But [this does] not [all occur] at the same time, but sometimes only the trunk and the branches have died, while different ones have grown up beside them; and when [the plants] are like this, [then] roots [that are] other [than the old ones] come into being from the existing [rootstock], and [the plants] continue ever in this way, with this [part] perishing and that one coming into being; wherefore they are also long-lived. And plants resemble insects, as was said before,[25] for after being divided they [still] live, and they become two or many from one. And insects have gotten as far as to live [after being divided], but they are not able [to live] for a long time, for they don't have [the necessary] organs, nor is the [ruling] beginning (*arkhē*) in each [section of the original insect] able to produce them. But the [ruling beginning] in the plant is able to; for [the plant] has both a root and a stem everywhere, potentially. Wherefore from this [beginning] there is ever going forth this [part that is] new while that one is becoming old, [with these] differing just a little, in being long-lived in this way, [from] the way plants derived from cuttings [are long-lived]. For someone might assert that in a certain manner the same [things] also happen in propagation from cuttings; for what is cut off is a certain part [of the plant]. Now then in propagation from cuttings this [i.e., the prolongation of life,] happens when they [i.e., the parts,] are separated, whereas in the former case [it happens] within the [plant that is still] continuous [i.e., one]. And the cause is that the beginning is present everywhere in [the plant], being in it as a potentiality. And [something that is] the same happens with the animals as well as plants. For among animals the males are longer-lived for the most part; and their upper parts are bigger than their lower [ones] (for the

25 467a11–12.

male is more dwarf-like[26] than the female), and heat is in the upper [part] and cold in the lower; and of the plants those whose heads
467b are heavy are longer-lived. And of such a sort are those that are not of a year's life, but [rather] tree-like; for the root is the upper [part] and the head of the plant,[27] while those of a year's life take their growth in the direction of their lower [parts] and the fruits. But it will be determined concerning these [things], and by themselves, in our [speeches] concerning plants. But now, concerning the others,[28] [the] animals, the cause[29] concerning magnitude of life as well as short-livedness[30] has been stated. It remains for us to contemplate concerning youth as well as old age and life and death. And when these [things] have been determined, our course of inquiry concerning the animals would have an end.

---

26 Cf. *On Memory and Recollection* 453a31–b2; *On the Parts of Animals* 686b3–11, 689b25–28.

27 Cf. *De Anima* 412b1–4, 416a3–5.

28 Mugnier would delete the word translated here as "others," though he has no manuscript authority for this. If that word were to be deleted, the prepositional phrase translated as "concerning the others, [the] animals," would be translated instead as "concerning the animals." That is admittedly an easier reading, but the received text that I have translated is a recognized, if slightly awkward, Greek expression.

29 Cf. nn.18 and 23 above.

30 The Greek word translated here as "magnitude" is *megethei*, from *megethos*, whose basic meaning, at least in Aristotle, is magnitude or size. It can, indeed, also mean greatness, in the sense of bigness as opposed to smallness (cf. 466a15–16). And in fact this is what one expects Aristotle to say. But unlike the title of the treatise, where the words *makrobiotētos*, or long-livedness, and *brakhubiotētos*, or short-livedness, are strictly parallel, Aristotle chooses here to couple the latter term with a term that refers primarily to length of life in general rather than to a great length of life in particular.

On Youth and Old Age and Life and Death and Breathing

Chapter 1 **467b**

We must now speak about youth and old age and about life and death; and at the same time, it is necessary perhaps to state the causes also concerning breathing; for [it is] on account of this that to live and not to live come about for some of the animals. And since distinctions have been drawn concerning soul in other [speeches], and it is [accordingly] clear that it is not possible for its being[1] to be body[2]—yet nevertheless [it is] manifest that it is present in some part of the body, at any rate, and this, one of the [parts] that have power in the parts.[3] Now as for the other parts or

---

1 The Greek word translated as "being" is *ousian*, a form of *ousia*, which refers primarily to an independent being, such as a dog or cat, that stands on its own and of which various attributes are predicated, but which can also refer, as it does here, to the "beingness" of such a being, as distinct from attributes that belong to it but that don't characterize it as the being or the kind of being it is.

2 By "other [speeches]" earlier in this sentence, Aristotle is referring above all to *De Anima*. And as for its not being possible for the soul's being to be body, see in particular *De Anima* 412a15–19, 414a14–22.

3 Since Aristotle has spoken of soul in *De Anima* as the form of a certain kind of body (412a15–21), adding that it is one with that body as closely as the shape impressed in a block of wax is one with the wax (412b6–9), it might seem surprising that he says here that soul is present in some part of the body, thus suggesting, at least, that it is not in them all. However, he has already said in *On Sense Perception and Sense-Perceptibles* that "the soul or the perceptive [faculty] of the soul is not at the extremity of the eye, but evidently inside" (438b8–10), and in *On Memory and Recollection* he has spoken of "that which comes into being through perception, in the soul and in the part of the body that has it" (450a27–29). Moreover, in *On the Motion of Animals* he goes so far as to say that "there is no need for soul to be in each [part], but with it being in some ruling beginning of the body, the other [parts] live by being naturally attached" (703a36–b1). Now in the first two of these quoted

powers of the soul, in whichever way one should call [them], let them be disregarded for now.[4] But as for as many [bodies][5] as are called animals and [as are said] to live, in those, on the one hand, that have obtained both of these (I mean by "both," to be [an] animal and to live), [it is] necessary that there be one and the same part in virtue of which it lives as well as in virtue of which we give it the name animal.[6] For [it is] impossible for the animal, as animal, not to live; but [insofar] as it lives, [it is] not necessary by this that "animal" belong [to it]; for the plants live, but they don't have sense perception, and we determine what is an animal as against

---

passages, soul seems to be identified with the perceptive faculty, and from the context of the passage in *On the Motion of Animals* (703b3–4), it is clear that Aristotle is using the term "soul" for whatever it is that, in its being present in some part of the body, is primarily responsible for an animal's voluntary motions. In other words, these passages identify soul with only part of the soul as it was spoken of in *De Anima.* But it does not seem at all implausible that Aristotle should have thought of soul in both a wider sense, as he speaks of it in *De Anima*, according to which every part of a living body is ensouled, and in a narrower sense, according to which soul is located in some particularly important part of the body. Moreover, the fact that Aristotle refers in this very sentence to the discussion of soul in *De Anima*—treating what was said there as a settled matter, even as he goes on to add that soul is manifestly present in some part of the body that has power in the parts—is strong evidence against the view that he saw any incompatibility between this assertion and the understanding of soul in that earlier treatise (consider, moreover, *De Anima* 408b13–18). And the fact that the main clause of this sentence is not a then-clause corresponding to its initial since-clause points on the other hand to his awareness that soul is being considered here from a somewhat different perspective than it was there.

4 By "the other parts or powers of the soul," Aristotle is referring above all to the intellect, or the reasoning and thinking power (cf. *De Anima* 413b24–27, 415a7–12), but also to the locomotive power and perhaps to an imaginative power as well. Cf. *De Anima* 414b16–17.

5 Cf. Aristotle's use of the word "body" at 469a19.

6 The particle translated as "on the one hand" earlier in this sentence normally calls for a parallel, contrasting statement, introduced by a particle meaning "on the other hand." But no such statement is present here. This somewhat unusual construction often signifies that a contrasting statement is to be supplied in thought (cf. *On the Motion of Animals*, n. 53). And in this case, that statement would presumably have spoken of plants, which Aristotle will indeed speak of in the next sentence as being alive but not being animal.

what is not an animal by [its] perceiving. So then [it is] necessary that this part be one in number, and the same, but more [than one], and [these] different, in [their what it is] to be (*tōi einai*).[7] Since, then, there is some one common sense organ of the particular sense organs,[8] into which [organ it is] necessary for the actual sense perceptions to come together,[9] and this would be [a] middle of what is called the front and [the] back (for "in front" is said of that [direction] toward which we have sense perception, whereas "in back" [is said of] the opposite), and [since] furthermore, the body of all the living [beings], on the one hand,[10] is divided in respect of the upper and lower (for they all have the upper [part] and the lower [part], so that even the plants [do]), [it is] clear that they

---

7 In other words, although this is a single part, what it is for it to be that by virtue of which a body is an animal is different from what it is for it to be that by virtue of which it lives. Now it might seem that these last two sentences, though they begin with the explanatory conjunction "for," have not given adequate support, if any, for Aristotle's claim that there must be one and the same part in virtue of which an animal lives and in virtue of which we give it the name animal (467b20–22). But however that may be, Aristotle will continue to consider the matter in the rest of this chapter as well as in the following chapters.

8 I take the Greek words translated here as "of the particular sense organs" (*tōn idiōn aisthētēriōn*) as objective genitives, i.e., as referring to the objects that the common sense organ perceives, and I interpret the whole expression as a reference to a sense organ by which one perceives the particular sense organs in their functioning, e.g., by which one sees that one sees. As for Aristotle's speaking of this perceiving of one's perceiving, and of the functioning of the particular sense organs more generally, as perceiving of those organs themselves, compare *De Anima* 425a12–25 (and a19–25 in particular). Compare also *On Sleep and Awakeness* 455b19–23, where this common sense organ is linked especially with the sense of touch, and consider n. 13 to that passage.

9 Cf. *On Sleep and Awakeness* 455a12–b2.

10 Here again, although this clause contains a particle meaning "on the one hand," it is not followed by a parallel, contrasting statement introduced by a particle meaning "on the other hand." Cf. n. 6 above. If there is a statement to be supplied in thought, it might be one about nonliving beings, or perhaps instead about what he goes on to speak of in the immediate sequel as "the surrounding whole"(468a3) or as "the all"(468a7).

468a would have the nutritive ruling beginning[11] in the middle of these;[12] for [the] part where the nourishment enters, we call upper, looking to [the body of the living being] itself, but not to the surrounding whole, whereas [we call] lower [the part] where [the living being] discharges the first residue.[13] But this [upper and lower] is [oriented] in a contrary manner for the plants and for the animals; for it belongs most of all to the human being among the animals, on account of its being upright, to have the upper part [directed] toward the upper [part] of the all, whereas [it belongs] to the other [animals to have that part directed] in between [the upper and lower parts of the all]; but for the plants, which are without motion and get their nourishment from the earth, it is necessary to have this part always lower [i.e., lower with reference to the surrounding whole]. For the roots, in the plants, are analogous to what is called the mouth in the animals, through which [organ] the former get their nourishment from the earth, while the latter [do so] through themselves [i.e., by their own efforts].

---

11 The Greek word translated as "ruling beginning" is *arkhē*. On this translation, see *On the Motion of Animals*, n. 3. In the continuation of this treatise, I will translate it as "ruling beginning" or else as "beginning" or "principle" (in these latter two cases, along with a transliteration of the Greek in parentheses).

12 Note that this sentence has claimed neither that the nutritive ruling beginning is in the middle of the front and the back nor that the common sense organ is in the middle of the upper and lower parts. Cf. n. 7 above.

13 By "first residue" Aristotle is referring to solid and liquid waste, which he speaks of elsewhere as the "residues from nourishment" (*On the Parts of Animals* 653b10–12, b13–15), thus distinguishing them from such products as semen and milk, which he also calls residues, but which he understands as coming from nourishment that has already been transformed into blood (cf. *On the Generation of Animals* 725a11–28, 726a26–28; 776a15–777a8). Or at least this is what he is referring to in the case of animals. As for plants, it is not clear to me that he thought of them as discharging any "first residue" at all. In *On the Parts of Animals*, at any rate, he says that plants have no residue—or no useless residue, as distinct from seeds and fruit—since the nourishment that they get from the earth has already been worked up by the earth's heat, which acts like a stomach. *On the Parts of Animals* 650a20–23, 655b32–36.

Chapter 2

There being three portions into which all the complete [ones] of the animals are divided, one where they receive the nourishment, one where they discharge the residue, and third, the middle of these, this [last], in the biggest of the animals, is called [the] chest, while in the others [it is] the analog [to it], and it is differentiated more in some than in others. And in as many of them as are capable of locomotion, there are attached also parts for this service, [parts] by which they carry their entire trunk, [namely,] legs as well as feet and those [parts] that have the same power as these. But the ruling beginning, at any rate, of the nutritive soul is manifest, both from sense perception (*kata tēn aisthēsin*) and from reason (*kata ton logon*), [as] being in the middle [one] of the three parts; for many of the animals, even though either of the [other] two parts is removed, [namely,] the [one] that is called the head as well as the [one] that is receptive of the nourishment,[14] [continue to] live with that [portion] where the middle is. It is clear in the case of the insects, wasps and bees for instance, that this happens. And also many of the [animals that are] not insects are able to live when divided, on account of the nutritive [part]. The part they have, then, [that is] of such a sort [is] actually one, but potentially more [than one]; for they are constituted in the same manner as the plants; for the plants too, if they are divided, live separately, and many trees come into being from one beginning (*arkhēs*). And as for the cause on account of which some of the plants are not able to live when divided, while others are propagated from cuttings, [there] will be a different speech (*logos*) [about it].[15] But the 468b
plants and the genus of the insects are similar in this respect, at any

14 Although Aristotle uses forms of the same word (*dekhesthai*, which means "to receive") both for the function of this part and for that of the portion of the body that I translated above (468a14) as "where they receive the nourishment," he is clearly not referring to the region of the mouth and head, as he was there, but to the stomach, which receives the nourishment that had first been taken in by the mouth, along with the part that receives the residue of that nourishment.

15 No such account by Aristotle has come down to us.

rate. And it is necessary also that the nutritive soul, in those [of these beings] that have [it],[16] actually be one, but potentially more than one. And likewise also the perceptive ruling beginning; for manifestly the divided [parts] of them have sense perception. But as for preserving their nature, the plants are able to, but these are not able to, on account of not having organs for preservation, i.e., [their] being in want, in some cases, of the [organ] that takes [in], and in others of the one that receives, the nourishment,[17] while in other cases [being in want] of other [organs] as well as both of these.[18] For those of the animals that are of such a sort seem like many animals that have grown together; but those of the animals that are constituted in the best way are not acted upon to this effect [i.e., when they are divided, their souls do not become many souls], on account of their nature being, to the greatest extent that admits [of being the case], one. Wherefore, when they [i.e., the insects and those constituted like them,] are divided, some of the parts also produce a small [degree of] sense perception, because they have a sort of soulish affection (*ti psuchikon pathos*). For although their internal organs are separated [from them], they produce [self-]motion,[19] for instance even the tortoises [do so], although their heart has been removed.

---

16 On the basis of the following sentences, in which the words "of them" in the next sentence, as well as the word "these" in the one after that, must refer to "those [of these beings] that have [it]," Aristotle is suggesting here that, among the living beings that become many from having been one, only those that have sense perception, i.e., insects and other such animals, but not plants, have "the nutritive soul." Now it is certainly difficult to understand what this suggestion might mean, but it is in keeping with a passage in *On the Generation of Animals* (731a33–b5), where, at least according to the best manuscript (Z), Aristotle clearly speaks of plants as among the beings that lack soul, even though he goes on to say in that very context that they are alive. Cf. n. 3 above.

17 Cf. n. 14 above.

18 Cf. *De Anima* 411b19–24.

19 I translate the word *kinēsin* here as "[self-]motion," rather than "motion," because the verb translated as "produce" is in the middle voice. Aristotle naturally considers self-motion, which is motion in pursuit of something or in avoidance of something, as a sign that sense perception (along with appetite) is still present.

Chapter 3

And furthermore, [it is] clear[20] in the case of the plants as well as in the case of the animals, in that of the plants, on the one hand,[21] if we consider their coming into being from seeds and also their graftings as well as their propagations from cuttings. For coming into being from seeds comes to pass for all [of them] from the middle; for [their seeds] are all double-leaved [i.e., they bring forth two embryonic leaves], and [these two leaves] are joined where they are united [to the stalk of the mother plant], and [that place] is the middle[22] of each of the two parts;[23] for [it is] from there [that] the stem as well as the root of the [plants] that are growing grow out, and the ruling beginning is the middle of them. And in graftings and propagations from cuttings this happens especially in connection with

---

20 This sentence reads somewhat awkwardly in Greek, since Aristotle doesn't specify the subject of its main clause, i.e., he doesn't say what it is that is clear. The immediate sequel suggests that what he has in mind is that the nutritive ruling beginning is in the middle of the bodies of the plants as well as of the animals. But that was not the theme of the immediately preceding passage, and so the reader has to be perplexed by this sentence, at least at first.

21 Here again, although this clause contains a particle meaning "on the one hand," it is not followed by a parallel, contrasting statement introduced by a particle meaning "on the other hand." (Cf. nn. 6 and 10 above.) However, in this case, the discussion of the role of the heart in the animals with blood ("And of the [parts of the] animals with blood, the heart..."; 468b28) may serve as such a parallel statement.

22 At 468b20, I read *hēi sumpephuken ekhetai kai to meson estin*," with manuscripts M, S, Z, and P, rather than *hēi sumpephuken kai to meson estin*," with Mugnier, whose reading is in accord with manuscripts L and X. Mugnier's text would be translated, instead of as "and [these two leaves] are joined where they are united [to the stalk of the mother plant], and [that place] is the middle," as "and where [these two leaves] are united [to the stalk of the mother plant] is also the middle." The reading that I have chosen in this difficult passage, a passage that has also inspired several conjectural emendations, is in accord with a parallel passage in *On the Generation of Animals* 752a18–23, with the word *ekhetai* corresponding to *sunēptai* at 752a21–22 and the words *hēi sumpephuken* corresponding to *prospephuken* at 752a23. Cf. *Aristotle* On Youth & Old Age, Life & Death and Respiration, trans. William Ogle (London, 1897), 110, n. 21.

23 As is suggested by the explanatory clause that immediately follows, the two parts referred to here are the stem and the root of the developing plant.

the bud eyes; for the bud eye is a sort of ruling beginning of the branch, and [it is] at the same time also a middle, so that they either cut this away or insert [the graft] into this, so that either the branch or the roots come into being from these,[24] which suggests that the ruling beginning of stem and root is from the middle. And of the [parts of the] animals with blood, the heart comes into being first. This [is] clear from what (pl.) we have seen in those [animals] that admit of being seen while they are still coming into being. So that also in those without blood [it is] necessary for what is analogous to the heart to come into being first. And that the heart is the ruling beginning of the blood vessels has been said before in our [speeches]
469a concerning the parts of the animals;[25] and [it has also been said] that the blood, for the [animals] with blood, is the final nourishment, from which the parts come into being.[26] [It is] manifest, then, that the power of the mouth performs one function in connection with the nourishment and the [power] of the stomach another. But the heart is most authoritative, and it adds the end.[27] So that [it is] necessary for the ruling beginning both of the perceptive and of the nutritive soul to be, for the animals with blood, in the heart; for the works of the other parts in connection with the nourishment are for the sake of the work of this; and that which is authoritative ought to keep on [working] toward that for the sake of which [i.e., the end], not [being held back] in the [things that are] for the sake of this, for instance a doctor [ought to keep on working] toward health. Then again, the authoritative [element], at any rate, of the senses, for all the [animals] with blood, [is] in this [i.e., the heart]; for [it is] necessary that the common sense organ of all the sense

24 At 468b27, I read *toutōn*, with Mugnier, who follows manuscripts L, S, and X, rather than *toutou*, the reading of manuscripts M, Z, and P. According to the alternate reading the word "these" would instead be "this." That reading is admittedly a bit easier to interpret, but it seems to me that Aristotle wanted to call attention to the fact that a plant has many bud eyes.

25 *On the Parts of Animals* 665b12–17ff., 667b13–15.

26 *On the Parts of Animals* 650a32–35, 651a12–15, 668a9–11, 678a6–9.

27 Cf. 480a5–7.

organs[28] be in this [place].[29] And we see two [senses] manifestly extending there, [namely,] taste as well as touch, so that [it is] necessary [that] also the others [do so]; for it is admissible for the other sense organs to produce [their] motion in this [place], but these [sense organs, i.e., those of taste and touch,] do not extend at all toward the upper place. And apart from these [considerations], if to live, for all [animals], is in this part, [it is] clear that [it is] necessary also [for] the perceptive ruling beginning [to be in it]; for we assert that [it is] as animal [that] it also lives,[30] and we say that [it is] as perceptive [that] the body is [an] animal. And why some of the senses manifestly extend toward the heart, while others are in the head—on which account also it seems to some that the animals perceive on account of the brain—the cause of these [things] has been stated separately in other [speeches].[31]

Chapter 4

And so as regards the appearances (*kata... ta phainomena*), [it is] clear from what has been said that the ruling beginning of the

28 Here again, I think that Aristotle is referring to a sense organ by which, among other things, one perceives that one perceives, and thus perceives all the particular sense organs in their functioning, as well as itself in its own functioning. Cf. 467b27–28 and n. 8 above.

29 I suggest "in this [place]" here, rather than "in this [i.e., the heart]," as I did in the first clause of this sentence, since the Greek word for "heart" is feminine, but the word translated here as "this" is masculine or neuter, and not feminine, as it was in the earlier phrase. Consider the expression "toward the upper place" at the end of the next sentence. Now this expression might also be translated as "in this [part]" rather than "in this [place]," since the Greek word for part is a neuter noun. But "this part" is not necessarily the heart in particular, but it would be better understood as the middle of the body more generally, for this is clearly what Aristotle is referring to in the sentence after the next one—where he is speaking of "all" animals, not only those with blood and a heart—by the words meaning "this part" (469a17; cf. 468a13–25, as well as the first sentence of the next chapter).

30 Cf. 467b22–23 above, "For [it is] impossible for the animal, as animal, not to live."

31 *On the Parts of Animals* 656a27–657a11.

perceptive soul, as well as that of the growth-producing and nutritive [soul, or power], is in this [place] and in the middle [one] of the three parts of the body. But as regards speech/reason (*kata ... ton logon*),[32] [we say] that we see nature in all [things] doing what is finest from among the [things] that are possible. And if each beginning (*arkhēs*) of the two is in the middle of the being (*ousias*), each of the two parts would most fully accomplish its own work, [namely,] the [part] that works up the final nourishment as well as the [part] that is receptive [of it];[33] for in this way it

32 Regarding the distinction in these two sentences between the appeal to the appearances and the appeal to reason, compare the similar distinction at 468a22–23. However, that statement concerned only the claim that the ruling beginning of the nutritive soul is in the middle of the three parts of the body, whereas here Aristotle is claiming that the ruling beginning of the perceptive soul is in the middle as well. Also, it may be significant that there he contrasted reason with sense perception, rather than with the appearances, as he does here. At all events, it seems to me that the first sentence of this chapter does not mean that rational argument has not contributed to its being clear that Aristotle's claim about the place of these two ruling beginnings is correct. But up to this point the arguments have had the form of saying what must be the case, given the appearances that he has called to our attention, whereas the one that follows argues instead on the basis of what, according to reason, would be the finest possible place for these two ruling beginnings, quite apart from any appearances or facts.

33 One might have expected Aristotle to mean by these two parts the stomach, which works up the nourishment, and the mouth, which receives it (cf. 468a14). But he has already referred to the stomach as "the [part] that is receptive of the nourishment" (468a24–25), thus allowing for some confusion. And more importantly, he has said at 468b31–469a5 that the *final* form of the nourishment is blood, and he indicated clearly there, and will say explicitly later (480a5–7), that the heart is the part of the body that works it up. So he must be referring here to the heart, rather than the stomach, as the first of these two parts. And as for "the [part] that is receptive [of it]," since what it receives is understood most naturally to be the final nourishment that has just been mentioned, the part that receives it would be the part of the body that receives the blood. But every other part of the body receives blood from the heart (cf. *On the Parts of Animals* 668a1–11). And so as it seems to me, the two "parts" mentioned here are not to be understood according to the previous division of the body into three parts, but are rather the heart, on the one hand, and the rest of the body, on the other. (In this I agree with Ogle, *Aristotle* On Youth & Old Age, 112–13, n. 31.)

will be[34] near each of the two [parts], and the place [consisting] of such a middle[35] is [the] place of a ruler.[36] Furthermore, that which 469b
uses and that which it uses ought to differ (just as with respect to their power, so, if it admits [of being the case], also with respect to their place),[37] just as flutes and that which sets the flutes in motion,

---

34 Since the word translated here as "it will be" is a singular form of the verb "to be" (and since the word for beginnings is not neuter, in which case "they will be" would indeed be expressed by that singular form), "it" cannot refer to both of the two beginnings mentioned at the beginning of this sentence. And from the sequel—most explicitly, from the conclusion in the sentence that follows the next one—it seems clear to me that Aristotle is not referring here to "each" of those two ruling beginnings, but to that of the perceptive soul alone. (As for the nutritive ruling beginning, the first part of this sentence has already suggested a clear argument as to why it should be in the middle, namely, so as best to distribute the final nourishment to the rest of the body.)

35 At 469a34, I read *hē tou toioutou mesou khōra*, in accord with manuscripts L, S, and H[a], rather than *hē tou toioutou merous khōra,* with Mugnier, who follows manuscripts M and Z. Mugnier's text would be translated, instead of as "the place [consisting] of such a middle," as "the place of such a part." By calling it the place consisting of "such" a middle, and saying that it would be "near" the heart (as well as to the rest of the body), it seems to me that Aristotle is denying that the place of this ruling beginning, i.e., "the middle of the being (*ousias*)," is limited by any one organ, including even the heart (cf. n. 29 above). In this connection, recall what he said at the end of Chapter 2 (468b12–15, and see n. 19 above) about tortoises from which the heart has been removed. And as for the fact that this ruling beginning would not be, strictly speaking, "near" the heart, since it is also "in" it (cf. 469b5), see n. 37 below.

36 The word translated here as "ruler" (*arkhontos*) is derived from the word *arkhē*, which I have been translating as "beginning (*arkhē*)" or as "ruling beginning."

37 At 469b2, I read *topon*, with manuscripts L and Z, rather than *tropon*, with Mugnier, who follows manuscripts M, S, and P. Mugnier's text would be translated, instead of as "also with respect to their place," as "also with respect to their manner"; but this doesn't make any sense to me. On the other hand, the difficulty with the reading I have chosen is that if, as it seems reasonable, "that which uses" is the perceptive ruling beginning and "that which it uses" includes the sense organs, including the one common sense organ of the particular sense organs (cf. nn. 8 and 28 above), these would not differ, or not entirely, at any rate, with respect to place (cf. 467b27–30, 469a10–12, and n. 8 above). But note that Aristotle has said only that these ought to differ with respect to place if it is admissible (i.e., possible) for them to do so, and so it seems to me that he is indicating here that this is not entirely possible in the case of animals.

the hand[, differ in these respects]. If, then, the animal is defined by its having the perceptive soul, [it is] necessary for the [animals] with blood to have this ruling beginning in the heart, and for those without blood [to have it] in the analogous part. Now all the parts, and all of the body, of the animals have some inborn natural heat; wherefore, when [the animals are] alive, they are manifestly hot, but when they come to the end and are deprived of living, [they are] the opposite. It is necessary, then, for the beginning (*arkhēn*) of this heat to be in the heart, in the case of the [animals] with blood, and in the analogous [part], in the case of those without blood; for all [the parts] work on and cook [i.e., digest,] the nourishment by means of their natural heat, but especially the most authoritative [part does so]. Wherefore, even though the other parts are chilled, living remains, but if the [heat that is] in this [i.e., in the heart, is lost], they perish altogether, on account of the beginning (*arkhēn*) [of living] for all [the parts] being dependent on the heat there, and because the soul has been kindled, as it were, in these parts, in the analogous [part] of the [animals] without blood, and in the heart of those with blood. [It is] necessary, then, for living and the preservation of this heat to be present together, and for what is called death to be the destruction of this [heat].

Chapter 5

Yet we see two [kinds of] destructions of fire, at any rate, [namely,] dying out as well as being put out. And we call the [destruction caused] by itself "dying out," whereas that [caused] by its contraries [we call] "being put out," and [we call] the former "[destruction] because of old age," whereas the latter [we call] "violent [destruction]."[38] But [in fact] it happens that both of the destruc-

38 Mugnier brackets the words translated as "and [we call] the former, '[destruction] because of old age,' whereas the latter [we call] 'violent [destruction],'" even though they appear in all our manuscripts, thus indicating that he regards them as an interpolation by some ancient scribe. Presumably, he does so on the grounds that they apply to the extinguishing of the natural heat in animals in particular, rather than to that of fire in general, which is

tions come to be on account of the same [thing]; for when the nourishment fails, because of the heat not being able to take hold of the nourishment, there comes to be a destruction of the fire. For on the one hand, that which is contrary [to the heat of the fire], putting a stop to its cooking [i.e., its assimilating of the nourishment], prevents it from being nourished; but on the other hand, it sometimes happens that it dies out when too much heat gathers, on account of [the fire] not breathing [i.e., taking in air,] and [so] not being cooled; for also in this way the heat, gathering together in great quantity, quickly uses up its nourishment, and uses it up before the exhalation has formed.[39] Wherefore not only does the smaller fire next to the larger one die out,[40] but also the lamp's flame, itself in itself, burns up when it is placed in a larger flame,[41] just as [does] **470a**
any other of the combustibles whatsoever. And [the] cause [is] that the greater flame takes hold of the nourishment that is in the flame [of the lamp], [doing so] before [any] different [nourishment] comes in, and the fire continues ever coming into being and flowing like a river, but [this process] escapes notice on account of its speed.

---

otherwise the theme of this chapter. But even if these words are indeed meant to apply only to animals, I see no reason to believe that Aristotle himself didn't write them, since his main concern in this chapter is clearly to understand the cause of animal death (and life). And whether or not he makes this concern explicit here, he does make it explicit later in the chapter, most especially with his mention, at 470a5–7, of what is required in order to live.

39 The exhalation that Aristotle has in mind here, at least in the case of a wood fire, is exhalation of smoke (cf. *Meteorologica* 387a30–b1). Now elsewhere he speaks of smoke as being the nourishment of fire (*On Long-Livedness and Short-Livedness* 465b23–25; cf. *On Coming into Being and Perishing* 331b25–26). And though I am not certain of this suggestion, let me suggest that he is thinking here of smoke as the burning wood in its elaborated form, the form that it acquires as part of the fire (like blood in animals), and that he is treating the exhalation of some residual smoke as a sign that the elaboration is taking place.

40 Perhaps Aristotle is thinking of what happens to a smaller fire next to a larger one in a confined space.

41 Cf. *On Long-Livedness and Short-Livedness* 465b21–25, where in describing the same phenomenon Aristotle says that the smaller flame is burned up by the larger one, "by concomitance."

[It is] clear, then, that if the heat must be preserved (and this is necessary, if [an animal] is going to live), some cooling of the heat in its ruling beginning must come to be. And it is possible to take an example of this, [namely,] what happens in the case of coals that are damped; for if they are covered up continuously by what is called a damper, they are put out quickly; but if someone brings about, in close succession one after another, the removal and the putting on [of the damper], they remain on fire for a long time. And banking [i.e., covering with ash,] preserves the fire; for on account of the porousness of the ash, [the fire] is not prevented from breathing out [and thus expelling its excess heat], and [the ash] serves as a screen against the [cold] air around [the fire] in order that, with the amount of heat that is present in it, it not be put out [by it]. But concerning this cause, [namely, the cause of the fact] that contraries happen to the fire that is banked and [to the one] that is damped (for the latter dies out, whereas the former persists for a longer time), it has been spoken of in the *Problems*.[42]

Chapter 6

Since every animal has soul, and it [i.e., soul,] itself is not present without natural heat, as we have said,[43] for the plants, on the one hand,[44] the help [that] comes to be through their nourishment and [through] what surrounds [them] is sufficient for the preservation of their natural heat. For also the nourishment produces cooling[45] when it enters, just as [it] also [does] for human beings[46] when they

42 There is no such account in Aristotle's *Problems* as it has come down to us.

43 469b6–9.

44 This statement about plants, introduced by the particle translated as "on the one hand," is apparently answered by the statement about animals at 470b1–2 ("But of the animals...").

45 On the need for cooling in order to preserve a fire's heat, compare the account in the previous chapter, especially at 469b27–470a7.

46 Mugnier indicates by the use of brackets that he would exclude the words translated here as "when it enters, just as [it] also [does] for human beings." This is in keeping with manuscripts M, Z, P, and S, which do not contain

first take [it] in; but fasts cause heating and produce thirst; for the air [in the body of the living being], if it is unmoved, always becomes hot, but by being set in motion when the nourishment enters, it is cooled, until [the nourishment] has received its cooking [i.e., digestion]. But if the surrounding [air] is excessive in coldness on account of the season, with there being hard frosts, the strength of the [plant's natural] heat withers away, while if hot spells occur[47] and the moisture that is being drawn up from the earth is not able to cool [the plant], its heat dies out and perishes, and the trees are said to be blighted and to become sun-scorched at these times. Wherefore [people] put under the roots both certain kinds of stones and [also] water in vessels, so that the roots of the **470b** plants may be cooled. But of the animals, since some [are] aquatic while others pass their lives in the air, [it is] from these [surroundings] and through these [that] they procure their [own] cooling, the ones by means of the water and the others by means of the air. But as for in what manner and how [they do this], we must speak (*lekteon*), giving closer attention to the reasoning (*ton logon*).

---

them. I include them, though without any strong conviction that they are not an interpolation.

47 At 470a27, I read *ean de to periekhon*, with manuscripts M and Z, rather than *ean de ē to periekhon*, with Mugnier, who follows manuscripts L, S, and P; and at 470a29, I read *hē tou thermou iskhus, an de sumbainēi kaumata*, again with manuscripts M and Z, rather than *ē tou therous iskhura sumbainēi kaumata*, with Mugnier, who follows manuscripts L, S, and P (although L and S have *sumbainei* instead of *sumbainēi*). Mugnier's text—although its structure is somewhat irregular—might be translated, instead of as "But if the surrounding [air] is excessive in coldness on account of the season, with there being hard frosts, the strength of the [plant's natural] heat withers away, while if hot spells occur," as "But if either the surrounding [air] is excessive in coldness on account of the season, with there being hard frosts, they [i.e., the plants] dry out, or [if] in the summer there occur severe hot spells." The reading that I have chosen has the advantage of having both parts of this sentence speak explicitly about a loss of the plants' natural heat.

Chapter 7[48]

Now a few of the earlier students of nature have spoken about breathing. However, for the sake of what [end] it belongs to animals, some have not offered any opinion, while others have spoken, but they have not spoken finely, but in a way [that shows them to have been] somewhat inexperienced regarding the [things] that happen [in this connection]. Furthermore, they assert that all the animals breathe; but this isn't true. So [it is] necessary to discuss concerning these [thinkers] first, so that we may not seem to make a baseless accusation against [men who are] absent. Now with regard to as many of the animals as have a lung, that they all breathe [is] manifest. But even of these, as many of them as have a bloodless and spongy lung are less in need of breathing; wherefore they are able to remain under water for a long time, [viewed] in relation to the strength of their body. And all the [animals] that lay eggs, for instance the genus of frogs, have a spongy lung. Furthermore, hemydes[49] as well as tortoises remain under water[50] for a long time; for their lung has little heat; for they have one with little blood; therefore, when inflated, it itself, by its motion, cools [them] and makes [them able] to remain [under water] for a long time. However, if someone does [them] violence by holding them down for

48 Some modern editions divide the treatise *On Youth and Old Age and Life and Death and Breathing* into two separate treatises, with the one called *On Youth and Old Age and Life and Death* and the other *On Breathing.* In these editions, the treatise *On Breathing* begins with this chapter as Chapter 1, and the subsequent chapters are numbered accordingly.

49 The hemys was a soft-shelled animal (cf. *On the Parts of Animals* 671a31) akin to the tortoise. According to Ogle (*Aristotle* On Youth & Old Age, 116, n. 45), it was probably what is now called the *testudo coriacea*, or leatherback sea turtle, which is common in the Mediterranean.

50 The expression translated as "under water" is *en tois hugrois*, which means literally "in what (pl.) is wet." Now I don't see a reason for Aristotle's choice of this expression rather than one with the word *hudōr*, i.e., "water," which he used just above (*en tois hudasi*, 470b15). But since he might have had a reason that I don't see, I will include a transliteration of the Greek, in the remainder of this treatise, whenever I translate some form of the word *hugros* as "water"—or as "liquid." Cf. *On Sense Perception and Sense-Perceptibles*, n. 65.

an excessively long time, they all suffocate; for none of the [animals] of this sort takes in water, as fish [do]. All the [animals] that have a bloody lung are more in need of breathing because of the amount of their heat; but of the others, [namely,] as many as don't have a lung, none [of them] breathes.

Chapter 8

Now Democritus of Abdera and some others of those who have spoken about breathing have made no affirmations concerning the other animals [i.e., those without lungs], yet it looks as if they speak on the assumption that all [animals] breathe; but Anaxagoras and Diogenes, asserting that [they] all breathe, [also] say, concerning fish and oysters, in what manner they breathe. And Anaxagoras asserts that whenever they expel water through their gills, fish breathe 471a by drawing in the air that comes to be in their mouth; for [he asserts] that there is no void; whereas Diogenes [asserts that] whenever they expel water through their gills, they draw in air, by means of the void [that then comes to be] in their mouth, from the water that surrounds their mouth, on his assumption that there is air in the water.[51] But these [assertions] are impossible. For in the first place, they take away half of the matter (*tou pragmatos*), on account of the common [term] being used [by them] for one alone of its two [parts]. For it is called breathing (*anapnoē*), but one [part] of this is breathing in (*eispnoē*) and the other breathing out (*ekpnoē*), concerning which, [namely,] in what manner such animals breathe out, they say nothing. Nor do [their assertions] admit of their saying [this]. For whenever [these animals] breathe [in], they have to breathe out again by that [same passage] by which they breathed [in], and [they have] to do this always in succession, so that it turns

51 Aristotle had not bothered to say that Anaxagoras also held that there is air in the water surrounding the fishes' mouth (which is why, in his view as well, air comes to be in their mouth when they expel water through their gills), perhaps because Anaxagoras was famous for the assertion that everything is mixed in everything. Cf. *Metaphysics* 1009a25–27.

out that they take water into their mouth and breathe out [air] at the same time. But [it is] necessary for the one [i.e., the water taken in,] to obstruct the other [i.e., the air breathed out,] as they meet. Next, whenever they expel the water, they are at that time breathing out [air] from their mouth or from their gills, so that it turns out that they are breathing out and breathing [in] at the same time; for they [i.e., Anaxagoras and Diogenes,] assert that [it is] then that it [i.e., the animal in question,] breathes [in]. But [it is] impossible to breathe [in] and breathe out at the same time. So that, if [it is] a necessity for the [animals] that breathe to breathe out and breathe in, and it is not admissible that any of them breathe out, [it is] manifest that neither does any of them breathe.

Chapter 9

Furthermore, to assert that they [i.e., fish,] draw in air from their mouth or from the [surrounding] water by way of their mouth [is to assert the] impossible; for they don't have a windpipe, on account of their not having a lung, but their stomach is right next to their mouth, so that [it would be] necessary that they draw [the air in] by means of their stomach. But [then] the other animals, too, would do this; but as it is, they do not do [it]. And those [animals, i.e., fish,] would be clearly seen doing it [i.e., drawing in air,] when they are out of the water; but it is apparent that they do not do it. Furthermore, in all the [animals] that breathe and draw in breath,[52] we see a certain motion coming to be [in or] of the part that draws [it] in, but [this is something] that doesn't happen in the case of fish; for they do not manifestly move any of the parts around the stomach except for the gills alone, both in the water and after having been thrown up onto dry land, whenever they are gasping. Fur-
471b thermore, [in the case of] all the [animals] that breathe, whenever they die by suffocating in water, there come to be bubbles of their breath as it goes out violently, for instance, if someone does violence

52 The Greek word translated as "breath" is a form of *pneuma*, which can also mean air.

to tortoises or frogs or any other of such kinds [by forcing them to remain under water]; but in the case of fish it doesn't happen, [even] for [people] trying [to make it happen] in every way, which suggests that they don't have any breath [drawn in] from outside.[53] Also, the manner in which they say that breathing comes to be for them [i.e., for fish], admits of occurring also for human beings when we are in water; for if fish draw in [air] from the water around their mouth, why wouldn't we human beings too do [this], and the other animals? They would also draw in the [air] from their mouth in the same way as fish. So that if those [things] were possible, these would be also; and since [these] are not [possible], [it is] clear that it isn't [possible] in the case of those [i.e., fish,] either. In addition to these [considerations], on account of what cause do they die in air and manifestly gasp, like those who are suffocating, if indeed they breathe? For [it is] not from a lack of nourishment, at any rate, [that] they suffer this. For the cause that Diogenes states [is] simple-minded; for he asserts that they draw in too much air [when they are] in the air, but a moderate amount [when they are] in the water, and that they die on account of this. For [if that were so,] it ought to be possible for this to happen also in the case of land animals; but as it is, no land animal suffocates because of excessive breathing. Furthermore, if all [animals] breathe, [it is] clear that even the insects, among the animals, breathe; but many of them manifestly live when cut apart, not only into two parts but even into more, for instance the so-called millipedes; how or by what [organ] is it possible for them [i.e., the resulting parts,] to breathe? But [what is] most responsible for [what is said by these thinkers] about them [i.e., about such animals,] not being spoken finely [is] their being inexperienced regarding the parts [of the animals in question], the internal ones, and their not taking it [to be the case] that nature does all [things] for the sake of something;

53 Aristotle speaks here only of breath drawn in from outside, since he holds that all animals have innate or inborn breath (*sumphuton pneuma*), which is not drawn in from outside, and which enables them, among other things, to move themselves. Cf. *On Sleep and Awakeness* 456a6–24; *On the Motion of Animals* 703a9–19; *On the Parts of Animals* 659b15–19, 668b33–669a1.

for by investigating for the sake of what [end] breathing belongs to animals, and by examining this with reference to their parts, for instance gills and [the] lung, they would have rather quickly discovered the cause [of breathing].

Chapter 10

Democritus does say that something [advantageous] to those [animals] that breathe results from breathing, since he asserts that it
472a prevents the soul from being squeezed out; however, he said nothing about nature having produced it for the sake of this; for in general, like the other students of nature, he too does not touch upon that sort of cause at all. He says that the soul and what is hot [are] the same [thing], [namely,] the primary shapes among the spherical[ly shaped bodies]. He asserts, then, that when these are being pressed together by what surrounds [them] and squeezes them out, breathing comes to be [as] a help; for in the air there are a large number of such [bodies], as he calls intellect and soul; so then, when [an animal] breathes and the air enters, these [bodies], by entering along with it and holding back the squeezing, prevent the soul that is in the animals from going out;[54] and on account of this, living and dying depend on breathing [in] and breathing out; for whenever what surrounds [the spherical bodies within the animal] prevails, squeezing [them] together, and [a portion of it] is no longer able, by entering in from outside, to hold back [the squeezing], since [the animal] is not able to breathe, at that time death results for animals; for death is the departure of such shapes from the body as a consequence of the squeezing out by what surrounds [it]. But the cause, why ever for all [animals, it is] necessary to die, [and] not, moreover, at some chance time, but in accord with nature in old age, whereas [death] by violence [is] contrary to nature, he has not made clear at all. And yet he should have, since this [i.e., death in accord with nature,] manifestly comes to be at one time,

54 Cf. *De Anima* 403b31–404a16.

and manifestly doesn't at another time, whether what is responsible is from without or within. And neither does he speak about the ruling beginning of breathing, [namely,] what [is] the cause, whether it is from within or from without; for certainly the outside intellect[55] doesn't watch over [it, providing] the help, but the ruling beginning of breathing and of its motion comes to be from within, not because what surrounds is doing it [some] violence. And [it is] also absurd that what surrounds [the body] should at the same time squeeze [it] together and, by entering in, distend [it]. And so these are pretty nearly the [things] that he has said and how [he has said them]. But if one must hold that the [things] said earlier [by us] are true, i.e., that not all animals breathe, one must take it to be the case that the cause has been stated [by Democritus, in his stating] this [one], not concerning all death, but only [death] in the case of

55 The only suggestion I have seen regarding the meaning of the expression "the outside intellect" (*ho thurathen nous*), a suggestion made already by the medieval commentator Michael of Ephesus, is that it is a reference to the spherically shaped atoms, which Democritus called intellect or soul, in the surrounding air (cf. 472a7–8). This suggestion is indeed in keeping with the supporting argument that follows. However, it fails to account adequately for Aristotle's speaking of "the outside intellect" in the singular, let alone for his speaking of it as something that might watchfully provide help, which Democritus would never have imagined that his soul atoms could do. And so let me suggest that Aristotle may be referring instead to an outside intellect that he speaks of elsewhere in his own name, even using these same words in a passage where he says that "the intellect," in those animals that possess one, may be something divine that enters into them "from outside" (*thurathen*), presumably from a single intellect as their common source (*On the Generation of Animals* 736b5–29; cf. 744b16–22). And on this interpretation, the conclusion of the sentence would be arguing that if such an intellect were responsible for breathing, breathing would not come about, as it does in fact, by nature—which Aristotle defines as an internal ruling beginning (cf. *Physics* 192b20–32)—but only as a result of that intellect causing the surrounding air to force its way inside the animal. Now the thought that an external intellect is the cause of breathing would seem to be so obviously wrong as not to be worth mentioning, even in jest. But by referring to this alternative, and thus eliminating a possible misunderstanding of the claim he suggested, at the end of the previous chapter, that nature does all things for the sake of something, Aristotle may be calling attention to the serious question of what precisely it does mean.

the [animals] that breathe. And indeed [it has] not [been stated] finely even in the case of these. [This is] clear from the [things] that happen, and [in particular] from those of such a sort as we all have experience of. For in hot spells, as we are being made warmer, we are also more in need of breathing and we all breathe more rapidly; but when what is around [us] is cold and our body is drawn together and condensed, [what] happens [is] that we hold our breath. And yet at that time, [according to Democritus,] what enters
472b from outside ought to prevent our being squeezed. But as it is, the opposite comes to be; for when too much of what is hot is gathered together [in the body], because [people] aren't breathing out, [it is] then [that] they are in need of (*deontai*) breathing; and [it is] necessary (*anangkaion*) that they breathe by breathing in. And they breathe a lot when they are hot, [which suggests] that they breathe for the sake of cooling, when, [as] the saying [goes], it makes fire on fire [i.e., when it is very hot].

Chapter 11

The circular pushing [as] described in the *Timaeus*[56] has in no way determined, concerning the other animals, in what manner the preservation of the hot [in them] comes to be,[57] whether [it is] in

56 Plato, *Timaeus* 79a5–e9.

57 Preservation of "the hot" in an animal, i.e., of the heat or of what is hot in it, is that for the sake of which, according to Aristotle, breathing occurs (cf. 469b27–470a7 and 474b10–24, together with 475b15–19; 479a7–28). But it is not clear why he speaks of this here in connection with the *Timaeus*. It is true that Plato's Timaeus, unlike the students of nature whom Aristotle has been discussing so far (cf. 470b6–9, 471b23–29), does speak of that for the sake of which breathing occurs. But the end he speaks of, as that for the sake of which the god or gods contrived the entire system that includes breathing, is not the preservation of the animal's heat, but is rather nutrition (cf. Plato, *Timaeus* 76e7–77c7ff., especially 77e7–78b3), and nutrition is not simply identical with the preservation of an animal's heat. Still, there is a considerable overlap between these two views regarding that for the sake of which breathing occurs. For on the one hand, according to Timaeus, the first product of the nutritive process is blood, and he speaks of blood as being like a stream of fire,

the same [manner] or through some other cause; for if the [process] of breathing belongs only to land animals, one must state the cause of [its belonging to them] alone; whereas if [it belongs] also to the others, but the manner is another [one], one must determine also concerning this [manner], if indeed [it is] possible for all [animals] to breathe. Furthermore, the manner of cause [given in the *Timaeus*] is contrived. For he [i.e., Timaeus,] asserts that when the hot [breath] goes out through the mouth, the surrounding air, being pushed and [thus] set in motion, sinks through the flesh, which is porous, into the same place [as that] from which the hot [breath] that had been inside went out, on account of there being no void when they replace one another; and when [the air entering through the flesh has been] heated, it goes out by the same place [as that by which it entered] and pushes around, [so as to drive] inside through the mouth, the air that was going out [from the mouth, as] hot; and [the animals] always keep on doing just this, breathing [in] and breathing out. But it turns out, for those who have this supposition, that breathing out comes to be before breathing in. But the opposite is [the case]. And a sign [is this]: for these come to be one after the other, and when [animals] come to the end, they breathe out, so that it is necessary that the beginning [be] breathing in. Furthermore, regarding that for the sake of which these belong to animals (I mean breathing [in] and breathing out), those who speak in this manner have said nothing, but they make a statement [about it] merely as about some

---

which is to say that, for him, the process that includes breathing leads in the first place to the renewal or preservation of what is hot within the body (cf. *Timaeus* 80d1–81a2; 79d1–2); and on the other hand, Aristotle speaks later in this treatise of the animal's natural heat, or rather of its natural fire, as being necessary for the soul's nutritive power, without which its other powers cannot exist (474b10–14ff.; cf. *De Anima* 416b26–30). And so the difference, or at least the important difference, between Aristotle's understanding of breathing and that of Plato's Timaeus would not concern the end for the sake of which breathing occurs, but rather what Aristotle here calls the manner, or the cause, through which the animal's heat, and thus its nutritive power, is preserved.

concomitant.[58] And yet we see [that] these [are] decisive (*kuria*) for living and coming to the end; for when [animals] are not able to breathe, then it results that perishing comes to be for those that breathe. Furthermore, [it is] absurd [to assert in effect] that while the going out of the hot [breath] through the mouth and its going in again do not escape our notice, the going in of the breath into the chest and its going out again when it has been heated do escape notice; and [it is] absurd also that breathing is the going in of what is hot. For the opposite is manifest, namely, that what is breathed out is hot,[59] whereas what is breathed in is cold. And when it is hot
473a [outside, animals] pant as they breathe; for it happens [then] that they draw breath in a lot on account of what goes in not cooling [them] sufficiently.

---

58 Timaeus speaks of the entire system that includes breathing as having been contrived by the god(s) for the sake of something, namely, for the sake of distributing nourishment throughout the body (cf. the previous footnote, n. 57). But in his account it is not the air we breathe that serves this end, but rather fire that enters the body along with it, and not the fire, moreover, that enters and leaves the body through the mouth, i.e., not the fire that we might be said to breathe in and out, but rather the fire that, along with air, enters the trunk of the body through its porous flesh. For it is this fire that he speaks of as entering the stomach and there resolving food and drink into smaller parts, which it then drives throughout the body (Plato, *Timaeus* 78d1–79a4). In his account, then, the air (and fire) that we breathe in and out through the mouth—which he is referring to, I think, by his parenthetical reference just above to breathing [in] and breathing out—serve no purpose in themselves, but are merely necessary concomitants of the (closed) system that drives particles of fire in and out of the stomach. (At *Timaeus* 70c1–d6, Timaeus does speak of breathing, together with the lung, as having been devised by the gods in order to cool the heart. But the context makes it clear that the cooling of the heart that he speaks of there serves only an occasional, and not a truly vital, function.)

59 Although Timaeus does not speak of the air breathed in as being hot, and indeed states explicitly that it is heated after it enters the body (and also that breath in the lung serves to cool the heart), an important feature of his account is that breathing involves the entrance of fire, along with air, into the body (cf. Plato, *Timaeus* 78d1–79a4, along with the two previous footnotes, nn. 57 and 58). Perhaps this is what Aristotle has in mind here by attributing to Timaeus the claim that breathing is the entrance into the body of what is hot.

Chapter 12

But again, one must also not take it to be the case that breathing comes to be for the sake of nourishment, on the assumption that the fire inside is nourished by the breath, and that when one breathes [in, it is] like throwing fuel on a fire,[60] while when the fire has been nourished, there comes to be breathing out. For against this speech (*logos*) too we will again say the same [things that we said] against the previous ones; for this, or what is analogous to it, ought to happen also in the case of the other animals; for all [animals] have vital heat.[61] Next, in what manner is one to say that becoming hot [results] from breath, [the very notion of its doing so] being a contrived [one]? For we see rather that this [i.e., becoming hot,] comes to be from nourishment [i.e., food and drink]. Also, it results [from that view] that [animals] receive nourishment and discharge its residue by the same [opening]; but we don't see this coming to be in the other cases [i.e., with food and drink].

Chapter 13

Empedocles also speaks about breathing; however, [he does] not [say] for the sake of what [it occurs], nor does he make it at all clear, concerning all the animals, whether they breathe or not. Also, in speaking about breathing through the nostrils, he supposes that he is also speaking about the decisive (*kurias*) [form of] breathing. [But this is false.] For there is breathing through the windpipe from the chest as well as that through the nostrils; and it is impossible to breathe by means of the nostrils themselves apart from that [i.e., the windpipe]. Also, when animals are deprived of the

60 This understanding of the manner in which breathing serves the goal of nourishment is not, as we have seen, Timaeus' understanding of how it does so, nor is it that of Aristotle (cf. n. 57 above). Thus, Aristotle is not denying, it seems to me, that breathing is for the sake of nourishment, but only the more specific claim that it serves this goal by providing the nourishment, or fuel, for the fire inside the body.

61 Cf. 469b6–8; *On the Motion of Animals*, n. 70.

breathing that comes to be through the nostrils, they don't suffer anything, whereas [when they are deprived of] that by the windpipe, they die. For nature uses breathing through the nostrils secondarily for smelling in some of the animals; on account of which, while nearly all animals share in smelling, they don't all have the same sense organ. But about them there have been clearer state-
473b ments in different [treatises].[62] Now he [i.e., Empedocles,] asserts that breathing [in] and breathing out come to be on account of there being certain blood vessels, in which there is blood, but [which] are not, however, full of blood, and [which] have passages to the air outside [that are] smaller than the [smallest] parts of the body, but larger than those of the air; wherefore, since the blood is of such a nature as to be in motion upward and downward, when it is in downward local motion, the air rushes in and there comes to be breathing [in], whereas when [the blood] is going upward, [the air] is driven outside and there comes to be the breathing out, [with him] likening what happens to [what happens with perforated] water-carriers.[63]

In the following way do all [animals] breathe [in] and
 breathe out. In all [of them]
Tubes of flesh that [to some extent] lack blood extend
 to the outermost [surface of the] body,

62 *On the Parts of Animals* 659b13–16; *On the History of Animals* 534a11–b10; *On Sense Perception and Sense-Perceptibles* 444a25–28, 444b7–28.

63 The Greek word translated as "[perforated] water carrier" is *klepsudra*. The Greeks knew of several varieties of the clepsydra. But the one referred to here was a kind of funnel-shaped strainer, with its broad base at the bottom covered by a disk containing many small perforations, and with a narrow cylindrical tube at the top. To carry water from one place to another, one would first hold its base under water with the tube open at the top, so as to let the water enter, and then cover its top with one's hand, lift the base out of the water, and carry it to the desired location before again uncovering the top, so as to release the water.

And at their mouths the utmost extremities of the nose[64] are pierced through
With closely packed pores, [sufficiently small] so that they keep in [the] blood,
But [so that] an easy path for air has been cut by the passages.
Accordingly, whenever the thin blood rushes away from there,
The bubbling air will descend with a furious swell,
But when [the blood] leaps back, there is breathing out again, as when a girl,
Playing with a [perforated] water-carrier of gleaming[65] bronze,
When, having placed the opening of the tube upon her well-shaped hand,
She dips [the vessel] into the soft frame of silvery water,
Not then does the water enter into the vessel, but the mass

64 The Greek word translated as "nose" is *rhinōn*, the genitive plural of *rhis*, which can be used in the plural to mean "nose" or "nostrils." This translation is in keeping with Aristotle's interpretation of the passage, since he treats Empedocles as speaking here, if not exclusively, at least primarily, of breathing through the nostrils (cf. 473a17–19, 474a7–18). It is however hard to understand how one could think that the "pores" at the extremities of the nose, if these are the nostrils, would be small enough to hold blood inside the body. Accordingly, some modern editors and translators understand Empedocles to be using the word *rhinōn* not as a form of *rhis*, but as the genitive plural of *rhinos*, which means "skin," and to be speaking not of breathing through the nose, but of cutaneous respiration through the pores of the skin (a form of respiration that, as we have seen, also played a role in Timaeus' account of breathing; cf. 472b13-20). And though this is a tempting suggestion, I choose to follow Aristotle's interpretation of the passage and to translate the word as "nose." As for the difficulty regarding the size of the nostrils, perhaps Empedocles meant by the "pores" at the extremity of the nose not the nostrils themselves, but smaller openings in the wall of the nasal cavity.

65 At 473b17, I read *diipeteos*, in keeping with manuscripts M and Z, rather than as *di eupeteos*, with Mugnier, who follows manuscript L. According to Mugnier's text, the words translated here as "of gleaming bronze" would be translated instead as "of light [i.e., not heavy,] bronze." That reading is certainly possible, but it is not the one accepted by Diels-Kranz. Empedocles, frag. 100 Diels-Kranz, 1:348.

Of air, falling upon the closely packed perforations from inside, keeps it out,
Until she uncovers the compact stream [of air]; but then,
As the air leaves, a fitting [i.e., equal, amount of] water enters.
And so likewise, when water occupies the depths of the bronze,
With the [tube's] opening and passage having been covered by her mortal flesh,
And the air outside, seeking eagerly [to get] inside, holds back the water,
Controlling its surface, at the gates of the ill-sounding strainer,[66]
474a Until she lets go with her hand; then back again, in reverse from before,
As the air rushes in, a fitting [amount of] water runs out.
Thus likewise [in the case of] the thin blood, surging through the limbs,
Whenever it rushes back within, away [from the pores],
A stream of air descends immediately, raging in a swell,
But when [the blood] leaps up [to the pores], an equal [amount of air] is breathed back out again.[67]

And so he says these [things] concerning breathing. But as we said, the [animals] that manifestly breathe, breathe through the windpipe, together with [their breathing] through the mouth or through the nostrils. So that if, on the one hand, he is speaking about this breathing, [it is] necessary to investigate how the account (*logos*) of

66 At 473b27, I read *ēthmoio*, with manuscripts S and P (and Diels-Kranz, 1:348), rather than *isthmoio*, with Mugnier, who follows manuscripts L and M. According to Mugnier's text, the words translated as "the ill-sounding strainer" would be translated as "the ill-sounding neck [of the strainer]" and would refer to a gurgling sound presumed to come from the open tube of the clepsydra. But it seems false that any gurgling would come from there, at least not so long as the clepsydra were held with the tube above the base.

67 Empedocles, frag. 100 Diels-Kranz.

the cause that has been given [by him] will fit [with this]. For it is manifest that the opposite happens. For by raising up the place [that receives the breath, i.e., the chest], as [men expand] bellows in forges, [animals] breathe [in]; and [it is] reasonable that heat cause [it] to rise, and that blood have the role of heat; and by making [the chest] collapse and driving [it] down,[68] as there [men do to] bellows, [animals] breathe out. Except that there they don't take the air in and let it out again by the same [passage], whereas those who breathe [do so] by the same [passage]. But if, on the other hand, he is speaking only about [breathing] by way of the nostrils, he is much mistaken; for breathing is not peculiar to the nostrils, but [the breath goes] along the channel near the uvula at the extremity of the vaulted roof in the mouth, [and] since the nostrils are connected [to this passage], part of the breath proceeds in this way [i.e., through the nostrils], but part of it [proceeds] through the mouth, likewise as it goes in and as it goes out. And so the [things] said by the others concerning breathing have such, and so many, difficulties.

Chapter 14

Since it has been said earlier[69] that living and the having[70] of soul is [bound up] with a certain heat; for neither is digestion, through which nourishment comes to be for animals, either without soul

---

68 At 474a15, I read *kataplēttontes*, with manuscripts M and Z, rather than *katapneontes*, with Mugnier, who follows manuscript L. According to Mugnier's text, instead of "driving [it] down," the translation would read "blowing upon [it]" or 'blowing over [it]," or perhaps even "blowing down," but none of these make much sense.

69 469b6–20, 470a5–6, 470a19–22.

70 The Greek word translated as "having" is *hexis*, which more commonly means "state" or "condition" (cf. *On Sense Perception and Sense-Perceptibles*, n. 2). Accordingly, the expression "the having of soul" (*hexis psuchēs*) might also have been translated as "the state of soul," which in the context would presumably mean "the state [of the body] that is soul." (On this interpretation of the expression "of soul," which translates the Greek genitive form *psuchēs*, cf. Smyth, *Greek Grammar*, para. 1322.)

or without heat; for it is accomplished in all cases by means of fire; wherefore in the first place in the body, and in the first part of this place,[71] in which it is necessary for the beginning (*arkhēn*) of this sort to be [located], there also [it is] necessary that the first, [i.e.,] 474b nutritive,[72] soul be present. And this place is the one in the middle of that which receives the nourishment and that where [the animal] discharges the residue [from it]. Now in the bloodless [animals, this is] without a name, but in those with blood, the heart is this part. For the [form of] nourishment from which the parts in animals directly come into being is the nature of blood. But [it is] necessary that there be the same ruling beginning of the blood and of the blood vessels; for the one is for the sake of the other, as [being its] container and receptacle. And the ruling beginning of the blood vessels is the heart for the [animals] with blood; for [these vessels don't extend] through this, but they are in fact all fastened from this. This [is] clear to us from the dissections.[73] Now [it is] impossible for the other powers of the soul to be present without the nutritive (on account of what cause [this is so] has been said earlier in our [speeches] concerning soul),[74] and [it is impossible for] this [power to be present] without the natural[75] fire; for nature has kindled it [i.e., the nutritive power,] in this. The destruction of fire, as has been said before,[76] is [either] being put out or dying

71 Aristotle uses the expressions "the first place" and "the first part of this place" in order to contrast this region, and especially this part of it, with those regions of the body in which it is also necessary for such a beginning (i.e., a certain heat) to be located, but merely because they are larger wholes that contain "the first place" and "the first part" of it among their parts.

72 On the nutritive soul as being the first, i.e., indispensable, soul, cf. *De Anima* 416b13–22.

73 Cf. *On Sleep and Awakeness*, n. 24.

74 *De Anima* 413a20–b2, 414a29–415a3.

75 Since all fire is natural, the word "natural" here, which appears to be a term of distinction, presumably means "belonging to the nature of the animal." And Aristotle has spoken earlier of the "inborn natural heat" and "natural heat" of animals, as well as of their "vital heat." 469b6–16; 473a9–10, together with *On the Motion of Animals*, n. 70.

76 469b21ff.

out. Being put out is the [destruction] by its contraries; for which reason [it is put out] in a mass by the coldness of its surroundings, and it is put out more quickly when scattered. Now this [sort of] destruction is violent, likewise in the [beings] with soul and in those without soul; for both when the animal is cut apart by instruments and when it is frozen by an excess of cold, they die. But dying out [occurs] because of [the] large amount of heat; for both if the heat around [it] is excessive and if it does not receive nourishment, that [which is] afire is destroyed, not by becoming cold but by dying out. So that [it is] a necessity for there to come to be a cooling down, if it is going to gain [its] preservation; for this [is what] helps against this [sort of] destruction.

Chapter 15

Since some of the animals are aquatic and others spend their time on land, for those of them that are very small and those without blood, the cooling that comes to be from their surroundings, whether water or air, is sufficient for help against this [sort of] destruction;[77] for since the heat they have is little, they need little help. For which reason, also, nearly all such [animals] are short-lived; for since they are small, they [can] endure [only] a small push [on the scale of heat and cold] in both directions. As many of the insects as are longer-lived (for all insects are bloodless) are **475a**
split below[78] the midriff,[79] so that they may be cooled through the

77 "This [sort of] destruction" is that mentioned at the end of the previous chapter.

78 Since Aristotle understands "up" in animals and plants as referring to the region of the body that takes in food and "down" as that from which the residue from it is eliminated (cf. 467b32–468a7), the word translated as "below" (*hupo*) means what we would call "behind" or "to the rear of." Accordingly, the split or splits in question here are to the rear of the midriff.

79 The Greek word translated as "midriff" is *diadzōma*. Aristotle uses this word to refer to the diaphragm in animals with blood (cf. *On the Parts of Animals* 672b10ff.), and although it is not clear to me what he means by it in the case of insects, it may refer to the juncture between the thorax and the abdomen.

membrane, which is rather thin, [that covers this opening or these openings]; for since they are hotter, they need more cooling down, for instance bees (for some of the bees live as long as seven years) and the other [insects] that buzz, for instance wasps and cockchafers and cicadas. And indeed they produce their [buzzing] sound by means of breath, like those [animals] that are panting; for in the midriff[80] itself, raising [itself up] by means of the innate breath[81] and sinking down, it happens that there comes to be rubbing against the membrane [that we have just spoken of]; for they set this region in motion, as those that breathe [air] from outside do by means of the lung and [as] fish do by means of their gills. For [what] happens [with these insects is] similar [to what would happen] if someone were to suffocate one of the breathing [animals] by holding shut its mouth; for these too will produce this rising [i.e., heaving motion,] with their lung. But for these, this sort of motion does not produce sufficient cooling down, but for those, it [does produce] sufficient [cooling down]. And by this rubbing against the membrane they produce the buzzing, as we are saying, like small children [who blow] through reeds that have been

80 The word translated here as "midriff" is *hypodzōmati*, a form of *hypodzōma*. I might perhaps have translated it as "abdomen." However, a bit later in this chapter, at 475a20, Aristotle will speak of some cicadas as being split "under," i.e., behind, the *hupodzōma* (cf. n. 78 above); and since he is apparently referring there to the same openings that he spoke of in the sentence just before this one as being "under," i.e., behind, the *diadzōma* (cf. the previous footnote, n. 79), I prefer to treat the word *hupodzōma* there as an equivalent for *diadzōma* in that earlier sentence, and to translate it also as "midriff." Accordingly, I choose to translate it as "midriff" here as well, even though it seems to refer not to the junction between the thorax and the abdomen, but to the midsection or hind section of the insect's body more generally. Aristotle will use this word again, also after the preposition "in," at 475b4, where I understand it as referring to this same region of the insect's body and will again translate it as "midriff."

81 In *On the Parts of Animals* 659b13–19, Aristotle speaks of the innate breath (or "naturally inherent breath") as a form of breath that is not inhaled from outside, but that belongs to animals by nature. And in *On the Motion of Animals* 703a9–19, he has spoken of this breath as that which gives animals the power to move themselves. As for the naturally inherent breath in insects in particular, see also *On Sleep and Awakeness* 456a13–20. Cf. n. 53 above.

bored through, whenever they have placed a thin membrane over [the opening]. For [it is] also on account of this [that] those of the cicadas that sing,[82] sing; for they are hotter, and they are split below the midriff;[83] but in those [of the cicadas] that don't sing, this [part] is unsplit. And among the [animals] with blood and that have a lung, but that have [a lung] with little blood and [that is] spongy, some, on account of this, are able to live a long time without breathing, because their lung, since it has little blood or liquid (*hugron*), has [the capacity for] much rising; for its own motion suffices for a long time in cooling [the animals] down. But finally it is not able, but [the animals] are suffocated, if they are not breathing, as has been said before;[84] for [of the forms] of dying out, destruction on account of not being cooled is called suffocation, and we assert that the [animals] that perish in this way are suffocated. Now that, of the animals, insects do not breathe has been said before,[85] and this is manifest in the case of the small animals, for instance flies and bees; for they swim about in water for a long time, if it is not excessively hot or cold (although [among 475b the animals that breathe,] those that have little power seek to breathe more rapidly). But these perish and are said to suffocate when their stomach becomes filled and the heat in their midriff[86] perishes. For which reason also they revive if they spend time in ash.[87] And of the [animals] that live in water, as many as are bloodless [can] live for a longer time in air than those that have blood

82 According to Ogle, the cicadas that sing are the males, and the abdominal membranes through which, in the view of nearly all naturalists, they produce their buzzing sound are now known as their "drums." *Aristotle* On Youth & Old Age, 123, n. 88; cf. 36–37.

83 Cf. nn. 78, 79, and 80 above.

84 470b22–23.

85 471b19–23.

86 Cf. n. 80 above.

87 Apparently, Aristotle means by these two sentences that if their stomach becomes filled with water, these small insects can no longer raise and lower their midriff sufficiently to cool themselves down and thus preserve their heat, but if they are placed in warm ash for a time while they are still alive, their lost heat can be restored and they revive.

and that take in sea [water], as for instance fish [do]; for on account of their having little heat, the air is sufficient to cool them down for a long time, for instance in the case of the soft-shelled [animals] and that of the octopuses (but in the end, indeed, [the air that cools them] does not suffice for [their continuing] to live, on account of their having little heat); since even among fish, most[88] live in the earth—being motionless, however—and are discovered by being dug up. For as many [animals] as either do not have a lung at all or [have] a bloodless [one] need cooling down less often.

Chapter 16

And so concerning the bloodless [animals], it has been said that for some the surrounding air and for others the [surrounding] water helps toward [preserving] life. But for those with blood, i.e., those that have a heart, as many [of them], on the one hand, as have a lung all take in air and bring about their cooling down by breathing [in] and breathing out. And those that produce live offspring within themselves and not merely externally (for selachians[89] produce live offspring, but not within themselves) have a lung, as well as, among the [animals] that lay eggs, those with wings, for instance birds, and those with scaly plates, for instance tortoises and lizards and snakes. Now those [i.e., those that produce live offspring within themselves, have] a bloody [lung], but most of these [i.e., of the others just mentioned,] have a lung that is spongy, for which reason they make use of a less rapid breathing, as has been said before.[90] But they all do make use [of breathing], even as many [of such animals] as spend their time and lead their life in water, for instance the genus of water snakes and of frogs and of crocodiles and of hemydes[91] and [also] tortoises, those of the sea as well as those that live

88 Some modern editors, plausibly, read *polloi*, or "many," instead of the manuscripts' *hoi polloi*, or "most."

89 Selachians are cartilaginous fishes, such as sharks and rays.

90 470b13–15.

91 On the hemydes, cf. n. 49 above.

on land, and seals. For all these and those like them bring forth [their offspring] on dry land, and they sleep either on dry land or in the water, holding their mouth above [the water's surface] on account of breathing. But as many [of the animals with blood] as have **476a**
gills, on the other hand,[92] are all cooled down by taking in water; and the genus of what are called selachians and of the others [like them] that are without feet, have gills. And all fish are without feet; for in fact the [appendages] that they have, [people] speak of [using the word "fins" (*pterugiōn*)] on the grounds of their likeness to wings (*pterugōn*).[93] Of the [animals] that have feet, one alone of those that have been observed has gill[s], the one called a kordylos.[94] But no [animal] has yet been seen that has at the same time a lung and gills. [What is] responsible [for this is] that the lung is for the sake of being cooled down by the breath [taken in]—and it looks as if the lung (*pneumōn*) has gotten its name because of [its being] the receptacle for the breath (*pneumatos*)—whereas the gills are for being cooled down by means of the water [taken in]; and one organ [is] useful for one [task], and one [form of] being cooled down [is] sufficient for all [animals]. So that since we see nature doing nothing in vain, and [since] if there were two [organs for cooling] one would be in vain, on account of this, some [animals] have gills and others [have] a lung, but none [has] both.

92 Cf. "on the one hand" at 475b17.

93 At 476a4, I read *pterugōn* (or "wings"), with manuscripts L, M, P, and S, rather than *pterugiōn* (or "fins"), with Mugnier, who follows manuscripts Z and X. According to Mugnier's text, the phrase translated as "[people] speak of [using the word 'fins'] on the grounds of their likeness to wings" would be translated instead as "[people] speak of [in the way they do] on the grounds of the likeness of their fins [to wings]."

94 The kordylos was apparently either a tadpole or the larval form of some sea-newt.

Chapter 17

Since each of the animals needs, on the one hand, nourishment in order to be and, on the other hand, cooling down for preservation, nature uses the same organ for both of these, just as in some [animals it uses] the tongue for [tasting] flavors and for [vocal] expression, so in those that have a lung [it uses] what is called the mouth for the working up of nourishment as well as for breathing out and breathing [in].[95] But in those that don't have a lung and that don't breathe, the mouth [is present] for the working up of nourishment, whereas the nature of the gills is present for cooling down in those that need cooling down. Now how the power of the organs that have been mentioned produces cooling down, we will say later. But with a view to their feeding[96] not hindering [it], it happens similarly with the [animals] that breathe and with those that take in water; for when [those that breathe are] breathing, they don't at the same time take in food; otherwise, it happens that they choke when the food, either wet or dry, goes through the windpipe into the lung along with [the air]; for the windpipe lies in front of the esophagus, through which the food proceeds into what is called the stomach. And so for the quadrupeds with much blood,[97] the windpipe has a sort of cover,

95 The opening sentence of this chapter is awkward in the Greek as well as in the English translation. Regarding nature's use of one organ for two functions, compare *On the Parts of Animals* 659a13–23 and 683a20–25.

96 The word translated as "feeding" is *trophēn*, a form of *trophē*, which I have generally been translating as "nourishment." I will continue to translate it for the most part as "nourishment," though I will use the translation "feeding" (and also "nutriment" and "food") in those contexts where one of these seems more appropriate.

97 The Greek word translated here as "with much blood" is *enaimois*, which I would normally have translated simply as "with blood," in the sense of "having blood in them." But in the continuation of this sentence, Aristotle will contrast these quadrupeds with those that lay eggs, and yet he has made clear in the previous chapter, at 475b19–23, that there are quadrupeds, such as tortoises, that both have blood and lay eggs. However, since he also said in the continuation of that passage that those latter quadrupeds have a "spongy" as opposed to a "bloody" (*enaimon*) lung, I interpret the word *enaimois* here as referring only to those animals with a bloodier rather than a spongy or less

the epiglottis; but for birds and those of the quadrupeds that lay 476b
eggs, there isn't [such a cover], but they produce the same [result] by contracting [the windpipe]; for when taking in food, these contract [the windpipe], whereas those place the epiglottis over [it], and when [the food] has gone by, those raise [the epiglottis], whereas these open [the windpipe], and [then] they take in breath with a view to being cooled down. But those [animals] that have gills, after having expelled water through these, take their food in through the mouth. For they don't have a windpipe, so that they couldn't be harmed at all in this way by water's falling into [it] along [with their food], but [they could be harmed] by its entering the stomach. For which reason they bring about its expulsion and the seizing of their food quickly, and they have sharp teeth and nearly all [of them] are saw-toothed; for it is not admissible for them to chew their food [since while chewing, they would be swallowing too much water].

Chapter 18

Concerning the cetaceans, among the aquatic [animals], someone might be perplexed; but [the facts] with respect to them too are in accord with reason, for instance concerning dolphins and whales and as many of the other [animals] as have what is called a blowhole. For these don't have feet, but having a lung,[98] they take in sea water. But what has now been stated [is] responsible for this;[99] for they

bloody lung, and I try to convey this interpretation by translating it as "with much blood." Cf. *On the Parts of Animals* 664b20–25.

98 In other words, not having gills.

99 From the sequel, it would appear that by "this," Aristotle means the cetaceans' taking in sea water despite their having a lung rather than gills. For it is this fact that he goes on to explain, on the grounds they don't take in water for the sake of cooling down, but because it is necessary for them to do their feeding in water (cf. 476b23–24 and 477a7–10, together with 476b13). Aristotle might also, however, be thinking of the question of why these animals with a lung rather than gills don't have feet, i.e., why they are sea animals in the first place, a question that is implicitly raised at the end of the next chapter and in the following one. Contrast 476a2–3, read without my bracketed addition.

don't take in water for the sake of cooling down. For this comes to be for them when they breathe; for they have a lung. For which reason also they sleep holding their mouth above [the surface], and dolphins, at any rate, snore. Furthermore, if they are caught [underwater] in nets, they quickly suffocate on account of not breathing; for which reason such [animals] are seen coming to the surface of the sea, because of breathing. But since [it is] necessary [for them] to do their feeding in water, [it is] necessary [for them], after taking in water, to expel [it], and because of this they all have a blowhole; for having taken in water, these draw the water up [so as to expel it] at the blowhole, as fish [do] at the gills. The position of the blowhole [is] also a sign [of this]; for it leads to none of the [parts] with blood, but it has its position in front of the brain, and it expels the water. And on account of this same [reason] both the cephalopods[100] and the soft-shelled [animals] take in water, I mean [by these latter], for instance lobsters, as they are called, and crabs. For in fact none of them needs cooling down, for each of them has little heat and is 477a bloodless, so that it is sufficiently cooled down by the surrounding water (*hugrou*); but because of feeding [they take in water, which they immediately have to expel], so that the water (*to hugron*) not flow in [to the stomach] at the same time as they take [the food into it]. Now the soft-shelled animals, for instance crabs and lobsters, expel the water through the folds next to their shaggy [parts], whereas cuttlefish and octopuses [expel it] through the hollow above what is called the head. But it has been written about them more precisely in our inquiries concerning the animals.[101] So then concerning the taking in of water (*to hugron*), it has been said that it happens because of cooling down and because of the animals that are aquatic in their nature having to take in their food from the water (*tou hugrou*).

---

100 The Greek word translated as "cephalopods" is *malakia*. Cf. *On Long-Livedness and Short-Livedness*, n. 16.

101 By "our inquiries concerning the animals" Aristotle is referring to *On the History of Animals*. See, in particular, 524a9–12, 524b21–22, 526a26–27, 526b19–21, 527b18–22.

Chapter 19

After these [things] one must speak about cooling down, in what manner it comes to be for the [animals] that breathe as well as for those that have gills. Now it has been said earlier[102] that as many of the animals as have a lung [all] breathe. But [as for] why some have this part, and why those that have [it] need breathing, responsible for [some] having [it], on the one hand,[103] [is] that the higher (*timiōtera*) of the animals have obtained[104] more heat; for [it is] necessary that together with [their greater heat] they have also obtained a higher soul; and these are higher than the nature of plants.[105] For which reason also those [animals] that have an especially bloody and hot lung[106] [are] bigger in size, and the [animal] that uses the purest and the most blood is the most upright of the animals, [namely,] the human being, and it alone has its upper [part oriented] toward the

---

102 470b12–13.

103 The counterpart to this "on the one hand," i.e., Aristotle's response to his other question, that of why the animals that have a lung need breathing, would seem to come only in Chapter 21, though there the question that he explicitly addresses is not why they need breathing, but rather why they breathe. 478a11–25; cf. 478a28–31.

104 The Greek word translated as "have obtained" is *tetukhēke*, a form of the verb *tugkhanō*, from which the word *tukhē*, or "chance," is derived. Instead of "have obtained," I might also have translated it as "have happened upon" or "have as a matter of fact."

105 Several editors have emended the Greek word I have translated as "plants" so that it would be translated instead as "fish" (Biehl) or "cold [animals]" (Ross). But the word for plants occurs in all our manuscripts, and on the assumption that it is correct, the "these" that are higher than plants might well refer to animals in general, understood here as distinguished from plants by the presence of soul. And this clause, in claiming that it is soul that makes animals higher than plants, would thus support the implicit premise in the argument of the preceding clause ("for [it is] necessary") that it is the animals to which a higher soul has been allotted that are the higher animals. And if this suggestion is correct, it would not be the first time in this treatise that Aristotle has spoken of the possession of soul as characterizing animals as distinct from plants. Cf. 468b3ff. and n. 16 above.

106 Aristotle understands blood as being intrinsically hot. Cf. *On the Parts of Animals* 649b20–27.

upper [part] of the whole, on account of its having this part of such a sort [i.e., on account of its having a lung that contains the purest and the most blood]. So that one must posit it [i.e., this part, namely, the lung,] as responsible for the being (*ousias*)[107] [of the animals that have it], both for this [animal] and for the others [that have it], just as [one must posit this] for any other whatsoever of their parts. So then they have [it] for the sake of this [i.e., having such an *ousia*].[108] But one must hold that the cause [that acts] from necessity and [is the cause] of motion[109] has put together the [living beings] of this sort, just as it has also put together many [that are] not of this sort. For some are put together from [relatively] more earth, for instance the genus of plants, while others [are put together] from [relatively more] water, for instance the [genus] of the aquatic [animals]; and of the winged and land [animals], some [i.e., the former, are put together] from [relatively more] air, while others [i.e., the latter, are put together] from [relatively more] fire. And each [of these kinds] have their station in the places that are proper [to them, i.e., to their characteristic elements].

---

107 On this use of the word *ousias* (a form of the word *ousia*), cf. n. 1 above. Note also that the Greek word translated here as "responsible for" (*aition*) might also have been translated as "a cause of."

108 Despite the fact that cooling down is the announced theme of this chapter, but in keeping with Aristotle's separation of the question as to why some animals have a lung from that of why these animals need breathing, he does not say that they have a lung for the sake of breathing, which they need for the sake of being cooled down (cf. n. 104 above; also 478a27–34; *On the Parts of Animals* 668b33–669a13, 669b8–9). For that answer to the question of why some animals have a lung would lead to the question of why these animals are in need of being cooled down in this manner, and it is this more fundamental question that Aristotle addresses in this chapter.

109 In speaking here of a cause that operates from necessity and that is also the cause of motion, Aristotle is clearly using the term "motion" in its broad sense that includes "coming into being" (cf. *Physics* 201a3–18). Accordingly, he is implicitly distinguishing what he has just spoken of as that for the sake of which some animals have a lung, namely, to have the being (*ousia*) or the kind of being they have—which is indeed a kind of answer to the question of why they have a lung (though Aristotle hasn't used the word "cause" for it; contrast 477a23–24 and n. 107 above)—from the cause that necessitates the coming into being of animals, both those with and those without a lung.

Chapter 20

Empedocles did not speak of this [matter] in a fine way when he asserted that those of the animals that are hottest and have the 477b
most fire are aquatic, fleeing [thereby] the excess of the heat in their nature, so that since they are lacking in the cold and the wet,[110] they might be preserved by way of the place (*topon*), to which they are contrary; for [he asserts that] the wet is less hot than the air. Now in general [it is] absurd (*atopon*)—how is it admissible that each of them, having been born in the dry [place], should change its place [and migrate] into the wet [one]; for the majority of them are pretty much also without feet. But he, in speaking of their initial putting together, asserts that they came into being in the dry [place], but that, fleeing [it], they went into the wet [one]. Furthermore, they are not even manifestly hotter than the land animals; for some are entirely without blood, while others of them have [only a] little blood. However, what sorts of [things] should be called hot and cold have received an inquiry [from us] by themselves;[111] but concerning the cause that Empedocles has stated, in a way it is reasonable (*ekhei*... *logon*), [namely,] what [he says] is being sought [by these animals], yet what he asserts, at any rate, is not true. For while the contrary places and seasons preserve those who have excesses of their states (*tō*... *hexeōn*), their nature is preserved most of all in their proper places. For it

---

110 The Greek expression translated here (and for the remainder of this chapter) as "the wet" is *to hugron*, which I have sometimes translated as "water" (cf. n. 50 above). I might have translated it in this chapter too as "water," since this is surely what Aristotle is referring to, at least in the immediately following sentences. But I choose this more literal translation in order to emphasize that he is thinking primarily here of the contrary qualities wet and dry, and hot and cold, which he regarded as being more fundamental than the elements earth, air, fire, and water, elements that are each constituted by one of the possible pairs of these qualities (cf. *On the Parts of Animals* 646a12–17; *On Coming into Being and Perishing* 329a33–35, 330a30–b9). In keeping with this, I will also translate the contrary expression, *to xēron*, as "the dry" or "the dry [place]," rather than "land" or "dry land."

111 Cf. *On the Parts of Animals* 648b2–649b8.

is not the same: the material of the animals, from which each one is [constituted], and the states (*hexeis*) and conditions (*diatheseis*) of it [i.e., of that material].[112] I mean, for instance, if nature had put something together from wax, it would not have preserved it by putting it in a hot [place], nor if it [had formed] something from ice; for it would have quickly been destroyed on account of the contrariety; for the hot melts what has been put together by[113] its

---

112 In *Categories* 8b25–9a13, Aristotle speaks of states (*hexeis*) and conditions (*diatheseis*) as among the qualities that can belong to a being, and he distinguishes between them on the grounds that states are relatively long-lasting and stable, whereas conditions can quickly change. By his mention here, and only here, of conditions as well as states, he seems to be emphasizing that the states of the animals' material that he has in mind in this chapter are not qualities that can quickly change. Also, in the *Categories* passage, Aristotle is clearly thinking of states and conditions of composite beings, such as human beings, rather than, as here, states and conditions of the material aspect of their nature; accordingly, he mentions knowledge and virtue as examples of states, and heat, cold, disease, and health as examples of conditions. And how he understands the state, as distinct from the nature, of the animals' material (such as "the hot" and "the wet") is not easy to see. It is clear, however, that as a consequence of making this distinction, Aristotle avoids Empedocles' assertion that an excess of a quality, namely, heat, can be in, or belong to, the nature of certain animals. Cf. 477b2, 478a7–9.

113 The preposition translated as "by" is *hupo*. In speaking here of what is put together "by" the contrary of hot and, at the end of the sentence, of what is put together "by" hot and dry, Aristotle is treating these material constituents of things as also being the agents by which those things are put together from them. In other words, he is treating them as also fulfilling the function that he attributes elsewhere in this sentence to "nature." To make sense of this, it helps to recall that these material constituents are not inert. And who can say what might result, or have resulted, from the interaction of these motions of matter? In this connection, recall Aristotle's claim at the end of the previous chapter that "the cause [that acts] from necessity and [is the cause] of motion" has put together the kinds of animals with a lung as well as many others. For it now appears that he meant by this not merely some cause that that acts from necessity upon earth and water and the like, so as to put together from them the various kinds of animals, but rather earth and water and the like themselves, which, by being in motion and setting one another in motion in various ways, necessarily bring these animals into being. In this connection, consider *Physics* 200a30–32, where Aristotle says that "the necessary" in the things of nature is "that which is spoken of as material and the motions that belong to this."

contrary; nor if it had put something together from salt or nitre, would it have brought it into a wet [place] and put it [there]; for the wet destroys the [things] put together by hot and dry. If, then, the wet and the dry are the material for all bodies,[114] the [things] put together from wet and cold are reasonably in [places that are] wet (and if cold, they will be in a [place that is also] cold), but the [things] put together from dry [are reasonably] in a dry [place]. On account of this, trees do not grow in water, but in the earth. And yet it belongs to the same speech [i.e., that of Empedocles, to say that they go] into the water, because of their being excessively dry, just as he asserts that the excessively fiery [animals have done]; for [according to that speech] they [i.e., trees,] wouldn't have gone into it because of its coldness, but because [it is] wet. So then the natures of the [animals'] material, in whatever sort of place they are, are in fact of that sort, those in water [being] wet, those in the earth [being] dry, and those in the air [being] hot. However, the 478a
states [of their material], those that are excessive in heat, [are preserved more when put] in a cold [place], whereas those [that are excessive] in coldness are preserved more when put in a hot [place];[115] for the place equalizes the excess of the state toward the mean. So then this [process] needs to be sought for within their proper places[116] and in keeping with the changes of the season common [to those places]; for it is admissible that the states [of their material] be contrary to the places, but [it is] impossible that

114 Aristotle speaks here of the wet and the dry, rather than the hot and the cold, as the material for all bodies, since he presents wet and dry as the passive contraries and hot and cold as the active ones. Cf. *On Coming into Being and Perishing* 329b24–32.

115 Note that Aristotle speaks here of preservation of the excessive states themselves, not merely, as he did at 477a14–16, of preservation of the living beings whose material (sometimes) has the excesses of one of these states.

116 At 478a5, I follow manuscripts M and Z, which do not contain *hekastēs hulēs*. This is also in agreement with Mugnier, who brackets these words. They are present, however, in manuscripts L, P, S, and X, and if one were to read them, the phrase translated as "within their proper places" would be translated instead as "within the proper places for each [sort of] material." As it seems to me, the two readings do not differ significantly in meaning.

the material [be contrary to them]. So then that [it is] not because of heat belonging to their nature [that] some of the animals are aquatic, while others are land animals, as Empedocles asserts, let so much have been said, and [let so much have been said as to] why some [animals] don't have a lung while others have it.

Chapter 21

[As to] why the [animals] that have [a lung] take in air and breathe, and most of all as many of them as have a bloody [lung],[117] responsible for breathing, on the one hand, [is] the lung, since it is spongy and full of tubes. And this part, most of all among those that are called vitals,[118] is the bloodiest. As many [of the animals], then, as have a bloody one need their cooling down [to be] fast, on account of the turn of the scale being small for the soulish[119] fire [as to whether it is to continue burning], and [they need this cooling down, or that which produces it,] to enter everywhere into [the lung] because of the large amount of its blood and of its heat. And air is able to do both of these [things] easily; for on account of its having a nature that is thin, penetrating everywhere [into the lung] and [doing so] quickly, it thoroughly cools [it]; but water [is] the contrary [in its nature]. And why, accordingly, those [animals] that have a bloody lung breathe the most [is] clear from these [things];[120]

---

117 Though Aristotle goes on to say that the lung is the bloodiest of the parts that are called "vitals," he has nevertheless distinguished the animals with a bloody lung from those in whom it is "bloodless and spongy," and he has said that the latter do not need to breathe as much as the former do (470b12–16). Cf. n. 97 above.

118 The Greek word that, for want of a better term, is translated here as "vitals" is *splagkhnōn*, which refers to the heart, lung, liver, spleen, and kidneys—but not the stomach or intestines—and which originally meant those parts of a sacrificial animal that were reserved to be eaten by the sacrificers themselves.

119 The Greek word translated as "soulish" is *psukhikou*. Cf. *On the Motion of Animals*, n. 64.

120 Although this clause does not explicitly contain the usual word for "on the other hand," it corresponds to the clause at the beginning of the chapter (478a12) that contained the word translated as "on the one hand." Also, it is

for what is hotter needs more cooling down, and at the same time [as it cools the lung,] the breath also travels easily toward the ruling beginning of the heat in the heart [i.e., of the heart's heat].

Chapter 22

As for the manner in which the heart is connected by passages to the lung,[121] one must contemplate [this] from [specimens] that are being dissected and from the accounts of inquiries that have been written [by us] concerning the animals.[122] Now then the nature of animals in general needs cooling down on account of the kindling of the soul [that takes place] in the heart.[123] They procure this through breathing, as many of the animals as have not only a heart but also a lung. And those that have a heart but not a lung, as [is the case with] fish on account of their nature being aquatic, procure their cooling down by means of water through [the use of] their gills. How the heart is situated in relation to the gills, one must contemplate [this], with respect to [what] sight [can reveal], from the
dissections,[124] and with respect to precision, from the accounts of 478b
[our] inquiries; but to speak now, too, by way of summary, it is in the following manner. For the heart might seem not to be situated

---

worth noting, it seems to me, that Aristotle did not say of his response there to the first and primary question of the chapter, as he says here of his response to this second question, that it is "clear."

121 Aristotle means by these passages the blood vessels that, because of their close proximity (once they enter the lung) to the bronchial tubes, can be cooled by the air in those tubes.

122 Cf. *On the History of Animals* 496a19–33. Note that the Greek word *historia*, which is translated as "history" in the title of that work, is also the word whose plural form is translated here as "accounts of inquiries." Its primary meaning is inquiry, from which it comes to mean also the knowledge attained from one's inquiry or the written account of one's inquiry, and hence "history," whether natural history or history in its more usual modern sense.

123 Cf. 469b15–16, 474b12–13.

124 This may be another reference to actual dissections, as the mention at the beginning of the chapter appears to be, or else perhaps to a work of Aristotle that has been lost. Cf. *On Sleep and Awakeness*, n. 24.

in the same way in those of the animals that live on land and in fish; but it is [situated] in the same way. For [in the direction] toward which they incline their heads, there the heart has its pointed [end]. But since the heads don't incline in the same way for those of the animals that live on land and for fish, [it is] toward the mouth [that] the heart has its pointed [end].[125] And a tube consisting of a sinewy blood vessel extends from the pointed [end] of the heart to the middle [of the region of the gills], where all the gills are joined to one another. Now this [tube] is the largest, but from either side of the heart other [tubes] extend to the tip of each of the gills, [tubes] through which cooling down comes to be for the heart, inasmuch as water is always passing through the gills [and thus surrounding these tubes]. In the same way in the [animals] that breathe, the chest is in frequent motion up and down as they take breath in and expel it, [just] as the gills [are in motion] in fish. And the [animals] that breathe, [if they are] in air that is small [in amount] and [that remains] the same, suffocate[, as fish do in a small amount of water];[126]

125 Since "no fish has a neck" (*On the History of Animals* 504b17), fish are unable to genuinely incline their heads, or to move them in any direction other than that in which they move the whole body, and this is normally in the direction of the mouth, i.e., the direction in which they move for feeding. Furthermore, unless the main clause of this sentence applies only to fish—and nothing in the words themselves gives any indication that this was Aristotle's intention—he may have in mind, with regard to land animals, that one of the reasons they incline their heads is for feeding (cf. *On the Parts of Animals* 692b22–693a3, 693a8–10), so that the direction in which they incline them, namely towards the front, is also the direction of their mouths, not all the time, but when they are feeding. And at least to this extent, given that the pointed end of the heart is situated toward the head in fish and toward the front of the chest in land animals, it is true that in both these cases the pointed end of the heart is situated in the direction of the mouth.

126 I suggest that this bracketed addition be supplied in thought, even if Aristotle didn't write any such words, in order to make sense of the word translated as "each of the two" in the continuation of the sentence. The alternative would be to treat "air that is small [in amount]" and "air...[that remains] the same" as two separate instances of air. But it doesn't seem plausible to me that air that remains the same, if it is not also small in amount, would "quickly" become hot through contact with the animal's blood, as Aristotle goes on to say of the air in question. Cf. *On the History of Animals* 592a19–23.

for each of the two of them [i.e., the air and the water,] quickly becomes hot; for contact with the blood [or with the walls of the blood vessels] heats each of them. Being hot, the blood [in these cases] prevents the cooling down. And when the [animals] that breathe are unable to move their lung, and the aquatic [animals] their gills, on account of [some incidental] affliction (*pathos*) or on account of old age, [it is] then that the end happens.[127]

Chapter 23

So then common to all animals is coming into being and death, but the manners differ in kind; for perishing is not without differentiae, yet it has something common [to all instances of it]. Death is in some cases violent and in others according to nature, violent whenever its ruling beginning is from outside, and according to nature whenever [it is] in [the animal] itself. And the putting together of the part [of the body in which such a ruling beginning comes to be is] of such a sort from the beginning (*ex arkhēs*)[128] [as to receive it]; it [i.e., natural death, is] not something suffered adventitiously (*ti epiktēton pathos*). Now in plants this is called withering, and in animals old age. There is death and perishing equally for all [living beings] that are not incomplete; and similarly for these [i.e., the incomplete], but in another manner. I call incomplete, for instance eggs and the seeds of plants, as many as have not taken root. Now perishing comes to be for all [living beings] through the failure of a

127 At 478b21, I read *tote sumbainein tēn teleutēn*, in accordance with all the manuscripts, rather than *tote sumbainein dei tēn teleutēn,* with Mugnier, who follows Biehl in inserting *dei.* According to Mugnier's text, this last clause would read, instead of as "[it is] then that the end happens," as "then the end must happen."

128 At 478b26–27, I read *toiautē ex arkhēs*, with manuscripts M and Z (and in basic agreement with manuscripts P and X), rather than *ex arkhēs toiautēs*, with Mugnier, who follows manuscripts L and S. According to Mugnier's text, this phrase would be translated, instead of as "of such a sort from the beginning," as "from a beginning/principle that is of such a sort."

certain [sort of] heat,[129] and in the complete [ones], [through such failure] in the part in which the ruling beginning of their being (*tēs ousias hē arkhē*) is. And this [beginning] is, as has been said before, in the [part of the body] in which the upper [part] and the lower [part] are joined together,[130] in plants [the part] in between [a] shoot
479a and [a] root,[131] and in those of the animals with blood the heart, and in those without blood what is analogous.[132] Some of these have potentially many ruling beginnings, but not, however, actually. For which reason [i.e., because they potentially have many ruling beginnings,] both some of the insects live when divided, and, of the [animals] with blood, as many as are not exceedingly full of life live a long time with their heart having been removed, for instance tortoises, and they are in motion with their feet, if their shells are on, on account of their nature not having been put together well, but similarly to insects.[133] The ruling beginning of life fails in those that have [one] whenever the hot [part of the body] that shares in [or with] it is not cooled down. For as has been said many times, [that part] is consumed itself by itself.[134] Whenever, then, the lung in some and the gills in others are hardened, the gills in these and the lung in those drying up and becoming earthy on account of the length of time, they are not able to move, nor [in particular] to raise and lower, these parts. And finally, when a tightening comes to be, the fire dies out. For which reason when even small ailments (*pathēmatōn*) come upon [them] in old age, they quickly come to the end; for on account of their heat being little, inasmuch as the greater

129 Cf. n. 75 above.

130 Cf. 467b32–468a4, where, however, Aristotle said only that the "nutritive ruling beginning," i.e., the ruling beginning of the nutritive soul, and not "the ruling beginning of their being," is in the middle of the upper and lower parts of the body. He did however say in that context (467b20–22) that for an animal, "[it is] necessary that there be one and the same part in virtue of which it lives as well as in virtue of which we give it the name animal."

131 Cf. 467a20–30, 468b16–28.

132 Cf. 469a5–b20.

133 Cf. 468a26–b15.

134 466b28–33, 469b21–470a7, 474b13–24.

[part] of it has been breathed away in the long course of their life, whatever tightening there comes to be of the part [in which this heat, or this fire, is present], [the fire] is quickly put out; for since there is, so to speak, a fleeting and small flame in it, it is put out by a small motion. Wherefore death in old age is also painless; for [the old] come to the end even though no violent suffering (*pathos*) happens to them, but the release of the soul comes to pass wholly imperceptibly. And of diseases, as many as make the lung hard, either by means of growths or [secreted] residues or an excess of morbid heat, as in fevers, [these] make the breath rapid because [those afflicted by them] are not able to raise their lung up far or to lower it. And finally, when they are no longer able to move [it], having breathed out, they come to the end.

Chapter 24

Coming into being is the first having a share[, occurring] in that which is hot, of nutritive soul, and life is the continuation of this. Youth is the growth of the primary part capable of cooling down [the living being],[135] old age [is] the wasting away of this [part], and

135 It would appear at first that in speaking of "the primary part capable of cooling down [the living being]," Aristotle is referring to the lung and the gills, at least in the case of those animals that possess these organs. But it seems odd to claim that youth is the growth of these parts in particular. Moreover, Aristotle has said in *On Sleep and Awakeness* (455b34–456a11) that the ruling beginning of the breath, and of cooling down in general, is in the middle part of the body, or in the case of animals with blood, "the part around the heart," and he said nothing there about the lung in particular. According to that passage, then, the primary part capable of cooling down the living being would be the part around the heart, and hence would include the heart (and the chief blood vessels) as well as the lung. That passage ends with a promise of a fuller discussion later, a promise whose fulfillment in the present treatise is evidence that what Aristotle said there might well have a bearing on what he means here. In support of reading this passage in light of what was said in that one, one should consider that the lung can take in breath, and thus cool the animal, only so long as the animal is alive, and that its life depends on the heart and the chief blood vessels as much as it does on the lung. And further support for this interpretation will come in the final chapter of the present treatise,

the prime [of life] is [what is in] the middle of these. An end, i.e., perishing, [that is] violent, on the one hand, is the being put out and dying out of that which is hot (for it might perish [violently]
479b on account of both these causes),[136] while the [perishing that is] according to nature, on the other hand, [is] a dying out of this same [part], coming about because of the length of time and [its] completeness.[137] Now in plants it is called withering, and in animals, death. And of this [i.e., death], death in old age is the dying out of the part[138] because of an inability to produce a cooling down on account of old age. What, then, coming into being is, and life and death, and on account of what causes they belong to the animals, has been said.

Chapter 25

From these [things, it is] clear also on account of what cause it happens to those of the animals that breathe that they suffocate in water (*en tōi hugrōi*), and to fish [that they suffocate] in air; for to

---

where Aristotle treats the heart and lung as a (single organ and a) single part, a part that he seems to identify even with the chest. See 480a19–b5, and also the transition between Chapters 25 and 26 at 479b12–19.

136 Cf. 469b21ff. There, however, Aristotle had said that what we call violent perishing—of fire, at any rate—is what we also call being put out, i.e., destruction by contraries, as opposed to what we call perishing because of old age, which we also call dying out, i.e., perishing on account of itself.

137 At 479b2–3 I read *teleiotēta*, with manuscripts L, S, P, and X, rather than *teleiotatē*, with Mugnier, who follows manuscripts M and Z. According to Mugnier's text, the end of this sentence would apparently be translated, instead of as "coming about because of the length of time and [its] completeness" (i.e., the completeness of time), as "coming about because of the length of time and [being] most complete."

138 What Aristotle speaks of here as "the part" is presumably the part that he spoke of at the beginning of the chapter as "the primary part capable of cooling down [the living being]," i.e., the part around the heart, which includes at least the lung, heart, and blood vessels. In saying that this part dies out because of "an inability to produce a cooling down," he must mean that it dies out because of an inability to cool itself down, an inability, as it seems to me, that belongs to this central region as a whole rather than to any one organ in particular.

the latter cooling down comes to be by means of water, and to the former [it comes] by means of air, of which each of the two [classes] is deprived when they change their places. And the cause of the motion, for the ones of the gills, and for the others of the lung, [organs] which, when they rise and fall, these breathe out and breathe in, and those take in the water (*to hugron*) and expel it.[139] Furthermore, the putting together of the organ is in the following manner.

Chapter 26

There are three [things] that occur regarding the heart, which seem to have the same nature, but do not have the same [nature]: leaping and beating [of the heart] and breathing. Leaping [of the heart] is a being forced together of what is hot in it on account of a cooling down[140] brought on by residues[141] or by products of [morbid] liq-

139 The main clause of this sentence lacks a predicate also in the original Greek. At the beginning of Chapter 21, Aristotle said that, in the case of the animals that have a lung, the lung is responsible (*aition*) for breathing, since it is spongy and full of tubes, but he also indicated in that chapter that this answer was not sufficient to make it clear why these animals breathe (478a11–13; cf. n. 120 above). And his reluctance here even to try to give the cause (*hē aitia*) of the motion of the lung in breathing (and of the corresponding motion of the gills) seems to me to go together with his refusal in the previous chapter to specify a single organ as "the primary part capable of cooling down [the living being]" (479a31; cf. n. 138 above). For whatever motions one would specify as the moving causes of the lung's rising and falling (cf. *On the Parts of Animals* 669a13–14) take place in an animal only as it is actually breathing, and so one could not separate them as causes from their effects, or as parts from the whole to which they belong.

140 This initial definition of leaping of the heart is clarified to some extent in the sequel. 479b22–24, 480a13–14.

141 Aristotle defines "residue" as the surplus from an animal's nourishment, i.e., a product of food and drink that does not serve to preserve the animal that consumes it. Such residues include liquid and solid excrement (*On the Parts of Animals* 670b23–27, 675b2–22), but also such useful substances as semen and breast milk. *On the Generation of Animals* 724b21ff., 776a15–b3.

uefaction,[142] as in the disease called "palpitation"[143] and also in other diseases and in states of fright; for also those who are frightened are cooled down in their upper [parts], and what is hot [in those parts], fleeing [from them] and being concentrated [in the heart], produces the leaping [in question, by being] forced into a small [space] in such a way that sometimes animals are put out [like a fire] and die because of fright and because of [the] morbid *pathos* [associated with it]. What occurs [as] beating of the heart, which is always manifestly being produced continuously, is similar to growths, [i.e., to] the [throbbing] motion that they produce, together with pain, on account of the change in the blood being contrary to nature. And [the throbbing] goes on until, [the growth] having been concocted, there is a discharge of pus. And this affliction (*pathos*) is similar to boiling; for boiling goes on while the liquid (*tou hugrou*) is being turned into vapor by what is hot; for it rises up on account of its bulk becoming greater. And cessation in the case of growths, if they are not vaporized away as the liquid (*to*
480a *hugron*) [in them] becomes thicker, [is] putrefaction, whereas in the case of boiling [it is] the breaking out [of the liquid] through the containing [surfaces]. But in the heart, the swelling, on account of the heat [there], of the liquid (*tou... hugrou*) that is always coming to [it] from the nutriment produces [the] beating, as [the swelling] rises to the outermost covering of the heart. And this [i.e., the whole process,] is always going on continuously; for there is always flowing in, continuously, the liquid (*to hugron*) from which the nature of the blood comes to be; for it is fabricated first in the heart. And [this is] clear in the coming into being [of an animal] from the beginning (*ex arkhēs*); for even though the blood vessels have not yet

---

142 Aristotle defines "a product of liquefaction" as a secretion from the material of an animal's growth, in a process brought about by a decomposition that is contrary to nature. Unlike residues, products of liquefaction are always morbid. *On the Generation of Animals* 724b27–28, 726a21–22.

143 The Greek word translated as "palpitation" is *palmos*, which means primarily a quivering, twitching, or pulsating motion. Aristotle does not use the word elsewhere, and nothing is known with any certainty about the disease that was called by this name, other than the name itself.

been distinguished, it [i.e., the heart,] manifestly contains blood. And on account of this it beats more [often] in those that are younger than in those that are older; for the exhalation [that] comes to be [is] greater in those that are younger. And the blood vessels all beat [i.e., pulsate], and at the same time as one another, on account of their being fastened from the heart. It is always setting [blood] in motion; so that they too are always setting [it] in motion, and at the same time as one another, when it [i.e., the heart,] sets [it] in motion. And so leaping up is the [heart's] pushing back that comes to be [in reaction] against the forcing together [in it of what is hot, a forcing together that is the effect] of what is cold, whereas beating is the infusion with *pneuma*[144] of the liquid (*tou hugrou*) as it is being heated [or, more precisely, it is the heart's pushing back repeatedly in reaction against the expansion brought about by this infusion].

Chapter 27

Breathing comes to be when that which is hot,[145] in which the nutritive ruling beginning is [located], increases. For just as the other

---

144 The word translated here as "infusion with *pneuma*" is *pneumatōsis*, which I might have translated as "vaporization," in keeping with my translation above of a different form of the same word, in connection with boiling, as "being turned into vapor" (479b31). But in the case of the heart, Aristotle has spoken both of "swelling" (480a3) of the wet nutriment as it is being turned into blood, and of "exhalation" (480a10), which presumably means the exhalation of vapor from the blood. And I choose the translation "infusion with *pneuma*" here in order to stress the change, both in character and in volume, of the liquid nutriment that is being turned into blood, even apart from the emission of any vapor from it. In this connection, one should keep in mind that the word *pneuma* means breath, which can be the animal's innate breath as well as what is breathed in from outside. Cf. n. 52 above, and also *On the Generation of Animals* 755a14–22, 762a19–26.

145 By "that which is hot," Aristotle is speaking of blood. And by using this indefinite expression rather than the word for blood, he is perhaps inviting us to think of it as what he was just speaking of in the previous sentence, namely, the liquid, derived from nutriment, from the heating of which the nature of blood has come to be. 480a14–15; cf. 480a2–6.

[parts] need nourishment, so [does] that, and more than the others; for that is responsible for nourishment for the others too.[146] And [it is] a necessity that in becoming greater it raise up the organ. And one must take the putting together of the organ to be similar to bellows in forges; for neither the lung nor the heart is far [from these] with respect to taking such a shape; and such [an organ] must be double;[147] for the nutritive [part, or that which is hot,] must be in the middle of its natural power.[148] So then as it [i.e., the nutritive part,] becomes greater [in volume] it rises, and as it rises [it is] necessary that the part surrounding it also rise, which manifestly [is] just [what] those who breathe bring about; for they raise their chest on account of the ruling beginning that is in it, [the ruling beginning] of such a part,[149] doing this same [thing]; and as it [i.e., the chest,] rises, [it is] necessary that the air from outside, which is cold, enter in,[150] just as into bellows, and that by [producing a] cool-
480b ing down it put out the excess of the fire. And just as this part rose as it [i.e., the nutritive part,] increased, [it is] necessary that it fall as that diminishes, and as it falls, [it is necessary] for the air that had come in to go out again, coming in cold and going out hot be-

146 Cf. 469a1–2 and n. 26 above.

147 The Greeks had not only single bellows, but also double ones, which had two bags, each with its own inlet for air. Aristotle is apparently comparing the shape of such bellows to that of the double organ consisting of the lung and heart.

148 At 480a24 I translate the expression *tēs phusikēs dunameōs* as "its natural power," rather than as the more narrowly literal "the natural power," since Aristotle seems to be speaking here of the power of the lung and heart, together, as a single organ with a single nature. Cf. 479a30–31 and n. 138 above.

149 By "the ruling beginning...of such a part," I assume that Aristotle is referring to the nutritive ruling beginning in the blood, or rather to the portion of this ruling beginning that is in the chest. Cf. 480b14.

150 At 480a29 I read *eisphrein* (which Bekker suggested as an emendation without knowing that it is also the reading of the first hand of manuscript X), rather than *eispherein*, with Mugnier, who follows the other manuscripts. According to Mugnier's text, this passage would be translated, instead of as "[it is] necessary that the air from outside, which is cold, enter in," as "[it is] necessary [for it] to bring in the air from outside, which is cold"; but then that which, "by producing a cooling down," must "put out the excess of fire" would have to be the chest, rather than the air, and that doesn't seem right.

BIN TRAVERLER FORM

Cut By: Cesar Flores Qty 30 Date 9/24/26

Scanned By: ________ Qty ____ Date ____

Scanned Batch ID's

________ ________ ________

Notes / Exceptions

____

cause of its contact with what is hot in this part, and especially in the case of the [animals] that have a bloody lung; for [it is necessary that] it rush into the many channel-like tubes that are in the lung, alongside each of which there extend blood vessels, so that it seems that the lung is wholly full of blood. And the entry of the air is called breathing [in] and its exit breathing out. And this is always, then, coming to be, continuously, just as long as [the animal] lives and moves this part continuously. And on account of this, living is in [i.e., is dependent on,] breathing [in] and breathing out. Also in fish the motion of the gills comes to be in the same manner. For when that which is hot in the blood rises through the parts [of the fish], the gills also rise, and they let water go through;[151] but as it [i.e., what is hot in the blood,] descends toward the heart through the passages [connecting the heart with the gills],[152] i.e., as it is being cooled down [by its proximity with the water that surrounds these passages], they [i.e., the gills,] sink down and expel the water.

---

151 Aristotle appears to be saying here that when the gills rise, they allow water from outside to enter into the openings between them, in the same manner as the lung in animals that breathe allows air to enter from outside when it rises. But the expression "they let the water go through" does not say this with any precision. And in fact, Aristotle had said of the gills, in *On the History of Animals* (504b29–30), that they are that by which the fish expel water that they have taken in through the mouth. Even in this treatise, moreover, he has made it clear that, after having expelled water through the gills, fish do take water into the mouth, necessarily so when they are feeding (476b5–10; cf. 476b23–27). Also, he has at least indicated that this water would be capable of providing cooling if it came to be in proximity to bloody parts of the animal (476b18–477a1). Now he has also said, to be sure, that it is when the gills are raised that fish take in water (479b12–15), and this might suggest that they take it in through the openings between them. But it is not clear to me that at the time when he wrote this treatise, he had come to think that fish do take in water in this way. And if he didn't think this, or even if he did, if he thought that the water that they take in through the mouth also plays a significant role in cooling them down, his reluctance to say so explicitly might stem from a reluctance to call attention to the difficulty of reconciling either of these views—on the assumption, at least, that the mouth and the gills are different organs—with his earlier claim that "one organ [is] useful for one [task]" and that "if there were two [organs for cooling] one would be in vain." Cf. 476a11–13.

152 Cf. 478a34–b13.

And while that which is in the heart is always rising [toward the gills, among other parts], [the heart] is always taking [some of it] back as it is being cooled down. For which reason, [just] as for those [i.e., the animals with a lung,] the decisive determinant of living or not living is in breathing, so for these [it is] in taking in the liquid (*to hugron*). And so concerning life and death and the [matters] belonging to the same genus with this inquiry, just about all [of them] have been spoken of.[153] And [to speak] concerning health and disease belongs not only to a doctor but also to the student of nature, up to the point of stating their causes. But it must not escape notice where they differ and where they contemplate different [matters], although that their occupation is coterminous up to a point, at any rate, is testified to by the [following] fact: for of the doctors, as many as are clever and over-industrious say something about nature and think fit to get their principles (*arkhas*) from there, and of those who have occupied themselves concerning nature, those who are most refined just about come to the end with the principles (*arkhas*) that have to do with healing.[154]

153 Compare *On Sense Perception and Sense-Perceptibles* 436a12–17.

154 Cf. *On Sense Perception and Sense-Perceptibles* 436a17–b1. Also, the Greek expression translated here as "those who are most refined" is *hoi khariestatoi*. In the *Nicomachean Ethics* (1095b22), Aristotle speaks of *hoi kharientes kai praktikoi*, i.e., "those who are refined and active," as choosing a life in pursuit of honor, and he explicitly contrasts this way of life not only with that of the vulgar, who pursue bestial pleasure, but also with the contemplative life. It is true that Aristotle sometimes uses the expression *hoi kharientes* without any implicit contrast with a still higher class, as in *On Prophecy from Sleep* (463a5), where I translate it as "the higher class." But in that passage Aristotle is speaking of the highest class "among the doctors," and he goes on to contrast doctors, or skilled craftsmen in general, with those "who are examining something and philosophizing" (463a7). Aristotle's subtle indication, then, that it is not the highest class among the students of nature who "just about come to the end with the principles that have to do with healing" helps, I think, to explain why, so far as we know at least, he did not follow this treatise with one devoted to health and disease. Cf. also *On Long-Livedness and Short-Livedness* 464b31–33.